fourth edition

HANDBOOK
OF ADVERTISING
ART PRODUCTION

Richard M. Schlemmer

State University of New York
College at Farmingdale

With illustrations by
Ross H. Schlemmer,
Scott R. Schlemmer,
and the author

PRENTICE HALL, Englewood Cliffs, New Jersey   07632

Library of Congress Cataloging-in-Publication Data

Schlemmer, Richard M.
    Handbook of advertising art production / Richard M. Schlemmer ;
  with illustrations by Ross H. Schlemmer, Scott R. Schlemmer, and by
  the author. -- 4th ed.
      p.   cm.
    Includes bibliographical references.
    ISBN 0-13-380882-3
    1. Pictures--Printing--Handbooks, manuals, etc. 2. Commercial
  art--Printing--Handbooks, manuals, etc. 3. Advertising layout and
  typography--Handbooks, manuals, etc. 4. Photomechanical processes-
  -Handbooks, manuals, etc. 5. Graphic arts--Handbooks, manuals, etc.
  I. Title.
  Z257.S33 1990
  686.2--dc20   89-25554
                                                           CIP

Editorial/production supervision
  and interior design: F. Hubert
Cover design by the author
Manufacturing buyer: Mike Woerner

*This one
is for Virginia*

Printed in the United States of America

10 9 8 7 6 5 4 3 2

ISBN   0-13-380882-3

PRENTICE-HALL INTERNATIONAL (UK) LIMITED, *London*
PRENTICE-HALL OF AUSTRALIA PTY. LIMITED, *Sydney*
PRENTICE-HALL CANADA INC., *Toronto*
PRENTICE-HALL HISPANOAMERICANA, S.A., *Mexico*
PRENTICE-HALL OF INDIA PRIVATE LIMITED, *New Delhi*
PRENTICE-HALL OF JAPAN, INC., *Tokyo*
SIMON & SCHUSTER ASIA PTE. LTD., *Singapore*
EDITORA PRENTICE-HALL DO BRASIL, LTDA., *Rio de Janeiro*

CONTENTS

PREFACE

In 1965, the electric typewriter used to type the final manuscript of the first edition of this book was considered a technological marvel. In contrast to this, this fourth edition has been written and composed on a Macintosh SE personal computer, using the MacWrite program, and the illustrations were originally laid out with Super Paint. The results were then printed out on an ImageWriter II. The utilization of such sophisticated devices, which have become the stock in trade of contemporary advertising and graphic art production, does more than contribute to the speed in which printed matter can now be produced. Given the inclination, they also afford the opportunity to better craft, revise, and otherwise polish one's work. It is in the cause of competence and craftsmanship, as well as efficiency, that this text has been again rewritten.

This edition represents an attempt to keep pace with the incredible technological advances that have occurred over these intervening years, yet to do so without discarding knowledge and information which is still basic.

Due to its decline in popularity, letterpress printing has been deemphasized, and the photomechanical processes, both line and halftone, have been given a separate chapter.

The latest typesetting technology is examined, and there is an entire new chapter on computerized imagery.

Descriptions of the latest developments have been added to the chapters on the standard printing processes, as well as to the text that pertains to their production requirements.

viii   PREFACE

Importantly, there are a host of new diagrammatic illustrations, illustrations which have been made to graphically depict the conventions and modern technology of advertising art production. As usual, definitions are included at the beginnings of chapters, so that words or processes will have been defined in advance.

The new technology does not constrict the creative mind; it allows it to expand to parameters never before envisioned. The ability to cope with this technology does not come packaged with the hardware involved; it requires an even sounder knowledge of the basics. It is this author's hope that this volume will contribute to both.

ACKNOWLEDGMENTS

These people have given willingly of their time and effort: my son, Scott, who rendered the new illustrations; Mark Altman, currently with, and Frank Canonica, formerly with, Linotype; my colleagues Lynn Hansen, Paul Gustafson, Timothy Karda, Robert Midura, and Steven Serr of SUNY Farmingdale, as well as Robert Newman of Newsday. To Philip Reichmeider and Charles Straub of SUNY, Farmingdale, for their computer seminar, and to Marie Severino of Linotype for her Linotron course.

I still thank those acknowledged in former editions, whose material I continue to rely upon.

And most gratefully to my newest academic colleague, William Steedle, without whose unfaltering expertise and help, this text would have necessarily been written on a portable typewriter.

R. M. S.

CHAPTER 1
THE FUNCTIONS
OF THE ADVERTISING
ARTIST

Advertising, once considered the almost all-American profession, has literally burst upon the international scene, bringing with it some of the most sophisticated brands of graphic imagery ever witnessed. Worldwide mergers have expanded it into a multibillion dollar (or pound or franc or mark or yen) industry. The competition among its producers has become keener, and with it the need for the trained creative minds and producers of the graphic image has intensified.

As a result, today's successful advertising artist is not only expected to possess an acute sense of the aesthetic, but also to possess the capacity for dependability and consistent quality, to have an eye for efficiency and economy, and to be conversant with contemporary graphic technology.

Employment for the advertising artist usually occurs in one of three categories:

1. In organizations whose principal business is to supply art for a profit.
2. In departments whose function is to supply art to their parent firm, where no direct profit results from the sale of the art that has been produced.
3. In publishing firms that use art as a means of enhancing their product and that may provide art facilities as a service to their advertisers.

The first category includes art studios, art departments of advertising agencies, public-relations firms, display houses, producers of technical literature, package designers, printers, and producers of sales-promotional aids.

The second category includes the art, advertising, and/or sales promotion departments of any commercial enterprise; the public-relations department; and the publications department.

The third includes the advertising and editorial art departments of publishers of newspapers, magazines, and books.

The duties of a person involved with the production of advertising art will usually fall within the following categories:

Sales. Provides liaison with the client.

Research. Provides information for planning advertising.

Copy. Writes advertising copy.

Art. Designs art. Executes art. Purchases art.

Production. Supervises work of staff. Orders work from outside sources.

THE ARTIST'S WORKING ARRANGEMENT

Artists have various working arrangements with their employers. The following are typical:

Salaried Artists.   Salaried artists are staff members who are paid a weekly salary. Fringe benefits, including vacations, are generally provided by the employer, and there is extra compensation for overtime. The requisite for employing salaried artists is having sufficient work to keep them busy.

The Work-Space Arrangement.   "Work-space" is normally a semifreelance arrangement whereby artists are retained for a flat hourly wage (somewhat higher than the salaried artist) or on a per-job basis. The artist is provided with working space, but is provided with minimal fringe benefits and is not additionally compensated for overtime. Permitted more freedom of action than salaried artists, these artists may also solicit work from outside sources and perform it on the premises. This arrangement is usually made with the more experienced artist, whose higher earning capacity compensates for the lack of overtime pay.

Due to current tax structures, more and more employers are paying all their artists, *even beginners,* on a work-space basis, thus eliminating the need for overtime pay, tax-witholding, and many fringe benefits. This is not an "off-the-books" arrangement as might be suspected; the artist's earnings are still reported to the government as if the employee were on a work-space agreement. *Artists will do well to predetermine all of the conditions of their employment before accepting a job.*

Freelance Artists. Freelance artists are self-employed, specialized artists who work at a location of their own choosing. These are the specialists who are called upon to perform a specific function or assist when the workload is too heavy for the regular staff. The freelance artist is paid well, but only for work performed. Freelancers are expected to be their own salespeople, keep their own books, and provide their own fringe benefits. They function as an extra asset or an emergency factor to an employer who seldom owes them any contractual allegiance.

THE ART STUDIO

The principal function of an art studio is the production of art for a profit. The studio solicits work from any firm that is a potential purchaser of art. It may serve as an art department for a client who has no art department, or it may handle any overflow with which its client's own art department cannot cope. Artists are classified by the area of their particular skill: design, illustration, lettering, retouching, mechanical art, etc. An art studio is a group of such artists, usually hired because of overlapping talents. The studio business is highly competitive; a studio can ill afford to refuse an assignment, and a multitalented group precludes the possible need for doing so.

Following is a description of a typical studio organization:

The Owner(s). The studio may be a sole proprietorship, a partnership, or a closed corporation. Persons seldom become owners of an art studio without some degree of ability to solicit and retain business.

The Salesperson. Considered part of management, the salesperson solicits new accounts and services them once they have been acquired. Salespersons are generally hired in the anticipation that they can bring new business with them. They may also service "house accounts"—accounts that have been secured by the owners. A good salesperson should know production and be capable of supervising the execution of artwork.

The Production Manager. Sometimes known as the studio manager, the production manager is in charge of the scheduling, execution, and on-time delivery of all work passing through the studio. The production manager is directly accountable to management or to the salespeople.

The Layout Artist. Often called an "art director" or "designer," layout artists are responsible for the creative effort of the studio. They execute rough layouts, comprehensive (semifinished) layouts, or both and should be well versed in production. They may be provided with one or more assistants. These are probably the most highly paid artists in the studio.

The Illustrator. The illustrator produces drawings and illustrations, from simple black-and-white "spots" to full-color renderings. Most illustrators concen-

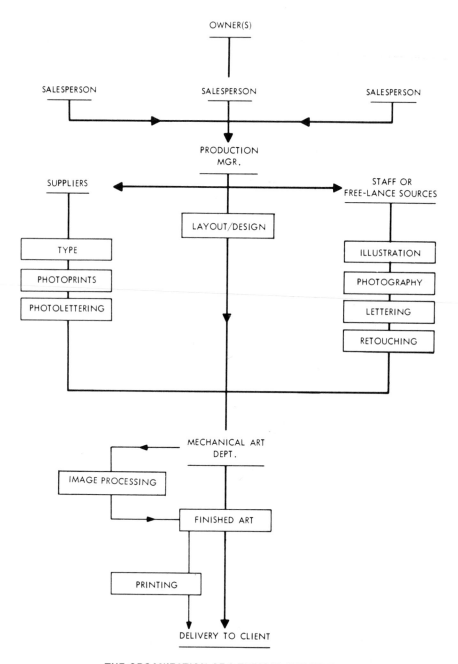

THE ORGANIZATION OF A TYPICAL ART STUDIO

trate their efforts within certain areas, such as story, decorative, fashion, still life, or product illustration. Some will develop expertise in areas of specific interest, developing a technique that becomes a hallmark that causes them to be sought after for specific assignments. If such is their degree of specialization, they will be employed on a freelance basis, unless the studio has considerable work requiring their special talent.

The Photographer. A source of original photography, both in black and white and in color, the photographer will shoot and process pictures, providing the client with finished photography. Some studios have their own photographic facilities, but many photographers prefer to establish their own studios and work for their clients on a freelance basis.

The Retoucher. The retoucher is an artist who specializes in the retouching and clarification of photographs in order to render them more suitable for reproduction. Traditional retouching is done on positive prints with airbrush and chemicals, but more modern techniques include both the retouching and montaging of positive transparencies, as well as electronic enhancement, alteration, and combination of digitally scanned images.

The Lettering Artist. The lettering artist is a person who designs and executes hand lettering. There are two varieties of hand-lettering: finished and comprehensive ("comp"). Finished lettering is rendered exactly as it will appear on the finished work. Comprehensive lettering—less tight—is used on semifinished layouts, and closely approximates the appearance of the finished work. Finished lettering has been almost totally supplanted by photolettering.

The Mechanical Artist. Mechanical art is the assembly of the specialist-produced elements of an ad or design into a unified composition—or "mechanical"—conforming to the layout and properly prepared for a particular process of reproduction. Since the elements are pasted in position on the mechanical, the operation is called paste-up, and the mechanical artist is often known as a "paste-up artist." The mechanical artist is also usually responsible for the execution of any required graphic elements—small spot illustrations, borders, bursts, cartouches, rules, etc.

Careers solely involving the production of paste-up art are being jeopardized by the widespread adoption of image assembly and page make-up systems.

Suppliers of the Studio

Suppliers are outside firms that furnish materials or perform services relating to the production of art or printed matter. They operate as independent businesses because of the specialized nature of their plant equipment. A substantial facet of production is the preparation for, and/or the ordering of, the customized work performed by these suppliers.

The Typesetter. The typesetter sets and arranges type into client-pre-scribed formats. The typesetter furnishes proofs on paper or film, plateready film, or input for image assembly systems.

The Photographic Laboratory. Not to be confused with the photographer, the photo lab duplicates, enlarges, or reduces photographs and produces prints, transparencies, dye-transfers, and a wide variety of other photographic functions.

The Image Processor. Formerly known as the "stat house," this service produces either photostats (a process employing paper negatives) or diffusion transfers (a chemically activated image-transferring system).

The Color Retoucher. Often a firm rather than an individual, color re-touchers alter and/or montage color photographic art—either photographically or electronically—prior to color separation.

The Color Separator. The color separator makes negative or positive film separations—either photographically or electronically—for full-color printing in the various printing processes.

The Printer. The printer produces multiple reproductions of the original art, employing one of several printing processes. Printing plants range from small shops with limited facilities to huge plants with multimillion dollar equipment.

The organization of a typical art studio is shown on page 4.

THE ADVERTISING AGENCY

The purpose of the advertising agency is to plan, prepare, and place (with media) advertising for its clients. The agency is also in business to produce advertising for a profit. The bulk of this profit comes in the form of a commission, paid by advertising media, for the time and space purchased by the agency on behalf of its client. Agency commission is generally 15 percent of the media cost, which, in view of some firms' multimillion dollar advertising budgets, is often considerable. Copy and creative art are provided by the agency as a service, while finished art, typography, plateready film, and special services are billed on a cost-plus-service charge basis. Existing variations abound.

Each department of the agency is organized to perform a specific function:

Account Management. Each account is managed by an *account execu-tive,* who acts as liaison between the agency and the client's advertising manager. Account executives draw upon the talents of the agency's staff and supervise the agency's part in the advertising program.

Creativity. The creative department is divided into two branches: copy and art. The copy department is responsible for writing all material that will be used in the client's advertising; the art department is responsible for the creation

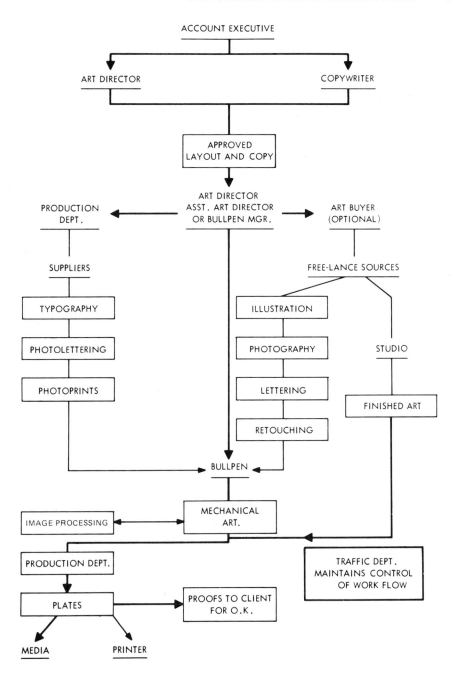

PRODUCTION IN A TYPICAL AGENCY

of the visual material. Such work is designed by the *art director*—a highly paid creative artist. The art director supervises the production of the finished art, which is executed by the agency's mechanical art department or purchased from studios or freelance artists.

Research. The research department provides the statistical information necessary for the planning of advertising. It provides data on subjects such as population and income distribution, buying habits, regional preferences, motivational factors, etc. The department may solicit outside sources in the compilation of market or psychological research.

Media Selection. The media department analyzes the reading, viewing, and listening habits of the potential consumer. It compiles statistics on the coverage, effectiveness, and cost of all the available media. Equipped with this information, the department can make recommendations to the client, selecting the effective placement of the advertising and advising as to the effectiveness, scope, and cost.

Production. The production department specifies and orders the necessary material or service for producing or reproducing the finished art, including whatever material is to be sent to print media for the publication of the advertisement.

Traffic. The traffic department assumes control over the scheduling and flow of work through the various departments of the agency.

Billing. The billing department keeps an accounting of the cost incurred in the preparation of the advertising material, and bills the client accordingly.

Production flow through a typical advertising agency is charted on page 7.

THE ADVERTISING DEPARTMENT

The advertising department is formed by the advertiser to oversee the firm's advertising program. If media is involved, the advertiser must employ an accredited advertising agency, because media will not accept direct placement from an advertiser. The advertiser may choose to produce some of its nonmedia advertising itself, thus the advertising department is faced with the choice of providing itself with a staff capable of satisfying its own requirements, purchasing from external sources, or a combination of both.

If the advertiser uses a considerable volume of art of a specialized nature, it may prove economical to include specialized artists on its staff. This is particularly true if the advertiser produces its own catalog, instructional material, or technical manuals.

Large retail stores employ no advertising agencies but place their advertising directly. Since such stores often advertise on a daily basis, there is no time to send work to an outside art source. Such firms employ their own fully staffed art

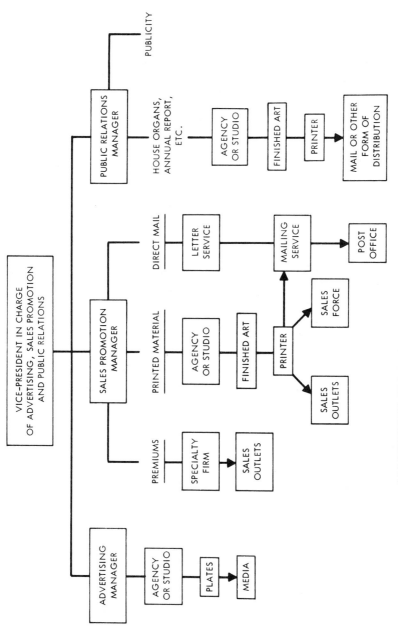

ORGANIZATION OF A TYPICAL ADVERTISING DEPARTMENT

9

departments. A typical advertiser might organize its own advertising department in the manner illustrated on page 9.

The title and function of the person in overall charge of advertising is governed by the size of the company and by the importance it accords its advertising program, but it is this person who is responsible for the advertising policy of the firm. Often a vice-president, this executive may also be in charge of sales promotion and public relations. In this case, the following department heads would report to this person and be responsible for the following areas:

The Advertising Manager.   The advertising manager is responsible for all the firm's consumer and/or retail advertising—advertising aimed at the buying public. An additional responsibility may be for the media advertising of producer goods—goods that will be used in the manufacture of other goods. The media of the advertising manager are principally print, radio, and television.

The Sales Promotion Manager.   The sales promotion manager is responsible for the purchase of all sales-promotional material—material presented to the potential purchaser in order to influence buying. Promotional material may be displayed at the point of purchase, presented by the advertiser's salesperson, or sent directly to the potential purchaser. Sales promotion is an ongoing effort, sometimes but not necessarily connected to a particular advertising campaign.

The Public Relations Manager.   Public relations managers are responsible for all matters pertaining to the image of the firm. Their tool is publicity, and their media are almost any facet of communication that can be called upon to serve their purpose. Among the specific items produced by the public relations department may be the house organ (the firm's external/internal magazine or newspaper) and the annual report.

ADVERTISING MATERIAL PRODUCED BY THE ARTIST

Advertising material may be generally classified in five categories:

1. Material that is presented to the consumer by means of an advertising medium.
2. Material that is presented to the consumer at the point of purchase.
3. Material that is presented to the consumer by mail or by some means of personal distribution.
4. Material that is produced either to instruct salespersons or aid them directly in selling the product.
5. Material that is produced to promote the corporate image.

This material may be produced by the advertising agency and its art department; the advertiser's advertising, sales-promotion, public-relations, or art department; an art studio serving in conjunction with any of them; or with a firm concerned with the production of specialized material. Some of the varieties of advertising material that fall within the province of the advertising artist are as follows:

Consumer Advertising

Consumer advertising is a sales message directed to the general public. Advertising by merchants selling products produced by others is known as *retail advertising*.

Consumer advertising is often developed around a theme or "campaign" presented to the consumer through various media: print, television, radio, transportation advertising, and billboards. The trial offer, the improved formula, and the results of tests are typical themes. The campaign may be based on the product's attributes: utility, economy, safety, durability, or status appeal. It may feature a contest, a giveaway, or a discount coupon. It may use the image of a celebrity or a contrived character to promote or endorse the product.

A firm may produce a group of unrelated items. A firm's product may be a service or represent an intangible commodity such as security, prestige, or reliability. The ethical nature of the product may render a competitive advertising theme inappropriate. Stressing the attributes of the firm or presenting a favorable corporate image is known as *institutional advertising*.

Print advertising is advertising which appears in magazines or newspapers.

Television commercials require complex film, animation, and computer-graphic techniques and are produced by specialized firms.

The radio commercial is verbal and requires no artwork.

The trade advertisement is a sales message directed to organizations or people who are not the ultimate consumer of the product, but who manufacture, distribute, sell, or provide service. With less emphasis on hard sell, these messages are placed in a trade publication, a publication seldom read by the general public.

The directory advertisement is prepared for insertion in a telephone directory, business directory, organizational and club directory, etc.

The transportation advertisement or "car card" is a printed poster that appears in or on buses, subways, and commuter trains. Advertisements that appear on station platforms and in timetables also fall into this category.

The outdoor advertisement or "billboard" takes the form of large paper posters, painted signs, and printed displays.

Sales Promotion

Sales-promotional advertising is advertising presented directly to the consumer in order to influence retail purchasing. Dealer-promotional advertising is directed to dealers, persuading them to stock specific merchandise. The medium employed for sales promotion is usually the printed image, although dimensional signs and displays are sometimes utilized. This material may be displayed at the point of purchase, mailed or distributed to the consumers, or presented by the advertiser's salesperson.

Point-of-purchase advertising is a sales message that appears at the retail level, designed to influence customers who are passing by or who are inside the store. The purpose of this type of advertising is to draw attention to sale items and act as an instigator of impulse buying.

Packaging. Package design involves not only the design of the individual package or container, but also the design of the carton and the shipping carton. *Industrial design* is the design enhancement of the actual product, although very often the two fields overlap. There are firms that specialize in this type of design.

Exhibits and booths. This type of design involves the creation and construction of stationary and traveling exhibits for shows, conventions, and fairs. This type of design is usually conducted by specialized firms.

Specialties, premiums, and free offers. These may take almost any form, and the artist's involvement depends upon the nature of the item, which may encompass anything from the imprinted balloon to the household appliance. The artwork required to produce any accompanying catalog, coupons, or other devices may be considerable.

Specialties are items given to regular customers, not necessarily in return for a specific purchase. *Premiums* are items offered in order to induce purchase of a product. They are generally given in return for proof of purchase. The rebate falls in this category. *Free offers* are items or samples given indiscriminately to the public. No proof of purchase is required.

Direct Response Advertising

Direct response is advertising that requires the consumer to respond directly to the producer in order to acquire the product. Direct mail and television are utilized heavily for this type of advertising.

Direct Advertising

Direct advertising is material presented directly to the potential customer.

Direct mail advertising is advertising sent to the consumer through the mail. *Nonmail direct advertising* is advertising matter presented directly to the consumer in some other manner, typically door-to-door distribution.

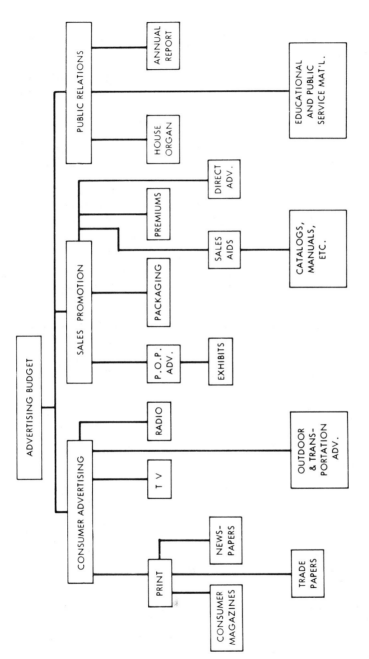

DISTRIBUTION OF ADVERTISING EXPENDITURES

Mail-order selling, now a part of direct response, is advertising specifically designed to elicit orders through the mail, using an attached order blank. *A mail-order house* is a firm that receives orders and delivers goods through the mail. Its sales tool is the catalog.

Any of this material may be modest or ambitious, depending on its particular purpose.

Sales Aids

Sales aids are materials furnished to the firm's sales staff in order to instruct or otherwise facilitate its sales effort.

Sales presentations are generally shown to a group. Designed to visually complement the sales message, they may take the form of charts, handmade or image-generated slides, motion pictures, or videotapes.

Sales manuals are manuals or handbooks used to instruct salespersons, providing sales and technical information about the product.

Technical manuals, also known as *service manuals,* contain technical information concerning the specifications, installation, maintenance, and repair of the product.

The catalog is a listing and description of the firm's products or merchandise offered for sale. There are two types of catalog: consumer and industrial.

The sales kit is a kit of informative material, often containing reprints of the firm's advertising, promotional material, catalog, etc., presented to, and often left with, an individual customer.

Public-Relations Material

Printed public-relations material is used for the promotion of the firm's corporate image, both externally and internally.

Stationery, consisting of letterheads, business cards, billheads, etc., is often designed with a unified theme intended to reflect the function and reputation of the company.

The annual report is the yearly statement of the financial status and progress of a corporation submitted to its stockholders and employees. This often takes the form of an elaborate brochure, the design of which is of great importance to management.

The house organ is a periodical publication designed to promote the interests of the company. There are two types: external and internal. One is to convey information to customers; the other is to do so for the employees.

The educational publication, distributed as a public service, serves to enhance the reputation of the firm.

CHAPTER 2
THE GRAPHIC
IMAGE

The history of printing is the history of production. While the duplication of the printed message remained in the hands of the monastic, there was no need for technical knowledge; the process of graphic communication was governed by individual artistry.

However, with the invention of movable type by Johann Gutenberg around 1450, printing came into the realm of mechanical technology, creating a situation in which the artistic and technical aspects of reproducing the graphic image became dependent upon each other and have remained so ever since.

The great innovation was not the invention of *printing*, but the invention of *movable type*. Early printing, dating from fifth century China, employed relief plates carved from wooden blocks, comprising entire pages of text and illustration, which, after use, were of no further value. Western woodblock relief prints were produced in the early fifteenth century. Movable type, first carved from wooden blocks as individual characters, soon came to be cast with molten metal in an individual mold or matrix. As such, it could be disassembled and stored after printing; retained for further use. Thus, while the invention of movable type brought incredible new flexibility in the printing from text, a process for reproducing illustrative matter—the wood block—was already at hand.

Letterpress (or relief) printing, the process utilizing movable type and wood engravings, remained the principal method of printing books, magazines, and newspapers for over four centuries.

Meanwhile, in 1798, Alois Senefelder, a Bavarian, invented lithography, a printing process based on the incompatibility of grease and water. Since in this process the artist was able to draw directly upon the surface of a flat stone, lithography soon became an artist's medium—the accepted process for printing "pictures."

The use of this process spread throughout Europe. Work was printed in black ink; additional colors were then applied by hand. In 1825 Goya executed his famous "bullfight" lithographs. By 1838, lithographs were being produced in many colors, and commercial work began to appear. This brought the medium into somewhat artistic disrepute, but it soon regained new heights as an art form in the hands of such masters as Manet, Daumier, Toulouse-Lautrec, and Whistler. The first American lithographic plant was established in 1832 at Hartford, Connecticut. Lithographs of the American scene found a ready market; the lithographic efforts of Currier and Ives have become a part of our national folklore.

Up to this time, there was no mechanical means of transferring an artist's work to a printing plate. Letterpress printing required the intervention of the wood engraver, and lithography required that the artist draw directly upon the plate. Both the wood engraver and the lithographic artist were required to draw backwards. A mechanical means for platemaking was needed; so was a more durable plate. Photography provided the answer.

Photography was invented in the early nineteenth century, and the photographic industry, as such, began in the 1870s. The advent of practical photography created two changes in the field of graphic art: (1) the ability to produce a factual image of the subject matter and (2) the ability to produce a printing plate, thereby eliminating the necessity for the artist to work directly on the plate.

To appreciate photography's contribution to printing, one must understand the difference between line and tone. *Line* is any solid stroke or area applied to a surface without tonal variation, such as a pen-stroke or a brush-stroke of undiluted color. *Tone* is diluted color applied to a surface—the dilution caused by the addition of a solvent, such as in oil or watercolor painting, or by lessening pressure, as in a pencil or a chalk (pastel) rendering. *Continuous tone* is the gradual flow of one tone into another, artistically known as "blending."

All three techniques existed in art before the advent of printing. So far, only the line technique had been suitable for reproduction. The raised surface of letterpress printed only solid lines and areas; semi-raised surfaces would not print middle tones, they would print nothing at all. Any tonal values had to be approximated by closely spaced lines or by crosshatching.

Photography is the result of the sensitivity of silver compounds to light. When silver bromide, deposited on a gelatin (film) surface, is exposed to light, it undergoes a chemical change that causes it to become *developable*. The developing process (immersion in a chemical solution) causes the exposed bromide to reduce to metallic silver, forming an image relative to the intensity of the light to which it was exposed. The resultant image—in which the lightest portions of the subject become the blackest areas of the film and the blackest portions of the subject become the lightest, more transparent areas of the film—is called a *negative*.

In order to obtain a *positive* image, with light and dark areas corresponding to those of the original subject, the negative must be printed. This is done by placing it in contact with a piece of sensitized paper and exposing it to light. The sensitized paper reacts to the light in the same manner as the sensitized film, but the light values, having become reversed on the negative, *become reversed again* on the sensitized paper, thus resulting in a *positive* image—one in which the tonal values correspond to the original. Since the middle tones (grays) of the positive constitute a chemical tinting of the emulsion (layer of sensitized coating) and represent a tonal gradation between the solid blacks and the whites, the resultant image is known as a *continuous-tone positive*.

The production of a photograph involved the following steps:

1. Camera exposure of the sensitized negative (film).
2. Development of the negative.
3. Fixation (to prevent further chemical activation).
4. Washing and drying.
5. Printing—exposure of the sensitized positive (paper). The resultant print need not be the same size as the negative, but may be enlarged or reduced (by *projecting* onto the printing paper) to any convenient size. *Contact printing* is placing the negative in direct contact with the paper in order to produce a print of the same size.
6. Development of the positive.
7. Fixation, washing, and drying.

The invention of photography produced yet another continuous-tone medium. At the time, no means for the printing of continuous tone had been perfected. However, when art originally executed in line is photographed, the resultant image on the film negative remains in line. Its light values are the reverse of the original but are either opaque or transparent; there is no tone. Thus, it became feasible to utilize a *line* photographic negative in the production of a *line* printing plate.

Instead of being printed onto photographic paper, the negative is contact-printed onto a printing plate coated with a light-sensitive emulsion, which is hardened by the light that has passed through the transparent areas of the negative. Some printing processes require the use of a film positive rather than a negative, but it is the printing plate of each process that differs, rather than the manner by which the printing image is deposited on the plate. Printing plates for all of the printing processes are now known as *image carriers*.

THE PHOTOGRAPHIC PROCESS

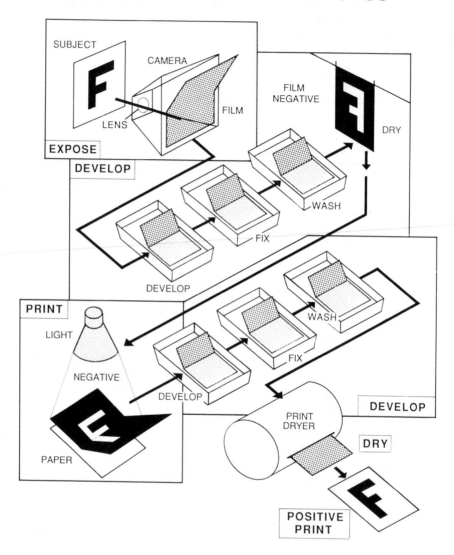

THE HALFTONE PROCESS

The photoplatemaking process posed no problem as a means of producing a metal plate by which any design composed solely of lines could be printed. However, duplication of the middle gray tones (neither white nor black) found in a *continuous-tone* original required the development of other techniques.

The eye, observing minute juxtaposed areas (dots) of black and white, will mix them and perceive them as gray tone—the darkness or lightness depending upon the ratio of black area to white area. Television, in which the image is caused by an electron beam scanning a phosphorescent screen in a pattern of thousands of fluorescent dots, is based on this same principle.

A method was needed that would break up the halftone areas into such a pattern of tiny dots—varying in size according to the value of the tone— and would optically reproduce the tonal effect when inked and printed with a single color.

The halftone screen, which provided the solution to this problem, was developed in the 1880s. It consists of two sheets of clear glass, each having parallel lines etched on one surface and filled in with black composition. The glass sheets are locked together in a frame with their lines at right angles to each other. The screen is placed behind the lens of the camera; each square thus becomes a miniature lens. The light reflected from the subject passes through the squares onto the film, producing a dot formation over the entire image. Each dot represents a minute portion of the image, and their size, shape, and proximity duplicate the tones of the original.

The fidelity (resolution) of the image is dependent upon the fineness of the halftone screen, which is dependent upon the number of ruled lines per inch.

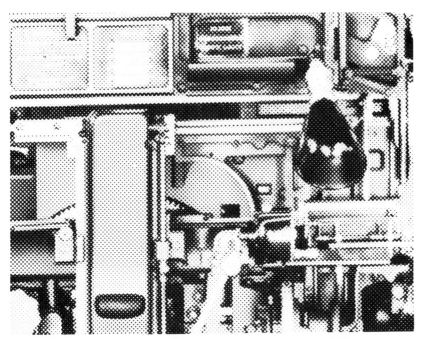

AN ENLARGEMENT OF THE HALFTONE DOT PATTERN

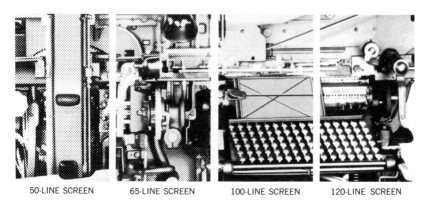

50-LINE SCREEN   65-LINE SCREEN   100-LINE SCREEN   120-LINE SCREEN

FOUR COMMONLY USED HALFTONE SCREENS

(EXAMPLES OF SQUARE HALFTONES)

Screen rulings range from 50 to as high as 600 lines per inch, with screens of 65 to 120 lines being used for normal printing purposes, depending in turn upon the surface of the paper involved.

Elliptical dots are oval-shaped halftone dots which provide a greater value range in the middle tone areas.

The double-dot halftone is a process in which two superimposed halftone images are printed with a single plate, thus producing a greater tonal range than a conventional halftone. One image accentuates the darks and highlights, while the other accentuates the middle tones.

It is often erroneously stated that the *halftone* process is a method of reproducing *halftone* art. Not so—the halftone process is a method of producing *continuous-tone* art.

Newspaper illustrations traditionally have printed 55- to 65-line screens—averaging 3,600 dots per square inch—on coarse, absorbent paper (newsprint). However, with so many newspapers now printing with offset lithography, screens of up to 100 lines are often acceptable. Magazine illustrations, printed on finer stock, are generally produced with 110- to 133-line halftones—containing some 17,000 dots per square inch. Some offset publications are accepting screens as fine as 150 lines per inch; illustrations in quality books are utilizing screens that are even finer.

Use of the glass halftone screen was superseded by the contact screen. This is a *photographic* screen pattern printed on a polyester base, which is placed in vacuum-held contact over the film in the back of the camera. The contact screen has been replaced to some degree by a photocell scanner, which in turn is being replaced with the laser scanner. These devices scan the copy with a beam of light, which then exposes the resulting dot patterns on either film or lithographic plate.

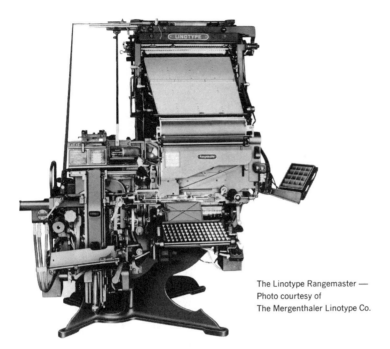

The Linotype Rangemaster —
Photo courtesy of
The Mergenthaler Linotype Co.

A SILHOUETTE HALFTONE

Many feel that halftone platemaking is an automatic, mechanical process where the human element functions to a minimal degree. This is hardly so. By altering the sizes of the dots, the halftone can be reworked to correspond to the full tonal range of the original art. Whether done manually, chemically, or electronically, human artistic discretion becomes the deciding quality factor in the production of the halftone image.

Photo retouching is, for the most part, an artistic attempt on the original photograph to minimize the need for dot alteration. The retoucher emphasizes the darks and highlights of the photograph with airbrush and chemicals. This compensates for the ensuing reduction of each by the halftone process. It is easier to work upon and evaluate a positive photographic print than on transparent film or a halftone plate.

In view of this, it becomes evident that the criterion of a suitable photograph for halftone reproduction is good definition of the middle values. The retoucher may readily affect the darks and the highlights, but it is almost impossible to alter—with any degree of subtlety—the middle values where the textural patterns occur.

THE COMBINATION PLATE

A combination plate is any processed plate that contains *both* line and halftone. Obviously, any plate that combines halftone illustration and text is a combination plate. If no line work touches or intrudes upon the halftone area, no special techniques are required for its production.

Line that appears *within* the halftone area poses a special problem and may take one or more of the following forms:

> *The Surprint*—Line work of the same color, *superimposed* or surprinted on the halftone area, appearing as a solid color on top of the halftone background.

> *The Dropout*—This is line work that has been removed or "dropped out" of the halftone, thus appearing as white (or the paper color) against the halftone background. The tonal value of the background must be light enough to support a surprint or dark enough to support a dropout. If a *different color* is to be surprinted on a halftone, the halftone area directly underneath must first be dropped out. This prevents the dots of the halftone from showing through and altering the surprinted color.

> *The Mortise*—A hole, regular or irregular in shape, which is cut out of the halftone in order to accommodate line work within it.

Suppose the letter "R" is to appear against a halftone background. If the letter is painted—or applied with rub-down lettering—on the original continuous-tone art, and the art is photographed through a halftone screen, the letter as well as the background art will receive the dot pattern, and the edges of the letter will

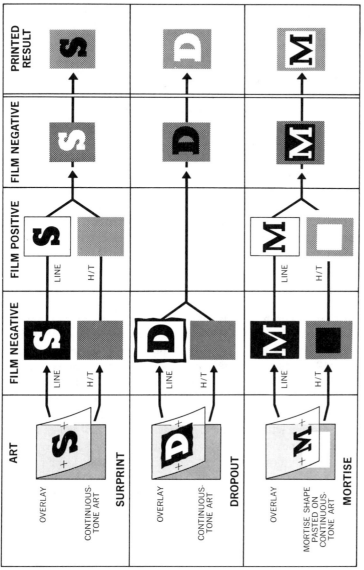

CHART SHOWING THE MANNER IN WHICH ARTWORK IS PREPARED AND FILM IS COMBINED TO PRODUCE A COMBINATION PLATE.

FILM POSITIVE (third column from left): A double exposure (double burn) of the negative directly onto the plate will eliminate the need for making an intervening film positive.

23

appear ragged. Therefore, in order to retain the sharp edges of the letter, each must be photographed separately—the background through a screen as a *halftone*; the letter, without the screen, as *line*. It is the way these two film images are combined that determines the nature of the plate and the printed result.

A dropout is made by using a halftone *film negative* and a line *film positive*, which are sandwiched together in order to expose the plate. Since the line positive duplicates the values of the original, it will appear black against a transparent background and will *block out* the dots on the halftone negative. When exposed to the plate, the values will reverse and the letter will appear on the plate as a nonprinting area against the halftone background. If the line copy is prepared in *reverse*—for example, a negative photostat positioned on an overlay—the resulting film negative will appear to be a positive and will block out the desired dots on the halftone negative (see combination plate chart on page 23).

A surprint is made by using a halftone *film positive* and a line *film positive*, which are sandwiched and reshot as a single film negative. The line positive blocks out the dots on the halftone positive. When both are sandwiched and converted to negative form, the line letter, which was *opaque* on the positive, becomes a *transparent area* on the combined negative. When exposed to the plate, the letter will become a *solid printing area*, and when printed, it will appear to be a solid letter superimposed on the halftone background. This may also be accomplished by *double burning*. This is a double exposure—one from each of the film negatives—and it eliminates the necessity for making film positives.

A mortise is made by dropping the desired shape out of the background and inserting the line copy within it. This may be accomplished in two ways: the mortise shape can be cut out of white paper and pasted in position on the original continuous-tone art. A film negative, shot from this art, will show the shape as a black, *opaque* area. A film *positive* is now made, showing the shape as a transparent area. A film *positive* of the line copy is positioned on the transparent area, and a combination *negative* is made. On the plate, the halftone background and the inserted line work will be a printing area; the mortised shape will not. When the plate is printed, a positive letter will appear inside a white shape which has been dropped out of the halftone background.

It is also possible to produce a *reverse mortise*; any black shape pasted on the art will appear as a transparent area on the film *negative*. A film *positive* of the letter is positioned in the transparent area. Sandwiched together, they are exposed to the plate. The resulting proof will show a black panel bearing a white (dropout) letter superimposed on the halftone background.

The disadvantage of a mortise it that the mortise's shape obliterates more of the background than if the type were printed directly on top of the background.

If the mortise shape is not provided on the art, it can be opaqued ("painted") on the halftone positive, which must then be converted to film negative form.

Combination plates need not necessarily use type as a line element. Drawings that employ line, surprinted or dropped out of a halftone background, are made as combination plates.

CHAPTER 3
LETTERPRESS
PRINTING

Although letterpress printing —which could once be described as "the standard to which all other printing methods aspire"—has declined almost to extinction, a description of it still remains pertinent, because of its place in the history of printing.

Letterpress printing—also known as relief printing—is printing from a raised, backwards-reading surface. In its original form, this raised surface was created by hand-carving away the areas around the printing surface, both for type and illustration alike. In later days, the raised image was deposited on the plate photomechanically.

Definitions

Engraving. A general term for any relief printing plate produced by hand, photo-mechanical, or electronic process.

Photoengraving. An etched relief printing plate produced for the letterpress process by means of photography. The process consists of exposing film negatives to sensitized metal, causing the image to become acid-resistant. The nonprinting areas are then etched with acid to the required relief.

Engraver. An artisan who executes hand-tool work on an engraving.

Etching. Biting an image into a metal plate by either chemical or electrolytic action.

THE WOOD ENGRAVING

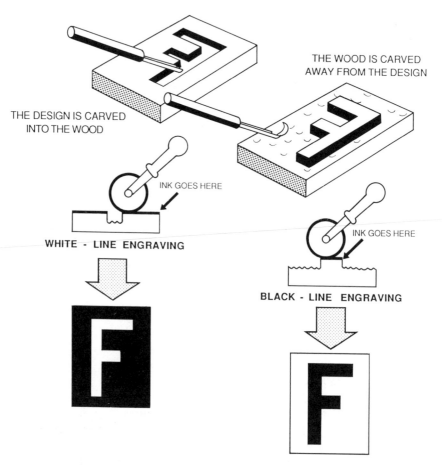

THE WOOD IS CARVED AWAY FROM THE DESIGN

THE DESIGN IS CARVED INTO THE WOOD

INK GOES HERE

WHITE - LINE ENGRAVING

INK GOES HERE

BLACK - LINE ENGRAVING

Line Engraving. The relief printing plate produced by the line etching process. Also known as a line plate or a line cut.

Flat Etching. The first acid application on a halftone plate, when the plate's entire surface is etched to the required printing depth.

Re-etching. The reworking of a flat etched plate in order to lighten desired areas by reducing the size of the dots.

Burnishing. The reworking of an etched plate in order to darken areas by enlarging the size of the dots.

The Line Etching Process

In letterpress, a film negative is made photographically and is contact-printed onto a sensitized metal plate, usually zinc, although plastic plates have

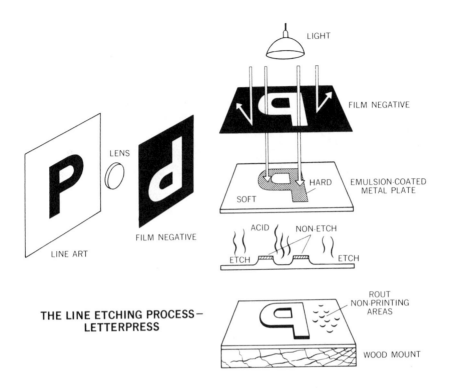

LIGHT

FILM NEGATIVE

LENS

EMULSION-COATED
METAL PLATE

HARD

SOFT

FILM NEGATIVE

LINE ART

ACID   NON-ETCH

ETCH   ETCH

**THE LINE ETCHING PROCESS —
LETTERPRESS**

ROUT
NON-PRINTING
AREAS

WOOD MOUNT

come into use. The image is exposed *backwards*. Since the light values of the negative areas are in reverse, the lines that will ultimately become the printing area are transparent. Light, passing through the transparent areas, strikes the sensitized emulsion, causing it to *harden*. This hardened emulsion forms a protective, acid-resistant covering over the printing area of the plate. When the plate is submitted to an etching process, the acid eats away the nonprinting areas, leaving a relief printing image on the surface of the metal. When inked, the image can be transferred to paper.

The Letterpress Halftone Process

A screened negative is produced, which is then contact-printed onto a sensitized copper plate. The plate is developed, leaving the light-hardened emulsion in place and removing it in the unexposed nonprinting areas. The plate is then submitted to an acid bath. This first etching (the flat etch) produces a flat image, well-defined in the middle values, but often devoid of the contrasting darks and highlights of the original continuous-tone art.

This contrast must be effected by hand by the photoengraver. The satisfactorily etched areas of the plate are coated to prevent further etching. Resubmitting the plate to the acid bath causes the highlight dots to become smaller, thus intensifying the strength of the highlight areas. This function is known as *re-etch-*

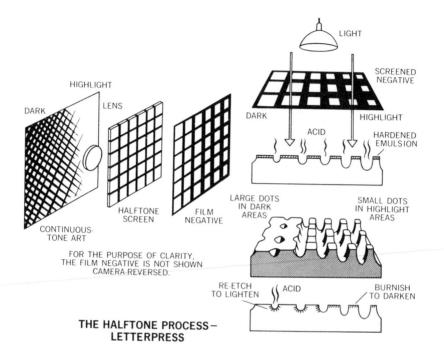

**THE HALFTONE PROCESS—
LETTERPRESS**

ing. Additionally, the photoengraver accentuates the dots in the dark areas by *burnishing* them with a buffing tool, spreading the dots to accentuate the dark areas.

There is a distinct difference between line and halftone etching. In line etching, it is necessary to faithfully reproduce every line on metal; in halftone etching, it is desirable to reproduce the *tonal effect* of the original copy. In order to faithfully duplicate the contrast and brilliance of good copy, considerable handwork is involved.

The metal plate is then routed (a further grinding down of the nonprinting areas), mounted, and proofed.

Electronic Engraving

A continuous-tone image may be converted directly into a letterpress printing plate. The original is "scanned" by scrutinizing the copy with minutely spaced, moving pinpoints of light. Each impulse of light is capable of evaluating the tonal value it perceives, breaking the subject into a dot pattern similar to that of the halftone screen. The perception of each impulse is transformed into electrical energy and transmitted to a diamond stylus, which engraves dot formations into the surface of a plastic printing plate. Not a line process, it is suitable for halftones in newspapers that still print letterpress.

Combination Letterpress Plates

In a letterpress combination plate, the depth of the halftone areas differs physically from the line areas—the line areas being considerably deeper. As a result, combination letterpress plates are expensive, because the plate's areas of line and halftone must be etched separately. At one time, mortise shapes were sawed out of the unmounted letterpress plates. The plate was mounted and type was inserted into the opening. This practice enabled changing of the type without having to change the background.

Duplicate Letterpress Plates

There are many reasons for producing duplicate letterpress plates:

Letterpress printing can be accomplished from a combination of cast type and photoengraved illustrative material, locked together in a press form. Cast type, especially a face that has delicate characteristics, is not durable enough for long press runs. Thus, it is often desirable to make a duplicate plate from the original in order not to subject the type to undue wear, and retain it for further use.

It is impossible to curve the flat printing form to fit the rotary press. Rotary press plates must be produced as a single unit so that they may be curved to fit the press cylinder. Duplicate plates, produced as a single piece, may be curved as desired.

Most letterpress printing—except newspaper work—is accomplished with plates photoengraved from mechanical art. This type of copper engraving is sufficiently durable for a long press run; however, if the ad is running simultaneously in several publications, it may be necessary to send them duplicate plates. Considering all of the necessary finishing procedures, it is too costly to reengrave from the original art. It is more practical to produce one finished engraving and make copies from it.

It may be desirable to have several impressions printing simultaneously (ganged up) in order to produce more copies or to shorten the press run. It may be necessary to preserve original plates to facilitate replacement in case of loss or damage.

The Electrotype

An electrotype—or electro—is a high-quality metal duplicate of a letterpress form of type and photoengraving(s) or of a photoengraved plate made from mechanical art.

The production of an electrotype—a process similar to chrome or silver plating—is based on the principle of electrolytic action: a bar of pure metal, immersed in an acid solution and subjected to an electric current, will decompose and deposit (plate) a metallic coating on the surface of another object suspended

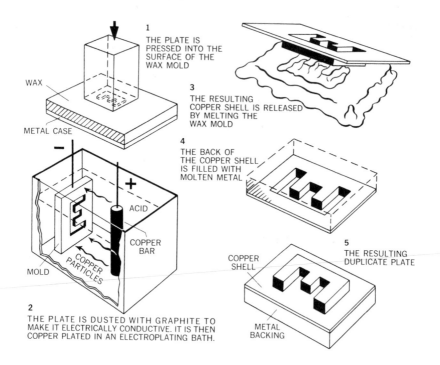

1
THE PLATE IS PRESSED INTO THE SURFACE OF THE WAX MOLD

WAX

METAL CASE

3
THE RESULTING COPPER SHELL IS RELEASED BY MELTING THE WAX MOLD

4
THE BACK OF THE COPPER SHELL IS FILLED WITH MOLTEN METAL

ACID

COPPER BAR

COPPER PARTICLES

MOLD

COPPER SHELL

5
THE RESULTING DUPLICATE PLATE

2
THE PLATE IS DUSTED WITH GRAPHITE TO MAKE IT ELECTRICALLY CONDUCTIVE. IT IS THEN COPPER PLATED IN AN ELECTROPLATING BATH.

METAL BACKING

THE WAX MOLD ELECTROTYPE

in the solution. In this case, the object is a molded impression of the original form or photoengraving. A copper shell is deposited on the mold, which, when removed and strengthened with a base metal, almost duplicates the quality of the original.

The variety of the substances used to produce the mold classifies the type of electro: *Wax-mold electros* are electroplated wax impressions of the original form or plate. *Lead-mold electros* utilize lead rather than wax as a molding material, the lead supplying a more faithful impression. Both molding materials have generally been replaced by plastic. In the event of an extremely long press run, electros may be nickel or chromium plated for greater durability. Flexible electros have been produced for wraparound printing.

The Stereotype

A stereotype (stereo) is a duplicate letterpress plate cast in type metal. The stereo is cast from a *mat* (matrix), a papier-mâché mold impressed from an original form or coarse-screen engraving. Molten metal is poured into the frontwards-reading mat, from which a backwards-reading letterpress plate may be cast and curved to fit the appropriate press.

Once considered an economical method for shipping a lightweight plate matrix to a multitude of newspapers, the stereotype finds little use in modern printing.

Duplicate Plastic Plates

Duplicate letterpress plates may be produced from thin plastic. Less expensive than electros, they do not stretch or shrink and are virtually indestructible.

Rubber Plates

See Chapter 6.

LETTERPRESS PRINTING EQUIPMENT

Traditional letterpress printing requires considerable preparation for the press run. The printing surface must be mounted on the press, and the press must be made ready to give a perfect impression. The cost and effort involved in this is one of the factors involved in the decline of letterpress printing.

Lockup.   Lockup is the positioning and securing of the elements of the composition (type and/or mounted engravings) prior to the printing operation. These elements are wedged into a rectangular iron frame known as a *chase*. The locked-up chase, now known as the *form*, is then positioned on the press.

Makeready.   Makeready is the process of adjusting the form to give a perfect impression. Ideally, all of the elements of the form should be precisely type-high (.918"). Seldom the case, the higher areas of the form will print dark, while the lower ones will print light. Thus, the press must be adjusted to compensate for this tendency. The process is time-consuming. *Pre-makeready* is the process of applying pressure to certain areas of the rear of the printing plate, in order to compensate for its unevenness *before* it is positioned on the press.

Letterpress Printing Presses

Letterpress printing machines range in speed from 1,000 to 25,000 impressions per hour, varying in capacity from postcard-size to 50" × 70" and even larger. Some presses are fed paper in individual sheets, while others are fed by large, continuous rolls of paper known as *webs*. *Perfecting* presses print both sides of the paper almost simultaneously. *Multicolor* presses will print two, three, four, or more colors in a single operation.

There are three types of letterpress equipment: platen, cylinder, and rotary presses.

The Platen Press.   This press utilizes a clamshell motion to bring the paper into contact with the form. As the press opens, inked rollers pass over the form, depositing ink on the raised printing surface. The paper is placed on the platen (the paper-bearing surface) and held in position by gauge pins. The platen and the inked form close together, depositing the inked image on the paper. Used mostly for the printing of cards, letterheads, and business forms, this type of press is readily adaptable for stamping, embossing, die-cutting, and creasing.

The Cylinder (or Flatbed) Press.   The cylinder press prints by means of a cylinder that rolls against the form. The paper passes between the cylinder and the inked form positioned in the flat bed of the press. The bed moves back and forth on its track, and, as the cylinder turns, the form advances with it. Only a small portion of the paper touches the form at one time, since the form is flat and the paper is wrapped around the cylinder. After the impression, the form returns to its original position, where it is re-inked.

There are four types of cylinder presses:

The Drum Cylinder makes one revolution per impression. The paper covers half the circumference of the cylinder. The other half is recessed, allowing the form to pass clear as it returns.

The Two-Revolution Cylinder prints during the first revolution and is lifted clear of the form during the second revolution to allow removal of the printed paper and the return of the form. The cylinder is only half as large as the drum cylinder, but the printing speed is considerably faster.

The Stop-Cylinder is arranged so that the cylinder stops after the impression and remains stationary during the return of the form.

The Perfecting Flatbed Press is a double cylinder press that prints both sides of the paper in a single operation.

Commercially, the flatbed press is obsolete. However, it is still often utilized when relief printing is being conducted as a fine art printmaking process.

The Rotary Press.   A rotary press is built for high-speed work. In the letterpress rotary, the paper passes between two cylinders, one of which holds a *curved* printing plate. In the cylinder press, the form must return to its original position, and the printing operation must be interrupted in order for it to do so. The action of the curved plate is continuous, since by the time the plate cylinder has revolved to the printing position the impression cylinder has fed new paper into place. Thus, the rotary is considerably faster and more efficient than any flatbed press. Rotary presses may be either sheet or web-fed and are inked by rollers that are in continuous contact with the plate cylinder. Letterpress rotaries, employed in magazine and newspaper printing, attained phenomenal speeds but have been almost completely supplanted by web offset presses.

The Cameron (or Belt) Press.   This type of press is a specially designed relief press used for book printing; its output is a finished book. Thin relief plates are secured to a moving flexible belt. Moving at high speed, the belt brings the plates into contact with the ink rollers and then the web. If properly

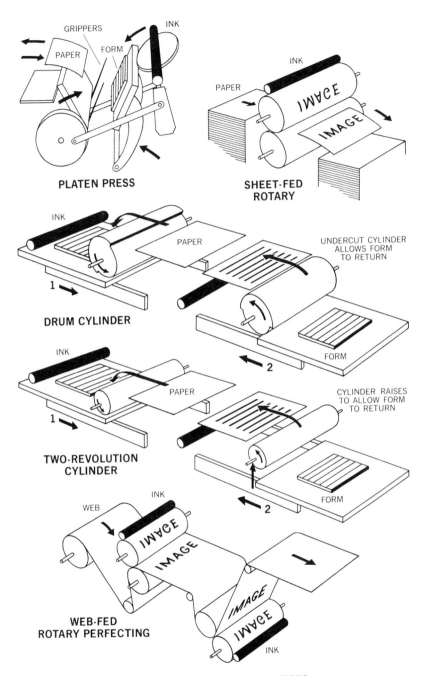

PLATEN PRESS

SHEET-FED ROTARY

DRUM CYLINDER

UNDERCUT CYLINDER ALLOWS FORM TO RETURN

TWO-REVOLUTION CYLINDER

CYLINDER RAISES TO ALLOW FORM TO RETURN

WEB-FED ROTARY PERFECTING

TYPES OF LETTERPRESS PRESSES

imposed on the belt, the paper can be cut, collated, and bound, all while still on the press.

DIRECT LETTERPRESS

Also known as wraparound printing, the direct letterpress process uses three cylinders: the plate cylinder, the impression cylinder, and the inking cylinder. It is difficult to adapt existing letterpresses for the process. The cylinder arrangement is similar to the offset press, suggesting that existing offset presses can be converted to this use, although there seems to be little inclination to do so. The flexible plate is wrapped around the plate cylinder and receives its ink from a cylinder of the same size, which inks the plate in one revolution. This type of inking system provides exceptional ink coverage in solid areas. The ink is distributed to the inking cylinder by means of rollers.

The plate image is backwards-reading and is transferred directly onto the paper, which is brought into contact with the plate by means of the impression cylinder. Wraparound printing has been successfully employed for such items as packages, labels, cartons, greeting cards, and magazine inserts. See also Chapter 6.

A Summary of the Letterpress Process

Letterpress printing is printing from a raised, or relief, surface. The printing surface is backwards-reading.

Letterpress printing can be accomplished from combinations of type and photoengravings (line or halftone), photoengravings of mechanical art, or duplicates produced from either.

Duplicate plates can be produced by a variety of methods. There is a plate suitable for almost any printing operation on a flat surface.

Both original and duplicate plates are expensive, but they can be resurfaced with special metals to withstand extremely long press runs. Their reuse is unlimited.

Letterpress plates can be converted for use in the lithographic process.

Since plates can be fabricated from a variety of substances, from heavy metal to light plastic, mailing and storage are variable factors.

Ease of correction is traditionally mentioned as an advantage of the process. Individual letters, lines of type, or individual engravings can be removed and replaced *if the printing is being done directly from the form.* In practice, however, most letterpress plates (newspaper and bookplates excepted) are photoengraved from mechanical art. A plate or an electro can be patched under certain limited conditions, but it is not universally practical. The correction must generally be made on the mechanical art and stripped into position on the negative, from which a new plate will be made. If the mechanical art is properly checked and proofread, this problem should not occur.

Proofs can be pulled directly from forms or plates. Proper proofing will indicate the quality of the finished product. Proofs can be submitted for approval before the plate is mounted in the press.

Makeready is an expensive, time-consuming process, but it gives the printer tighter control over the presswork.

Due to a number of factors regarding both cost and efficiency, offset lithography has all but supplanted letterpress as a major printing process.

CHAPTER 4
THE LITHOGRAPHIC PROCESS

Lithography has become the most prevalent form of printing. Newspapers, magazines, and books—publications traditionally printed with letterpress—have converted to offset lithography. Ease of platemaking, the ability of lithography to print fine-screen halftones on less expensive paper, the elimination of costly makeready, are all factors that have contributed to this transition. This has been further accelerated by the development of electrostatic and laser-scan offset platemaking.

The origins of lithography antedated photoengraving, stemming from the need for a printing process capable of printing pictures—directly reproducing the work of the artist without requiring the intervention (and often inadequate interpretation) of the commercial letterpress engraver.

Lithography, the planographic method, is a process in which the printing area is flush with the surface of the plate. This process, based upon the incompatibility of grease and water, was invented by Alois Senefelder, a Bavarian, in 1798. *Litho* means "stone," and *graphos* means "write." Lithography is, literally, "drawing on stone."

These steps are employed in making a stone lithograph:

1. The design is drawn, backwards, with *greasy* ink or crayon on a polished slab of fine-grained absorbent limestone. It may also be drawn frontwards on transfer paper, turned over, and transferred onto the stone.

2. The stone is sponged with diluted nitric acid and gum arabic. The acid decomposes the soap in the crayon or ink, releasing the grease. The gum prevents the grease from spreading.

3. The stone is dampened with water and inked. The ink, when applied with a roller, sticks to the greasy printing image but is repelled by the water on the nonprinting areas. This produces a printing surface which is in no higher relief than the thickness of the grease deposited by the crayon.

4. The paper is then laid atop the stone and the inked image is transferred onto it. After redampening and reinking, the stone is ready for another impression.

The use of this process spread throughout Europe. Work was printed in black ink; additional colors were then applied by hand. In 1825, Goya executed his famous "bullfight" lithographs, using blunt crayons and scraping with a knife to achieve the light areas. This and ensuing techniques established lithography as an artist's medium.

By 1838, lithographs were being produced in many colors, and commercial work began to appear. This brought the medium somewhat into artistic disrepute, but it soon regained new heights as an art form in the hands of such masters as Manet, Daumier, Toulouse-Lautrec, and Whistler.

The first American lithographic plant was established in 1832 at Hartford, Connecticut. Lithographs of the American scene soon found a ready market; the lithographic efforts of Currier and Ives have become a part of our national folklore. Early prints were colored by hand. Demand necessitating faster production, the hand-operated flatbed stone press gave way to the steam-powered press (1869) and output reached 600 sheets per hour.

As stones were scarce and expensive, easily damaged, and difficult to store, they began to be replaced by thin zinc sheets. The first rotary litho press (1889) featured such a plate on a cylinder, increasing production to 1,500 sheets per hour.

The development of the offset lithographic press (1904–1905), which transfers or offsets the image onto an intermediate surface before depositing it on the paper, opened up new areas of quality and quantity production for the lithographer.

In modern usage, there are two methods of depositing the design on the printing surface—by hand or photographically. There are two methods of printing—directly from plate to paper and by the offset method. Offset lithography is the most prevalent of all modern methods of printing.

Commercially, stone is no longer practical. Stone plates must be used on a flatbed press and are seldom employed except by individual artists who produce their own prints. Thin sheets of zinc or aluminum are currently used as plates. These metal plates are far less expensive, can be curved to fit rotary presses, and pose no difficulties for the artist who draws on them. In addition, the design can be readily deposited on the surface of a photosensitized metal plate.

Posters and billboards have traditionally employed direct lithography, using hand-drawn plates. However, with the current popularity of photography as an illustrative medium, and the universality of the rotary press, such methods have fallen into general decline and are employed only when the specific nature of the design requires their use.

Definitions

Lithography. The process of printing from a design deposited with greasy crayon or ink on a flat, polished surface. The process is based on the incompatibility of oil and water.

Stone Lithography. Lithographic printing in which a flat, polished slab of limestone is used as the printing surface.

Direct Lithography. Lithographic printing in which the impression is transferred directly onto the paper.

Offset Lithography. Lithographic printing in which the image is transferred to an intermediate or "offset" cylinder before being impressed on the paper.

Litho Stone. The flat slab of polished limestone used in stone lithography.

Litho Transfer. A design drawn or proofed from letterpress type on special paper used to transfer the image onto the stone of the press plate.

Litho Crayon. A greasy crayon made from soap, tallow, or wax, and lampblack; used for direct drawing on the stone or plate. The commercially available black pencil which is sharpened by unwinding a string is a litho crayon or "grease pencil."

Stripping. The assembly, in film negative form, of all the elements that are to appear on the lithographic plate; the act of producing a "flat".

Flat. The completed negative assembly, ready for the platemaking process. The equivalent of the letterpress "form."

Imposition. The assembly of the negatives of individual pages on the flat in proper sequence in the event that several pages are to be printed simultaneously.

Key Line. A thin line, or outline, placed by the artist on the mechanical art to indicate the location of various elements that are to be stripped into position. Usually drawn with red ink.

Dot-Etching. The tonal correction of halftone areas through chemically controlled dot alteration on the film negatives or the film positives.

Graining. The treatment of a lithographic plate with an abrasive in order to render the metal surface capable of water retention. This operation is performed by machine.

Surface Plate. A metal lithographic plate, with a light-sensitized surface coating, on which an image is formed by the action of light rays passing through the film negative.

Albumin Plate. A plate using the most common form of surface coating, made from a water-soluble protein found in egg whites. It is light-sensitized by the addition of ammonium bichromate.

STRIPPING

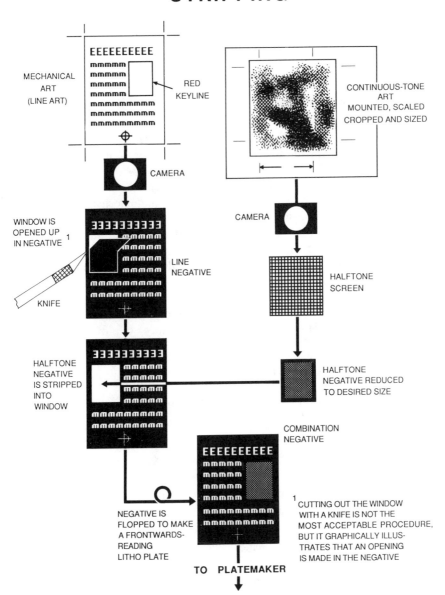

MECHANICAL ART (LINE ART)

RED KEYLINE

CONTINUOUS-TONE ART MOUNTED, SCALED CROPPED AND SIZED

CAMERA

WINDOW IS OPENED UP IN NEGATIVE [1]

CAMERA

LINE NEGATIVE

HALFTONE SCREEN

KNIFE

HALFTONE NEGATIVE IS STRIPPED INTO WINDOW

HALFTONE NEGATIVE REDUCED TO DESIRED SIZE

COMBINATION NEGATIVE

NEGATIVE IS FLOPPED TO MAKE A FRONTWARDS-READING LITHO PLATE

[1] CUTTING OUT THE WINDOW WITH A KNIFE IS NOT THE MOST ACCEPTABLE PROCEDURE, BUT IT GRAPHICALLY ILLUS-TRATES THAT AN OPENING IS MADE IN THE NEGATIVE

TO PLATEMAKER

Deep-Etch Plate. A metal lithographic plate in which the area beneath the printing surface has been *slightly* etched in order to prolong its ink-receptive quality for long press runs.

Developing Ink. A greasy liquid applied to the printing surface of the plate in order to make the image ink-receptive.

OFFSET LITHOGRAPHY

The word "offset" refers to an additional press cylinder known as the *blanket* cylinder, which receives the image from the plate before transferring it to the paper. Of necessity, the offset press is a rotary press. A thin metal (zinc or aluminum) frontwards-reading plate is wrapped around the plate cylinder. The greasy image, which has been deposited on the plate photomechanically, is inked and watered. The inked image is then brought into contact with, and transferred backwards-reading onto, the rubber-blanketed offset cylinder. Paper, fed to the press by the impression cylinder, comes in contact with the blanket and receives a frontwards-reading impression. The softness of the rubber blanket enables the offset cylinder to "lay" an impression on coarse-textured paper without the distortion that would be caused by squashed fibers, should similar paper be used in letterpress. Offset lithography enables fine-screened halftones to be printed on rough or uncoated paper stock, a feature that produces one of the economies inherent in the process.

Offset Lithographic Presses

The principal parts of the offset lithographic press are:

The Plate Cylinder. The cylinder around which the flat metal plate is wrapped.

The Blanket Cylinder. A fabric-based, rubber-surfaced cylinder that receives the image from the plate.

The Impression Cylinder. The cylinder that brings the paper into contact with the blanket cylinder, thus receiving the image.

The Feeder. The mechanism that feeds the paper into the press.

The Receiver or Stacker. The mechanism that removes and stacks the paper after the printing operation.

The Inking Mechanism. Rollers that apply ink to the plate.

The Dampening Mechanism. A device that feeds dampening solution from a storage fountain to soft flannel-like rollers that dampen the plate.

Due to the complexity of the feeding and receiving mechanisms and the presence of several ink and dampening rollers, the offset press seems an incredibly complex apparatus. However, its basic principle—the incompatibility of oil and water—remains the same as in the original stone lithograph.

Offset lithographic presses are described in a manner similar to letterpress presses—in terms of their maximum size capacity. When the press is discussed in terms of "number of colors," it refers to the number of printing units—ranging from one to six colors in capacity. Litho presses are either sheet- or roll (web)-fed. Because of the flexibility possible in the arrangement of printing units, a press can be set up to perform a great variety of printing combinations, either printing one side or perfecting (printing both sides simultaneously). For example, the six-color sheet-fed press—which consists of six individual printing units—can print six colors on one side of the paper or can be arranged as a web-perfecting press, printing four colors on one side and two on the other.

Offset lithographic devices are designed either as presses or as duplicators. A duplicator is designed for convenience, rather than for high-quality reproduction. A smaller machine, the controls and adjusters of a duplicator are not as precise as a press, and there are fewer ink and dampening rollers.

The Sheet-Fed Press. Sheet-fed offset lithographic presses can print from one to six colors in critical register and are the largest-sized of the offset presses. Perfecting presses print both sides of the sheets in one- to four-color combinations.

The Web-Perfecting Press. The web-fed press has the advantage of continuous feed, but critical registration is more difficult to maintain due to possible slippage of the web. There are three types of web-perfecting lithographic presses:

Blanket-to-Blanket. The blanket-to-blanket is the most common variety of web-fed press. A plate cylinder and its blanket cylinder are arranged in pairs. Each blanket cylinder acts as the impression cylinder for its mate. The paper passes between them and is perfected simultaneously. The web travels from the roll stand to the delivery mechanism in a straight line and is kept in lateral and directional control by various tension units.

Drum-Type. The drum-type press (or common impression cylinder) represents an attempt to maintain better web tension control than the blanket-to-blanket. Individual printing units (plate cylinder, blanket cylinder, inking, and dampening systems) are mounted in circular fashion around a large impression cylinder. The tension of the web around the large cylinder resists any tendency for it to follow the blanket cylinder. The web is completely printed on one side, fed through a drying unit and onto a second drum for perfecting.

The Unit-Type. The unit-type press is similar to the blanket-to-blanket, except that the web is perfected in a different unit. It is referred to as an "open" unit, signifying that each individual plate-printing unit can be handled separately and need not be paired, as in a blanket-to-blanket press.

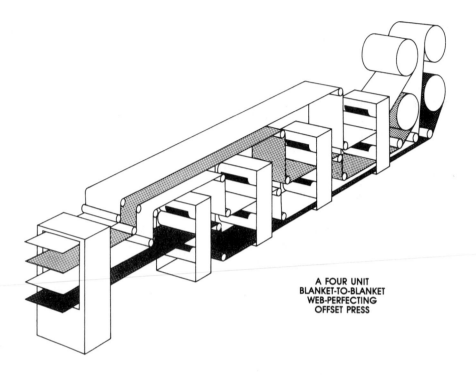

A FOUR UNIT
BLANKET-TO-BLANKET
WEB-PERFECTING
OFFSET PRESS

The Single-Plate Press. The single-plate press is used for high-speed printing of small, standard-sized handbills, throwaways, etc., which are printed on one side.

The Multilith. The multilith is a small, one-color offset press that works on the same principle as the larger ones. It is used primarily for small job printing. The "multi" utilizes presensitized aluminum, plastic, or paper plates. The plates may be made photographically, drawn by hand, or typed in much the same manner as the mimeograph stencil. They are available with basic business forms or letterheads already printed on them in reproducing ink. The machine's inking mechanism cannot handle a large flow of ink, and it takes a highly skilled operator to produce good halftone reproduction.

Letterset (Dry Offset). Letterset is the indirect method, utilizing the blanket roller without recourse to the dampening system. It is an offset, non-lithographic process. It is possible to convert existing offset presses to its use; all that is required is the undercutting of the plate cylinder so that it can accommodate the thin, flexible, shallow-relief plate.

The dry offset press has a triple-cylinder arrangement identical to the conventional offset press. The plate cylinder is undercut to receive the plate, which is inked with a series of rollers. The dampening system is either disconnected or removed entirely, and there is no limitation on the type of ink that can be used.

Driography. Driography is a process similar to lithography, but it utilizes no water. The process employs special aluminum plates coated with a diazo sensitizer (a photochemical used on presensitized litho plates) and silicone rubber. Processing removes the coatings in the image area, leaving the ink-resistant rubber in the non-image area. The ink thus adheres to the image area. Because normal litho ink has a tendency to smear over the printing surface, a special ink with low-spreading characteristics is used. The instability of such ink represents the major disadvantage of the process.

THE PREPARATION
OF THE LITHOGRAPHIC NEGATIVE

In modern usage, the terms "offset," "photo-offset," and "offset litho" appear interchangeably. There is no practical distinction among them, since the photographic process is the key to modern offset lithographic printing.

Offset photography utilizes a thin-base acetate film for normal work and a polyester or a polystyrene-base film for precision work; both use a silver-bromide emulsion. Litho film has an antihalation dye on the back of the film base to prevent halation (light-flare) and curling. The film is also overcoated with a protective anti-stress layer to protect the film from fingerprints and other marks.

In order to produce the offset plate, *all of the material that is to appear on the plate* must be assembled in the form of a photographic (film) negative. This negative is produced either by photographing mechanical art or as the output of an image-assembly system. Although litho platemakers would prefer to have all of the art in position on the mechanical, it is not always possible to do so. Photographs and illustrations, in their original form, may require enlargement or reduction to conform to the layout. Some image-assembly systems may not be capable of accommodating halftones. In this instance, the illustrations are supplied separately; their size and position is indicated on the mechanical by means of *key lines.*

It used to be said, humorously, that "there is no such thing as a type squeezer." There is. A *stretch–squeeze* lens can reduce an image in one direction (horizontally or vertically) while leaving the other dimension unchanged. Type can be stretched or squeezed as much as 8 percent.

An *image-reverser lens* can produce *frontwards-* or *backwards-*reading images at the touch of a switch. This lens can produce frontwards-reading paper halftones (Veloxes) in one step.

The process of negative assembly is known as stripping. The mechanical art is photographed, producing a film negative. The *separate art*—all art that is not pasted in position on the mechanical— is individually photographed to the required size and, in negative form, is stripped (mounted with red cellophane tape) into position on the negative of the mechanical art. This operation produces a *single negative assembly*, which will be used to produce the litho plate. This stripped-up assembly of film sections is called the *flat*.

The flats are assembled on a light-table; various devices are used for accurate alignment. Negatives can be taped together to form a flat, taped to a transparent plastic sheet, or mounted on a *goldenrod* supporting sheet. The goldenrod sheet is an opaque, orange-colored sheet that serves to block the light from the nonprinting areas. Openings are cut in the goldenrod, and the negatives are taped in position. All specks and imperfections are opaqued (obliterated with a reddish opaque paint) at the time of stripping. If several pages are to be printed simultaneously on the same sheet, the negative assemblies are positioned side by side (imposed) in negative form.

The flat is contact-printed (burned) onto the plate. A platemaking machine—often automatic—exposes the plate with a high-intensity light. Depending upon the variety used, plates may be burned with frontwards- or backwards-reading negatives, with the emulsion side up or down. Positives may also be used. Thus, it is important to consult litho-printing publishers' mechanical requirements in order to determine which kind of film is required.

The litho plate is a thin, flexible sheet of metal of insufficient thickness to provide any relief of the printing surface. Because of its minimal thickness, it is extremely inexpensive and therefore expendable. The thinness of the plate and the nonrelief of the printing surface defy any attempts at alteration. Should the plate prove defective or found to contain an error, the plate is discarded. The correction is rephotographed and stripped into the negative. A new plate is then produced.

LITHOGRAPHIC PLATES

The thickness of a lithographic plate ranges from .005" to .012" for small plates and .020" for larger ones. The offset plate must be grained—roughened in order for it to hold the necessary moisture provided by the dampening mechanism—either *chemically*, using an etching acid or an anodizing solution, or *mechanically*, using a graining machine that employs abrasive powder. The words "masters" and "plates" are used interchangeably, but master usually refers to duplicator plates.

There is a variety of lithographic plate materials:

Aluminum
Aluminum laminated on paper
Multimetal (bimetal and trimetal)
Plastic impregnated
Plastic on steel
Acetate
Paper (cellulose base)

There is also a variety of lithographic plates:

Surface Plates. In these, the printing image is deposited on the surface of the plate. *Direct-image plates* are made of paper, plastic, or foil and have no emulsion when purchased. The image may be either typed or drawn; letterpress type can be proofed onto the direct-image plate if a special ink is used. These plates can be coated with wipe-on solutions that will enable them to be imaged from either negative or positive film.

The surface lithographic plate is produced in the following manner:

1. The printing side of the aluminum or zinc plate is "grained" in order to render it capable of retaining moisture.

2. The plate is coated with a light-sensitive emulsion. The coating is done in a centrifugal "whirler," which spreads the emulsion uniformly on the surface. The coating is then dried with warm air.

3. The plate is then placed in a vacuum printing frame, and the negative flat is positioned over the plate. The image is contact-printed frontwards on the plate by exposing it under high-intensity lamps.

4. The exposed plate coating hardens and becomes waterproof. The coating on the nonprinting areas remains water-soluble and is washed off. Automatic processors are extensively used in modern platemaking; there is a processor for each type of litho plate.

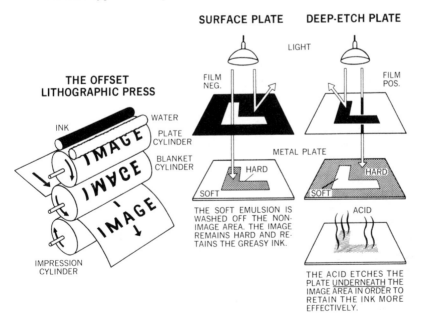

SURFACE PLATE   DEEP-ETCH PLATE

THE OFFSET LITHOGRAPHIC PRESS

LIGHT

FILM NEG.   FILM POS.

INK

WATER

PLATE CYLINDER

BLANKET CYLINDER

METAL PLATE

HARD   HARD

SOFT   SOFT

THE SOFT EMULSION IS WASHED OFF THE NON-IMAGE AREA. THE IMAGE REMAINS HARD AND RETAINS THE GREASY INK.

ACID

IMPRESSION CYLINDER

THE ACID ETCHES THE PLATE UNDERNEATH THE IMAGE AREA IN ORDER TO RETAIN THE INK MORE EFFECTIVELY.

LITHO PLATEMAKING

5. The remaining image is treated and developed. This leaves a greasy, visible, frontwards-reading image on the plate, which is now ready for the press.

6. Offset plates may be saved for reruns; they require little storage space. If the plate is not retained, the film is generally kept on file. Both plates and film are inexpensive to mail. Plates can be salvaged for reuse by grinding off the image and regraining them.

Presensitized plates are already coated when purchased. *Contact plates* are plates burned while in direct contact with the film image. *Negative-working plates*, the most common type of plate, are exposed to a flat consisting of film negatives. *Positive-working plates* are exposed to a flat of film positives or transparencies. The positives are stripped to a plate-sized sheet of acetate, using transparent tape, rather than to goldenrod with opaque tape. Its advantages are that:

1. Film positives from phototypesetters or image-assemblers can be stripped in directly.

2. Film positives are easier to register when stripping.

3. Continuous-tone film positives can be printed onto autoscreen film.

4. Ordinary film negatives will become reverses when stripped in.

5. Art can be drawn on acetate and stripped in.

Projection-printed plates receive their images from an enlarging/reducing device rather than a contact-printer.

Wipe-on plates are emulsion-coated in the shop.

Waterless plates (see page 43).

Diffusion-transfer plates form the image on an intermediate carrier sheet (high-contrast photographic paper) and transfer it onto the printing plate. The intermediate sheet can be exposed in a process camera or a scanner, thus bypassing normal film and stripping procedures (see pages 43–44). Diffusion-transfer plates are most often used on duplicators (see pages 119–21). *Transfer plates*, usually used for newspaper printing, employ an electrostatic process which makes a toner image of the mechanical art and transfers it to a litho plate.

Electrostatic plates are used in fast-copy systems, and their production is based upon the principle of xerography. Corrections can be easily made on the plates by removing the resin powder from unwanted areas. These plates are intended for short, medium-quality runs and are used extensively by the "instant printing" industry.

Laser facsimile plates are produced by the light emissions of a computer-controlled laser, which scans the artwork and in turn processes the printing plate. Since the platemaking laser is controlled by computerized signals, these signals may be transmitted over wire or through space to distant printing installations.

Deep-Etch Plates. The deep-etch plate is used for long runs and color work. The image is held in acid-etched areas *slightly* (.0005") below the grained surface. In this process, the area *underneath* the printing surface is etched in order to prolong the plate's ink-retaining qualities. This requires the use of a *film positive* rather than a film negative, thus exposing the *nonprinting* areas in order to protect them with a light-hardened coating while the printing areas are being etched. The ink is deposited onto these now recessed image areas, which reduces their tendency to wear away during the press run. The production of a deep-etch plate is a complex process, which because of cost, toxicity, and potential for water pollution has fallen into disfavor.

Bimetal Plates. These plates employ two dissimilar metals—one ink-receptive and one water-receptive. They are the most expensive of all litho plates. There are two types: copper plating on stainless steel or aluminum and chrome plating on copper or brass. The former is produced from film negatives, while the latter is produced from film positives, processed much as deep-etch plates are. Their advantage is their potential for high image quality and extremely long (in the millions) press runs. They, too, are coming into disfavor (replaced by photopolymer plates) for the same reasons as deep-etch plates.

Photopolymer Plates. Photopolymer (plastic) can be either positive or negative. They are usually processed automatically and can be heat-treated for extremely long press runs.

Relief Plates. Plates for dry offset and letterset are processed so that the nonprinting areas are removed to a substantial depth. The plate cylinders are undercut to receive the plates, and no dampening is required.

Dot-Etching

As in the photoengraving process, continuous-tone art must be screened in order to be reproducible. The halftone screens used in lithography are the same as those used in letterpress. They vary in fineness in proportion to the quality of the paper to be used. Unlike photoengravers, lithographers cannot go to the plate in order to enhance halftone reproduction. In lithography, the alteration of the dot size must be accomplished on the film.

Dot-etching is a process similar in effect to the reetching process in letterpress; it is utilized to chemically reduce the halftone dot in certain areas in order to provide greater contrast. It relies more on photographic control and less on handwork than does reetching. Attempting to etch directly on litho plates can endanger the image.

Dot-etching is a chemical process that can be very accurately controlled. It is effected on the film positive rather than the film negative. This is in keeping with the deep-etch process where positives are required for platemaking and is especially applicable in color lithography. It is possible to alter dots on halftone negatives, but positive dot sizes match the actual printing values and are thus easier to work with. For surface plates where negatives are required, the negatives are contact-printed from positives that have already been dot-etched. Intensification (enlargement of the dots) has limited usefulness; but it can be chemically effected by staining with light washes of dye or by using a spatter technique with an airbrush.

The practice of dot-etching has been curtailed by the advent of the electronic scanner. With the scanner, dot formations can be altered electronically *before* they are processed onto film, thus eliminating any necessity for working on the film itself. Sophisticated electronic equipment cannot only manipulate value, it is capable of *altering* color completely.

Combination Plates

There is no counterpart of the letterpress combination plate in offset lithography, although the same effect can be readily produced.

In photoengraving, the halftone area is processed in a different manner than the line area. As a result, there is an additional charge for halftone work in terms of the cost of producing the plate, over and above the necessary camera work. The generous use of halftone art can appreciably increase letterpress platemaking costs. In the lithographic plate, there is no difference between the line and halftone areas, since there is no depth of etch to be considered. The area of the plate that is occupied by halftone has no bearing on the cost of the plate. Exclusive of the cost involved in screening and stripping the negatives, a plate entirely covered by halftone costs no more than one with only a small halftone area in one corner.

Additionally, the litho plate can accept copy that *has been previously screened*. A screened proof from a magazine or other printed source can be pasted on the mechanical. The existing dot pattern will be accepted by the litho plate. There will be some percentage of quality loss, but this method is often feasible in instances where the original art is not available.

Surprints, dropouts, and mortises are produced by combining film in the same manner as in the letterpress process. However, once the proper combination has been made, no special attention to the plate is required. The plate will accept anything that is on the film—line, halftone, or a combination of both—without discrimination.

Considerable economies can be effected due to the inexpensive nature of the lithographic plate, particularly in work that requires the combination of line and halftone. However, this saving can be dissipated by the improper preparation of the mechanical art. So long as the platemaker understands what is wanted, it can and will be produced (at an additional charge) even if the art has been improperly prepared.

Production of the desired result in such cases may require the shooting of additional negatives, positives, or both, which would not have been required had the art been prepared properly. As a result, a thorough understanding of the intricacies of combination art is recommended for the artist who becomes involved in the production of art for offset printing.

DUPLICATE LITHOGRAPHIC PLATES

There is no counterpart of the electrotype or the stereotype in offset lithography. Duplicate plates are not made from original plates, but rather from film negatives (or positives). Once the stripping operation has been accomplished, it is a simple matter to produce any number of plates.

The Step-and-Repeat Machine

The step-and-repeat machine is a specially calibrated device equipped to produce multiple-image plates. The film negative (or positive) is placed in the machine. After exposure to the photosensitized plate, the film holder is moved, in perfect alignment, to the next position, and so on, until the desired number of exposures has been made.

LITHOGRAPHIC PROOFS

Since the correction of the negative is the critical factor, proofs of one- or two-color work are made directly from the negative. These proofs are produced by exposing the negative to light-sensitive paper similar to the architect's blueprint. These *blueprints* are characterized by the fact that everything appearing on them, even the background, appears as some value of blue. *Vandykes* are similar prints that are brown instead of blue. *Diazo papers* form a positive image when exposed to a film positive. *Instant image proofs* produce dry proofs without any equipment or chemicals, merely by exposure to ultraviolet light. Though giving no indication of the actual color of the printed piece, these prints still afford the opportunity to check copy, positioning of illustrative matter, and so forth, before the plate is made.

For color work, press proofs are the most desirable, but they require plate-mounting on the press, dampening and inking adjustment—the entire lithographic process—for their production. Therefore, color proofs—processed directly from the negatives or the positives—are often substituted.

3-M Color Key sheets—negative or positive acting—are transparent sheets that are contact-printed from the flats. The sheets are available in a variety of hues that can be used to visualize multicolor printing. When processed in the appropriate hues, they form an accreditable approximation of four-color process when viewed on a light-table.

Cromalin ®, manufactured by DuPont, produces opaque color proofs. Each separation is exposed and developed onto an opaque sheet. Color toners, used to tint the exposed images, are available in a variety of hues, which can be effectively matched to press inks.

LITHOGRAPHIC CONVERSIONS

There is no method in the lithographic process for printing directly from letterpress plates, nor is there any means of incorporating all or part of a letterpress plate into a litho plate. However, it is possible to rephotograph *proofs* of letterpress plates and deposit their image on the surface of a litho plate. This method of adapting letterpress for lithographic printing is known as *conversion.*

The simplest example of conversion is the reproduction ("repro") proof used on the mechanical art. The reproduction proof originally was an impression of cast metal type—the simplest form of letterpress plate. These proofs were pasted in position on the mechanical art and were photographed to become the line negatives used by the litho platemaker. Letterpress proofs pulled on transparent sheets or translucent paper can be used in converting to lithography. Photo and laser typesetting machines produce typography on transparent film, both in positive and negative form, which may be used directly in litho platemaking.

As previously discussed, any halftone proof may be copied with some degree of success by the litho camera. The halftone proof may be pasted on the mechanical art and photographed as if it were a Velox (see page 240). If care is taken and special proofs are pulled for the purpose of litho conversion, good results may be obtained. A typical example of conversion would be the reprinting, in lithography, of an old four-color letterpress advertisement whose plates were still available. Each of the four plates used in the advertisement is proofed in *black ink* on special proofing paper. Each separation proof is then photographed (without further screening) by the litho camera, preparatory to the platemaking process. Reduction of prescreened art is not practical, since a 50 percent reduction of a 110-line screen would produce a 165-line screen—too fine for normal usage. Enlargement can be tolerated, so long as an enlarged dot pattern does not offer an aesthetic problem.

A *Scotchprint* is a translucent proof of a letterpress plate, which may be contact-printed to produce a litho negative. A *Cronapress conversion* produces cameraless conversions by contact-printing translucent film to a letterpress plate, clarifying it, and rendering it negative with dye. *Brightype* is a camera process for converting letterpress plates to litho negatives. Since letterpress has become less popular, the need for conversion techniques has substantially diminished.

METAL LITHOGRAPHY

Offset lithography is especially suited for printing on metal, due to the softness with which the blanket roller lays the image on the unyielding metal surface. The metal sheets are printed flat and dried in special ovens before being formed into the desired product. Metal lithography is waterproof, which makes it suitable for beverage cans, bottle crowns, and screw caps—any container or closure that is subject to moisture due to freezing or refrigeration. Other typical applications are metal toys, decorated trays, metal signs, cans, and large drums.

The metal-decorating press is similar in principle to the offset lithographic press used for printing on paper. The only difference lies in the arrangement of the cylinders, in the mechanisms that feed the metal sheets to the press, and in the drying apparatus. Precision requirements are very high. There is no difference in the plates utilized, other than that they must be produced to withstand extremely long pressruns. The mechanical art and the stripped film flat are prepared in the same manner that would be employed for paper printing.

SCREENLESS OFFSET

It is currently possible, using special continuous-tone lithographic plates, to do screenless printing with a lithographic press. This technique is an outgrowth of collotype printing, also known as the photogelatin process. Its advantage is that there is no moiré pattern and the colors are purer because there are no gray-appearing paper spaces showing between the dots.

When a bichromated (light-sensitized) colloid such as gelatin is exposed to light passing through a film negative, the light hardens the gelatin where it receives much light, and the areas that receive less light remain relatively unaffected. When the exposed plate is placed in water and the sensitizer is washed out, an image composed of hard and soft gelatin is left on the plate. This gelatin image will absorb glycerin and water in the same proportion as the hardening action, determining the amount of ink it will accept. The darker, less glycerin-impregnated areas can accept more ink.

In the collotype process, no halftone screen is required. It is a true screenless printing method.

Screenless printing is an ideal process for the reproduction of fine photographs, paintings, photographic posters, displays, and picture postcards. Screenless reproductions may be enlarged to any practical size. Since there is no screen pattern, the enlargement will still effect continuous tone. In quality booklet printing, it is possible to print the illustrations with photogelatin and then run the sheets through an ordinary offset litho press in order to print the copy.

A Summary of the Lithographic Process

Lithography is printing from a flat surface, in principle based on the incompatibility of oil and water.

The design is deposited on the printing surface either by hand or photographically. Printing may be accomplished directly from plate to paper or by the intervention of an offset or "blanket" roller. The use of the blanket facilitates printing on less expensive paper. Offset lithography is the most prevalent modern method of printing.

Offset lithographic plates are one-piece, inexpensive metal plates that are not easily corrected. These plates are readily curved to fit rotary presses. They are easy to store and inexpensive to mail. Deep-etch plates rival letterpress for long press runs. Bimetal plates excel them.

Copy for offset lithography must be created as either mechanical art or as photographic output from an image-assembly system.

The offset plate is produced either by exposure through photographic film or imaging with a laser, both of which deposit a frontwards-reading image on the plate. If necessary, additional elements of the design, as well as pages, can be stripped together in negative form known as a flat, ready for plate-making. Necessary corrections are stripped in a similar manner. Either prints or transparent color sheets made from the film or proofs pulled from the plates are submitted for client approval.

Due to the level, even nature of the plate, makeready does not pose a serious problem in lithography. In order for the lithographic press to print properly, the dampening mechanism must be adjusted correctly. Too little moisture causes the ink to adhere to the nonprinting areas and streak, while too much moisture will cause the paper to buckle.

Duplicate plates are inexpensive and easy to produce. Multiple images are economically projected onto the plate by the step-and-repeat machine.

Because offset presses are rotary presses, they are faster than flatbed letter-press presses. It takes less time to produce plates, duplicate plates, and multiple images.

Offset lithography will print well-defined halftones on less expensive paper than is required for good letterpress halftones.

It is possible to reprint previously printed line or halftone with the lithographic process. Well-defined halftone proofs can be pasted on mechanical art and copied without recourse to further screening.

Lithography is especially appropriate for large-sized work. It is easily applied to materials other than paper, since the blanket lays down an ink film of uniform thickness.

CHAPTER 5
THE GRAVURE PROCESS

Simultaneously with the development of the wood engraving, another method of printing illustrative matter was becoming popular—the *intaglio* method. Intaglio means "cut in" or "incised." In this form of printing, the ink is held in an incised area *beneath* the surface of the plate. Paper, placed on the plate, draws the ink from the incisions by capillary action.

This method enables the artist to cut the design—either with a tool or with acid—directly into the plate, rather than having to cut away the areas around the line, as in the black-line wood engraving. Although cut into the plate, as in the white-line wood engraving, the ink is held in the incisions rather than on the surface. This produces a black-line positive image.

Since the recessed (intaglio) printing surface is incompatible with the raised printing surface of type, it is not acceptable to the letterpress process. As a result, intaglio printing was reserved for the production of individual prints that were used for decorative purposes or pasted in books on blank pages inserted for their mounting.

The five methods of hand-producing an intaglio printing plate are described in the following sections:

The Etching

Etching originated in the shops of the armorers. It appeared as a printing process in the latter part of the fifteenth century and was practiced by Dürer and others in the sixteenth century. Lines are etched (eaten) with acid into a polished metal plate—usually copper—which has been covered with a protective film called the *etching ground*. Steps in the execution of an etching are:

1. The acid-resisting ground, a wax composition, is rolled onto the plate with a roller.
2. The plate is smoked so that the artist can see the drawing while scraping through to the bare metal. The drawing is done with a sharp etching needle or any other tool capable of cutting through the wax and baring the metal. The image is drawn backwards-reading.

MAKING AN ETCHING

AS A FINE-ART PROCESS

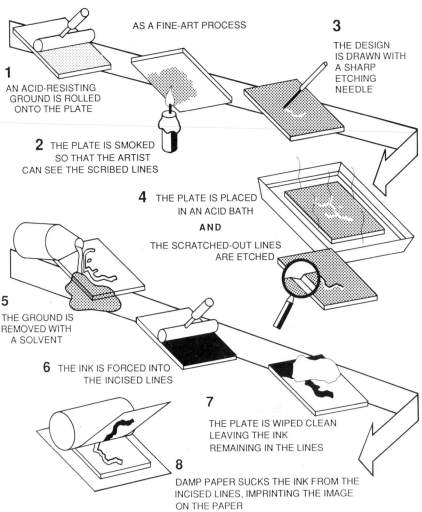

1 AN ACID-RESISTING GROUND IS ROLLED ONTO THE PLATE

2 THE PLATE IS SMOKED SO THAT THE ARTIST CAN SEE THE SCRIBED LINES

3 THE DESIGN IS DRAWN WITH A SHARP ETCHING NEEDLE

4 THE PLATE IS PLACED IN AN ACID BATH

AND

THE SCRATCHED-OUT LINES ARE ETCHED

5 THE GROUND IS REMOVED WITH A SOLVENT

6 THE INK IS FORCED INTO THE INCISED LINES

7 THE PLATE IS WIPED CLEAN LEAVING THE INK REMAINING IN THE LINES

8 DAMP PAPER SUCKS THE INK FROM THE INCISED LINES, IMPRINTING THE IMAGE ON THE PAPER

3. The back of the plate is sealed with wax in order to protect the metal while it is immersed in an acid bath.
4. The plate is placed in an acid bath. The depth of the lines—which will control their darkness—is controlled by the length of time the plate is kept in the acid bath.
5. The ground is removed with a solvent.
6. The ink is forced into the incised lines.
7. The surface of the plate is wiped clean with tarlatan—a stiff, transparent muslin—leaving the ink remaining in the lines. The ball of the palm also may be used.
8. Damp paper is placed on top of the plate and subjected to heavy rolling pressure. The damp paper sucks the ink from the incised lines, resulting in a black line or positive image being imprinted on the paper.

Etching achieved its highest development in the seventeenth-century works of Rembrandt. It declined in the eighteenth century, but was redeveloped in the nineteenth century through the work of Whistler and the Frenchman Meryon. It is currently enjoying considerable popularity as a graphic art medium.

Drypoint Engraving

In drypoint, the lines are scratched, backwards-reading, into the metal plate with a diamond or a pointed piece of steel. The tool is *drawn* across the plate, rather than pushed. The point raises a burr that is not removed. In printing, the burr, which holds ink, imparts a rich, velvety effect to the line. Drypoint is often used to reinforce an etched plate.

The Aquatint

The aquatint is an etching process that combines line and tone. The tone, or tint, is produced by etching through a porous ground of resinous powder sprinkled evenly on the surface of the plate. The acid finds its way through the porous ground, effecting tonal variations in the plate.

The Mezzotint

In executing the mezzotint, the artist works from a dark base to the highlight areas. Using a tool called a "cradle" or a "rocker," the artist roughens the entire surface of the plate. If printed, this burr would produce a uniform black surface. The picture is made by removing the burr with a mezzotint scraper. In the highlight areas, the plate is burnished so that no ink can be retained. The resulting print is characterized by its rich velvety tones rather than by a line effect. The mezzotint process is identified with eighteenth-century England.

Metal or Line Engraving

Metal engraving consists of cutting into a polished plate of copper or steel with a burin or an engraving tool that is *pushed* by the hand. The intent of line engraving is extreme clarity of line; as a result, the burrs are removed with a scraper. No acid is involved. The image is transferred to the paper, under pressure, in the same manner as etching and drypoint. Steel engraving attained a high degree of perfection in the United States during the nineteenth century.

It is important that this type of engraving not be confused with the term "engraving" as it is applied to letterpress photoengraving. Steel engraving finds modern use in the printing of currency, postage stamps, letterheads, business cards, and formal announcements. This is an intaglio process wherein the design is *cut,* backwards-reading, into the plate by hand or by an engraving machine. Photography's part in the operation may be to introduce the design onto the plate in order to serve as a guide for cutting, but there is no acid involved in the process.

Genuine steel engraving, which has come to symbolize the highest quality of printing, is characterized by the slightly raised or embossed effect of the image. It can be readily identified by the indentation (debossing) of the blank image on the reverse side of the paper. This debossing is due to the printing pressure the paper is subjected to, forcing it slightly into the recessed areas of the plate.

The status accorded the steel engraving, with the distinctive quality of its raised letters, has given rise to the less expensive process of *thermography*— sometimes known as "fake engraving." Thermographic printing is accomplished with a relief plate or type, using a dense ink. After printing, the surface is dusted with a low-melting powdered resin. Application of heat causes the resin to fuse and the image to raise above the surface of the paper. Thermography is shiny and less delicate than genuine engraving; it can be readily detected. The image is easily scraped off, and there is no characteristic debossing on the back of the paper.

THE GRAVURE PROCESS

Gravure, the "intaglio" printing method, is a commercial printing process in which the printing area is incised photomechanically beneath the surface of the plate. Gravure is characterized by its soft velvety appearance, by the subtlety of its tonal values, and by the apparent absence of the halftone dot. This is accomplished by the combined use of a fluid ink and a highly absorbent paper. Gravure can be printed on a cheaper grade of paper (newsprint) than is normally used for fine-screen letterpress or lithography.

Definitions

Photogravure. The original gravure process was executed by hand, except for the necessary original photography, and effected without the use of the halftone screen. Too slow for commercial purposes, it is used only to a limited degree in modern times.

Sheet-Fed Gravure. A gravure process in which individual sheets of paper are fed to a rotary press. This process is employed for the printing of high-quality color reproductions, utilizing 150- to 200-line screens. Sheet-fed presses are limited in the number of hourly impressions they can produce and are used for short runs from 10,000 to 100,000. The sheet-fed presses can accommodate a wider variety of printing papers than the faster, web-fed rotary presses.

Rotogravure. A gravure process in which a continuous web of paper is fed to a high-speed rotary press. Rotogravure can turn out four-color pages, printed on both sides, at the rate of 15,000 to 20,000 impressions per hour. This process is used to print newspaper supplements, magazines, and folding boxes.

Conventional Gravure. Both monotone and a few color gravure plants use the conventional gravure process, which employs the 150-line gravure screen. "Conventional" refers to the screen arrangement. Conventional gravure is still rotogravure, because rotary presses are utilized. The screen breaks up the plate into "pits" that do not vary in size—only in depth. Conventional gravure printing produces an effect of continuous tone, characterized by softness, especially in the extremities of the value range. Plates are made from continuous-tone positives and the gravure screen.

The Variable-Area–Variable-Depth Process. In conventional gravure, the darker the tone, the deeper the ink-retaining pit formed by the gravure screen. In the variable-area–variable-depth process, the continuous-tonal effect of conventional gravure is combined with the halftone process. Thus, the pits formed by the variable area/depth process vary in *both* size and depth, permitting more subtle variation of light, shade, and color. In the finished product, the halftone dot is more evident than in conventional gravure, but not nearly as much as in letterpress or lithography. Plates are made from continuous-tone positives, superimposed over halftone positives.

The Direct-Transfer Process. The image dots in this process vary in area, but not in depth. Since this process limits the available tonal range, it is used for printing packages and textiles.

Coloroto. Rotogravure, printed in color.

Pit. The recessed area, below the surface of the plate, that holds the ink in the gravure process.

Film Positive. A transparent image whose values are the reverse of the negative. Though transparent, these values are positive as in the actual image. Any print from a transparent positive—on paper or on metal—results in a negative image.

Carbon Tissue. A light-sensitive, paper-backed gelatin tissue used in the gravure platemaking process.

Four-Color Process. Four-color process is the printing of a full-color image by superimposing the impressions of halftone plates inked in the three physical secondary hues— magenta, yellow, and cyan—plus a black plate. Color printing will be fully discussed in a later chapter, but this basic fact should be understood at this point.

Color Separation. In order to produce the necessary plates for process printing, the original full-color art (or photograph) must be photographically separated into the four basic color components.

Register. A printed image is "in register" when it is in its correct position on the sheet of paper. Color impressions are in register when they are correctly positioned on top of each other in order to produce the desired combined effect. Register is a critical factor in color printing. It is accomplished by the precise alignment of crosshair register marks located in exactly the same position on each plate.

In the gravure process, exclusive of photogravure, the *entire* printing surface is screened. There is no counterpart of the line engraving or the combination plate. A 150-line gravure screen is generally utilized—one in which the *lines* are transparent and the *spaces between them* opaque. The image is transferred to a copper plate, which is etched by acid. The deepest etched areas, or *pits*, correspond to the darkest areas of the original copy and the shallowest areas to the lightest.

The etched plate is mounted on the cylinder of the press. The cylinder is enclosed in the ink fountain, and as it revolves, it receives a spray of fluid ink. A thin steel blade—the *"doctor"* blade—wipes the surface of the cylinder, leaving ink deposited in the pits but not on the surface. A rubber roller feeds the paper against the cylinder, and capillary action transfers the ink to the paper.

Gravure was invented in 1879 by Karl Klic (or Klietsch), a Viennese photographer, in order to provide a satisfactory method for reproducing works of art. He also developed rotogravure, which was introduced in England in 1895. The process was brought to the United States in 1903 and was first used by *The New York Times* in 1914 to print its Sunday supplement section. These early Sunday supplements were printed in a single color—dark brown—and came to be known colloquially as the "brown papers." In 1924, the *Chicago Tribune* was capable of printing four-color rotogravure.

Modern Sunday newspaper supplement sections are printed in four-color rotogravure. Several popular consumer magazines now utilize the process. The effect of a continuous tone—with its minimization of the halftone dot—is a characteristic of the gravure process. As a result, most "fan" magazines use gravure, since pictures of the stars can be printed to closely resemble photographic prints. Food and home decoration magazines often rely on gravure because of the rich, almost photographic, quality it imparts to pictures of culinary creations and room settings. The same is true for catalogs.

Gravure plates are very expensive. One justification for the expense lies in the saving of paper costs that can be made on an extremely long run; consequently, many manufacturers are printing their packages in direct-transfer gravure.

Photogravure

Photogravure, as originally developed by Klic, is a hand process, except for the necessary photography. Its output is a mere 500 sheets *per day*. The following steps are involved in the production of a photogravure print:

1. A thin layer of powdered resin is deposited on a polished copper plate, much as with the aquatint.
2. The art is photographed, and a film positive is made.
3. The positive is printed onto a carbon tissue—a light sensitive, paper-backed gelatin surface. The action of the light hardens the gelatin, rendering insoluble the portions which receive the most light. The darker areas, having received less light, remain water-soluble. After washing, an image formed in varying thicknesses of gelatin remains on the paper-backed surface.
4. The gelatin is squeegeed onto the plate on top of the layer of resin; then the paper backing is soaked off. The plate is etched with acid (perchloride of iron). The acid eats through the thin (dark) areas of gelatin more readily than through the thicker (light) areas. Thus, deeper pits will be etched in the darker areas.
5. *No screen is used.* The etching acid finds its way between the particles of the resinous ground. This breaks the tonal areas into minute irregular shapes, not perfectly aligned as are halftone dots, but nevertheless just as effective.
6. The plate is inked by hand, forcing ink into the depressions. Multicolor photogravure is seldom, if ever, attempted.
7. The surface of the plate is wiped clean by hand.
8. Dampened paper is positioned on the plate, and capillary action draws out the ink. Since the pits in the dark areas are deeper, they contain more ink. The ink in these areas floods onto the paper, obliterating the pattern of the resin particles and producing the effect of smooth continuous-tone. Photogravure is utilized for the fine printing of photographs and works of art.

Rotogravure

Rotogravure is essentially the mechanical version of the photogravure process. The 150-line screen is considered sufficient for most commercial purposes, but finer screens may be utilized for high-quality printing. The plates are curved so that they can be used in the faster rotary press. The press may be sheet- or web-fed. The following steps are employed in the production of positives used to make a rotogravure plate:

1. Film negatives of the artwork are made and developed.
2. The negatives go to the retoucher. These are continuous-tone negatives—they have not been screened. Tonal values are *added* with dye or *reduced* with cyanide. At least 75 percent of the retouching is done on the negatives.
3. Negatives of individual elements of the artwork are stripped together to form a continuous assembly.
4. Continuous-tone positives are made from the negatives. A continuous-tone positive print is also made for the purpose of examination. The positives are returned to the retoucher for the retouching of defects too slight to be observed on the negatives. The positives are used for platemaking, and the positive prints are submitted to the client for approval.

There are three types of gravure plate: *Flat plates* are used on sheet-fed presses for document-type printing. *Wraparound* plates are thin, flexible wraparound plates similar to an offset plate, which are used to print books, brochures and catalogs, art reproductions, and packaging. *Cylinders* are copper-clad cylinders which are actually mounted on the press. These are used for printing newspapers and specialty items.

GRAVURE CYLINDERS

The Diffusion-Etch Process

In order to etch gravure cylinders, the printer must be supplied with continuous-tone positives of the artwork. The positives are used for the production of the cylinders in the following way:

1. The positives are contact-printed onto the light-sensitive carbon tissue. In the conventional gravure process, the 150-line gravure screen has been previously contact-printed onto the carbon tissue. This screen provides the structure of the pit—the lines form the walls and the squares form the pits themselves. The intensity of the color value will be regulated by the depth of the pit.

    The continuous-tone positive is then surprinted, in exact register, onto the screened carbon tissue.
2. After exposure, the carbon tissue is squeegeed onto the copper plate and the paper backing is soaked off. This process is similar to the adhesion of a decal. Where the gelatin of the tissue has been exposed to much light, it has hardened and become water-insoluble. The gelatin under the darker portions has become relatively more soluble since the unhardened gelatin has been washed away with hot water. Adhesion to the plate forms a relief image, in gelatin, which is thickest in the highlights and thinnest in the shadows.

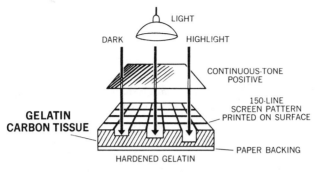

LIGHT

DARK   HIGHLIGHT

CONTINUOUS-TONE
POSITIVE

150-LINE
SCREEN PATTERN
PRINTED ON SURFACE

**GELATIN
CARBON TISSUE**

PAPER BACKING

HARDENED GELATIN

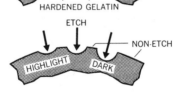

THE CARBON TISSUE
IS SQUEEGEED UPSIDE-DOWN
ONTO THE CYLINDER

PAPER AND SOFT GELATIN
WASHED OFF

COPPER CYLINDER

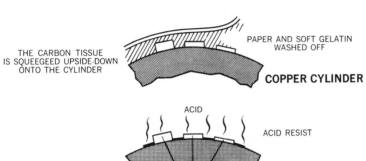

ACID

ACID RESIST

HARDENED GELATIN

ETCH

NON-ETCH

HIGHLIGHT   DARK

THE GRAVURE PLATE

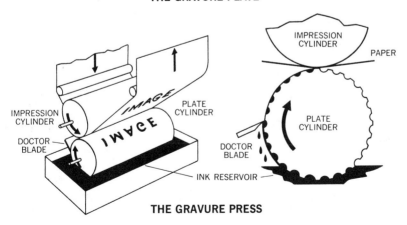

IMPRESSION
CYLINDER

PAPER

IMAGE

PLATE
CYLINDER

IMPRESSION
CYLINDER

IMAGE

PLATE
CYLINDER

DOCTOR
BLADE

DOCTOR
BLADE

INK RESERVOIR

THE GRAVURE PRESS

3. The etcher paints the nonprinting areas of the plate with black asphaltum as further protection against the acid. The acid (perchloride of iron) is then applied. Where the gelatin is thinnest, the etch is deepest. The etch is shallower in the thicker areas. This variation in depth of etch of the pits accounts for the tonal gradations of the printed image.

   The curved plate is now ready for the sheet-fed press. In large newspaper presses, a cylinder accommodating 16 pages may weigh as much as a ton. In such presses the carbon positive is squeegeed onto the copper-surfaced cylinder and etched by pouring acid directly over the surface. After the press run, the cylinder can be stripped and replated by immersion in an electrolytic copper bath. For extremely long runs, the cylinder is chromium-plated. If this plating is worn down during the run, the cylinder may be removed, replated, and the run continued.

4. The plate, mounted on the press cylinder, is sprayed with ink. As the cylinder rotates, the doctor blade wipes the nonprinting surface clean and forces the ink into the pits. The ink, which is very fluid, is held in each pit in a varying quantity depending upon the depth of the pit. The paper is soft and absorbent; its capillary action sucks the ink out of the pits and floods it onto the surface.

This surface flooding obliterates the impression of the individual pit, producing a printed proof that has the appearance of continuous-tone.

The Variable-Area–Variable-Depth Process

A *halftone* screen-positive is made, which is then printed onto the carbon tissue. This produces a variation in *both* the size and the depth of the pits, thus giving more critical control over ink distribution. Since the pits are *smaller*, as well as shallower in the lighter areas, there is less tendency to flood, and the pit (dot) pattern is more evident. This tendency toward lesser flooding allows the production of a more subtle tonal range, which is the characteristic quality of the process.

The Direct-Transfer Process

A light-sensitive coating is applied to the cylinder. A halftone positive is wrapped around the cylinder and exposed directly to it, rather than separately as in diffusion-etch. Development removes the unexposed coating and the cylinder is etched, resulting in a pit structure that varies in area, but not in depth. The process is used for package and textile printing.

The Electromechanical Process

This process is similar to that of an engraving machine. A beam of light scans the copy, computerizes the information, and transmits it to the action of a cutting head. A diamond stylus cuts into the slowly rotating copper gravure cylinder, translating the original image into appropriately sized pits.

The Laser-Cutting Process

A series of pits is chemically etched over the entire surface of the copper cylinder. The pits are filled with plastic, which resmooths the cylinder surface. The copy is light-scanned. The impulses are transmitted to a tiny laser, which removes appropriate parts of the plastic from the pits in order to obtain the desired pit configuration.

Gravure cylinders are chrome-plated for longevity.

Combination Plates

There is no combination plate in the gravure process—all the copy, even the typography, is screened. In gravure, if a letter image were to consist of a single pit for the entire letter, it would contain too much ink, and the resultant flooding would obliterate its original shape. Consequently, the selection of type for the gravure process is a critical factor, since type that is too small or too thin tends to have a fuzzy-edged appearance and becomes difficult to read. This characteristic fuzziness of the type, caused by the screen, is one of the first indications for determining if a piece has been printed by gravure. Some publications print partially in letterpress and partially in gravure in order to overcome this problem.

Duplicate Plates

In gravure, there is no counterpart of the electrotype or the stereotype—one gravure plate cannot be used to produce another gravure plate. If an advertisement must run simultaneously in several gravure publications, a set of master negatives is produced, from which the required number of positives can be made. A preliminary set of plates is prepared so that proofs may be submitted for client approval, as well as for guides to the various publications. A set of carbon-tissue positives is sent to each publication that will print the advertisement. In some cases, the continuous-tone positives may be shipped to the publication.

Conversions

There is no method of converting halftone letterpress and lithographic plates or proofs to gravure, because continuous-tone positives are necessary for gravure platemaking. Also, commercial letterpress and lithography seldom employ the 150-line screen. Proofs, pulled from *line* letterpress or litho plates, can be utilized for gravure art. For example, the mechanical art for a gravure advertisement necessarily contains pasted-up type proofs—which are line letterpress proofs. In practice, it is often less complicated to make individual mechanical art for the gravure advertisement.

Uses for Gravure

Gravure printing is divided into three categories:

1. *Package printing*—cartons, boxes, bags, labels, etc.
2. *Publication printing*—rotogravure is used for newspaper supplements, magazines, catalogs, etc. Sheet-fed gravure is used for fine books and other prestige printing.
3. *Specialty printing*—is used for printing wallpaper, floor covering, textiles, etc. It is an ideal process for printing any type of seamless material.

A Summary of the Gravure Process

Gravure is printing from an incised surface in which the ink is held in pits beneath the surface of the plate.

In the gravure screen, the lines are transparent, and the spaces between the lines are opaque.

In diffusion-etch gravure, which utilizes the gravure screen, the depth of the pits controls the darkness of the tone. In variable-area–variable-depth gravure, the addition of a halftone screen controls both the size *and* the depth of the pits. In direct-transfer, the pits vary in area, but not in depth.

Gravure plates are expensive, but they are extremely durable. The paper (mostly newsprint) used in gravure is comparatively inexpensive. The saving in paper costs in a long press run compensates for the extra cost of the plates. Also, there is very little paper waste in gravure.

The ink is fast drying.

There is no counterpart of the electrotype or the stereotype in gravure.

If additional plates are required, additional carbon tissues or additional continuous-tone positives must be produced.

Once a gravure cylinder is etched, it is impossible to make any but the most minor changes.

Makeready does not pose a serious problem. Gravure is a simple, extremely fast process, with rapid start-up procedures and direct press controls. It is difficult to maintain hairline register in gravure that is printed on high-speed rotary web presses.

Rotogravure is an unexcelled medium for the reproduction of the color photograph, due to the minimization of the dot pattern. It is also an excellent medium for the production of monotone halftone when speed is a requisite—as in the newspaper supplement—or when high-quality reproduction is desired.

Rotogravure is an economical process when an extremely long press run is involved. It is poor economy to use gravure for line reproduction unless a particular publication prints only in gravure. Many publications printing gravure also contain sections printed in letterpress or lithography so that existing one-, two-, or four-color plates can be utilized.

The use of gravure for short press runs is neither practical nor economical.

CHAPTER 6
THE FLEXOGRAPHIC PROCESS

Flexography is a rotary letterpress printing process that utilizes fast-drying inks and flexible rubber printing plates. Developed at the turn of the century, it was originally known as aniline. The process printed on paper with aniline-dye inks dissolved in alcohol. The original process was used for printing paper bags; little was demanded in terms of quality or speed.

Cellophane and later plastic materials rendered the use of traditionally printed oil inks unsuitable. Aniline, now known as flexography, utilizing rubber plates and solvent inks, provided the medium for printing on such surfaces.

Flexography is now designed to print on such substrates[1] as:

Paper	Cardboard
Cellophane	Corrugated board
Plastic	Laminates (polycoated paperboard, etc.)
Foil	

As a result, it is an ideal process for printing:

Flexible paper bags	Decals
Flexible film packaging	Milk cartons

[1]Substance that is being printed on.

Folding cartons	Multiwall bags
Corrugated containers and	Envelopes
displays	Paper cups
Pressure-sensitive tapes	Books—both paperback and hardbound
Tags and labels	

Flexography is now able to print high-quality, 150-line screen, four-color process at commercial speeds, even though in the 1950s it was generally conceded that no rubber plate was capable of printing four-color process.

The future of flexography seems assured; it has been evidencing a rapid growth. As a source of employment it remains promising, because while the possibility of automation exists in so many areas of printing, flexography, because it does not print a standard, predictable product, must necessarily remain an individualized operation.

FLEXOGRAPHIC PLATEMAKING

A relief plate is made from zinc or magnesium in the manner of a letterpress photoengraving (see pages 26–27).

A matrix of thermosetting resin must be formed from the original plate. A sheet of the plastic material is positioned over the plate, preheated, and subjected to pressure. The resulting frontwards-reading matrix is removed, dried, and baked.

The matrix is then covered with a sheet of unvulcanized rubber. Heat and pressure cured (vulcanized) the rubber for about ten minutes. The rubber is then removed, cooled, and trimmed. The resulting backwards-reading relief plate is virtually indestructible.

The plate is then mounted onto the plate cylinder, using double-sided tape. Rubber plates are inexpensive and are easily stored.

The newest platemaking process uses a laser to engrave flexographic rollers and plates, the laser removing the rubber in the nonprinting areas.

FLEXOGRAPHIC PRESSES

There are three types of flexographic presses: stack, common impression, and inline. These are all web-fed rotary presses, having one to six or more print stations (units); the classification refers to the way these stations are arranged.

Each station has three basic parts: an inking unit, a plate cylinder, and an impression cylinder.

Solvent inks—inks that contain highly volatile solvents and dry very rapidly through evaporation and/or absorption—are used in flexographic printing. In the inking unit, a rubber-covered fountain roller picks up ink from the fountain pan

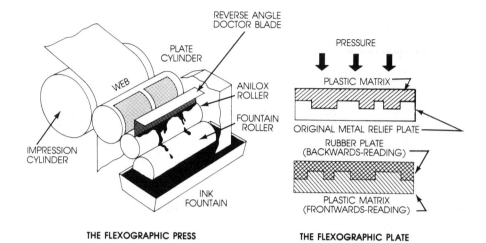

THE FLEXOGRAPHIC PRESS   **THE FLEXOGRAPHIC PLATE**

and transfers it to the form or anilox[2] roller, which in turn transfers it to a rubber plate mounted on the plate cylinder. Unlike offset lithography, this is an *ink* transfer, not an *image* transfer. The impression cylinder (much larger than the plate cylinder) supports the web and brings it into contact with the inked plate.

The difference between flexography and lithography/letterpress/gravure is that, while they print mostly on paper (litho on metal, perhaps), a single flexographic press will be required to print on a wide variety of substances. Therefore, flexographic presses are equipped with their own dryers, as well as sophisticated feeding, tension, and ink-viscosity controls. A reverse-angle doctor blade (acting as a squeegee and opposing the revolution of the anilox roll) is used for the precise metering of ink during speed changes—mainly in process printing.

A continuous web requires repetitive images, the spacing of which may be determined by the closure of the printed object; thus, the plate cylinder often contains multiple plates, imposed laterally, vertically, or both. As a result, the circumference of the plate cylinder is determined by the imposition of the image that is required.

Since the plate cylinder can be removed from the press, plates can be mounted, registered, and proofed in advance, without hindrance to the operation of the press.

Offset Gravure.   Offset gravure is produced by converting a flexographic press. The anilox roller is replaced by an image-bearing gravure cylinder, which is wiped by a doctor blade as in gravure. The plate cylinder of the flexographic press is covered with a solid (imageless) rubber plate that functions as a blanket roller, picking up the image from the plate and transferring it to the substrate. Wraparound plates are being developed for offset gravure.

[2]Chrome-plated engraved steel.

The process is currently used for packaging and for the printing of wood grains used in furniture, wallboard, and so on.

Heat Transfer Printing. In this process, images are first printed on paper and then transferred to the substrate by pressure and heat. The process uses inks that contain special heat-transferable dyes; it was developed specifically for printing on polyester fabric. Heat transfer uses gravure for long runs and flexography for shorter ones. Silk screen and offset lithography may also be utilized under specific circumstances.

A Summary of the Flexographic Process

Flexography is printing from a raised, backwards-reading surface, utilizing a rubber printing plate. No longer a stepchild of letterpress, flexography has come into its own as a major printing process.

The rubber plates must be made from relief plates, molded from an intervening matrix plate. Duplicate plates can be readily molded. Flexographic plates are inexpensive and extremely durable, but correction is time-consuming.

Modern flexography can print quality 150-line screen, four-color process.

Fast-drying inks facilitate the process's use in conjunction with high-speed wrapping and packaging mechanisms. Water-soluble inks that comply with governmental antipollution regulations may be utilized.

Plate cylinders are removable and can be mounted, registered, and proofed off-press, thus keeping makeready costs low.

Flexography is an ideal medium for printing on the wide variety of plastic, laminated, or corrugated materials used for modern packaging.

CHAPTER 7
THE SILK-SCREEN
PROCESS

The silk-screen process differs radically from other printing processes. Letter-press, lithographic, and gravure printing are accomplished with a plate; silk-screen printing is accomplished with a stencil.

The principle of the silk screen is a simple one. Silk, or some other finely woven fabric, is capable of supporting ink unless it is forced through the interstices between the threads. If the nonprinting areas are blocked with some nonporous material, the stretched silk fabric provides a surface through which pigment can be forced onto a printing surface. In this manner, the screen functions as a stencil.

In the conventional stencil, any free-standing, nonprinting area—such as the center of the letter "O"—must be connected to the surrounding nonprinting area in order to secure it in place. These connecting lines are characteristic of stenciled lettering. With the silk-screen stencil, it is not necessary to connect such free-standing areas; the silk fabric holds them in position. Because of this, silk screen is a stencil medium not subject to the artistic limitations of the conventional stencil.

Silk-screen printing is accomplished in the following manner:

1. The silk is stretched on a wooden frame having sufficient depth to serve as a reservoir for the ink. The frame is hinged to a flat surface upon which the material to be printed will be placed.

2. The stencil design is applied to the silk. It may be applied by painting directly on the screen with a liquid capable of blocking the pores of the silk; it may be cut from prepared stencil film and attached to the silk; or it may be produced photographically. The stencil blocks out the nonprinting area; the printing areas are the untouched silk.

3. The silk, stretched across the underside of the frame, forms a shallow receptacle into which the ink (or paint) is poured. Silk-screen frames have permanent blocked-out areas on all sides. It is in one of these areas that the ink stays when the frame is lifted. Normally the ink will not pass through the exposed silk in the printing areas unless it is forced through, but thin inks will run through the silk mesh if allowed to stand.

4. The frame is lowered into contact with the surface to be printed.

5. The ink is forced through the mesh of the silk with a squeegee. This is a rubber blade similar to a windshield wiper or a window-washer's tool. The ink is scraped with the squeegee held at a 45-degree angle. The motion of the squeegee covers the entire length of the frame; a single "pass" is sufficient to transfer the image onto the printing surface. Little pressure is required.

6. The frame is raised, and the printed image is removed and racked for drying.

The silk screen is not to be confused with the halftone screen. Although the pigment is forced through the spaces between the fibers, no dot pattern results. The silk-screen and stencil prints *solid* areas, similar to the line plate.

There is no record of the origin of silk-screen printing. The Egyptians have been credited with having used some form of stencil-printing. The early Japanese developed a cut-paper stencil in which the free-standing areas of the design were held in position with strands of human hair. This can be considered the ancestor of the modern silk-screen stencil, in which finely woven fabric is used to hold the free-standing areas in place.

Woven silk was used in Europe for this purpose during the 1870s. The silk used, known as *bolting cloth* in the sugar refineries, was originally made for the sugar industry. A patent for a silk-screen printing process was granted to an Englishman, Samuel Simon, in 1907, but it was not developed commercially. Full-scale commercial development of the process came about in the United States in the 1920s.

Silk-screen printing is basically a hand operation. Its great advantage as a commercial process lies in the fact that it can be applied on almost any surface. Silk screen can print on paper, metal, or glass, of any thickness. It can print on a flat or a curvilinear surface. Due to its versatility, the process has come into wide use. Since wide use implies volume production, special equipment has been designed to facilitate the printing of specialized applications.

The commercial development of the process has hinged upon the solution of two problems: the sharpness of the stencil image and the drying of the resulting prints.

Early silk-screen printing was characterized by ragged edges, caused by the inadequacy of the materials used to block out the nonprinting areas. In 1929, a knife-cut stencil tissue was developed. This tissue, known as *Profilm*, eliminated the fuzzy quality of the stencil image. A more easily cut version, called *Nufilm*, was developed several years later.

Early silk-screen inks dried too slowly to keep up with the output of the printing equipment. Drying is one of the inherent problems of the process. Printing equipment is compact; most of the available space in the silk-screen shop must be used for drying the prints. If the ink dries too fast, it will clog the pores of the screen and render it useless. It if dries too slowly, the shop will become overrun with drying prints, and production must be halted until there is room for more. Since silk-screen printing has become a large enough industry to warrant the attention of paint and ink manufacturers, formulas have been developed that are capable of being air-dried in minutes or mechanically dried in seconds.

Traditionally, silk-screen stencils are cut by hand. The development of the photographic stencil—in which the stencil material is photographically deposited on the screen—has widened the scope of the process. The photographic screen makes possible the printing of designs—especially type—too small to be cut practicably by hand.

Currently, the silk-screen process is enjoying widespread popularity, especially for the talented amateur who is capitalizing upon the universal popularity of the printed T-shirt by screen-printing non–mass-produced designs on a small scale. At the same time, sophisticated equipment has enhanced the process's ability to print on complex shapes.

Silk-screen printing, practiced as a fine-art medium, is known as *serigraphy*. The word is a combination of *seri*, meaning "silk," and *graph*, meaning "print." The process attracted public attention as an art medium in 1938, when Anthony Velonis organized a group of serigraph artists under the auspices of the New York City WPA. Through the work of such modern artists as Harry Sternberg, Adolph Dehn, and others, serigraphy has attained a high degree of prominence as a medium for the graphic artist and the printmaker.

THE SCREEN

Screen Fabrics.   Traditionally, silk is the fabric of the process. It has great strength and its weave is uniform and durable, enabling it to last for many thousand impressions. The finest grade is imported from Switzerland; less expensive but nevertheless practical fabrics are produced domestically and in Japan. In modern use, silk is not the only fabric employed. Organdy, nylon, dacron, and wire-cloth screens can be used effectively.

Organdy is an inexpensive substitute for silk, but it has neither the durability not the uniformity of weave. It may not remain as tightly stretched on the frame as does silk, especially under damp conditions.

The synthetic fibers nylon and dacron possess excellent tensile strength, but their high polish does not provide as effective an anchor for the stencil as does silk.

Wire thread, particularly stainless steel, can be woven into an extremely fine uniform mesh that will last indefinitely. Such screens are used for the printing of glass, electrical circuits, and many varieties of packaging where a large run is required. Metal screens are not easily stretched on the frame, nor do hand-cut stencils adhere to them as well as to silk.

Stretching the Screen.   The silk, or other fabric, must be stretched drum-tight across the frame. It is tacked to the wooden frame with tacks or staples; the edge of the silk is often faced with cloth tape in order to prevent the tacks from ripping the silk.

The fabric is bound to the edges of the frame in order to prevent leakage of the ink. This is accomplished by lacquering the tacked edges and covering them, when dry, with gummed paper tape. The tape is then coated with lacquer to protect it during the printing and the washing out of a glue stencil.

Several mechanical screen-stretching devices, as well as special frames that require no tacking, are available.

New fabric generally has a surface deposit of wax or some other sizing agent. This is removed after the screen has been stretched by scrubbing the fabric with a pumice-type detergent. The scrubbing roughens the fibers, causing better adhesion of the stencil. Synthetic fabric should be scrubbed with the powdered cleanser, while genuine silk should be degreased with a specifically prepared liquid.

Cleaning the Screen.   In order to prepare the screen for reuse with a new stencil, all the leftover ink and the previous stencil must be removed with an appropriate solvent. The reusability of the screen is governed less by the nature of its fabric than by the thoroughness with which it has been cleaned; proper cleaning will prolong its life.

THE STENCIL

There are five methods of preparing the stencil. The first two are more applicable as art techniques than for commercial printing.

The Blocked-Out Stencil.   In the blocked-out stencil method, the non-printing area of the screen is masked with lacquer, shellac, or glue. After the design has been traced onto the screen, the liquid is applied to the screen with a brush. The liquid is painted around the outline of the design. When dry, the liquid blocks the pores of the screen, preventing the passage of ink. A reverse image may be obtained by coating the design itself with the blocking liquid.

Since the blocking liquid is difficult to manipulate with a brush, particularly when intricate detail is required, this method has little application commercially. After printing, the screen is cleaned with a solvent capable of dissolving the particular blocking liquid.

The Tusche-Glue Stencil.   The tusche-glue method is, like lithography, based upon the incompatibility of oil and water. Tusche is a black, free-flowing, oily liquid, soluble in kerosene or turpentine. The design is painted onto the screen with the tusche. When the tusche sets, the entire screen is covered with a solution of equal parts of glue and water. When the glue dries, it forms a hard covering over the screen, trapping the tusche underneath. The screen is then washed down with kerosene. The kerosene has no effect upon the glue alone, but it loosens the tusche and causes the glue coating over it to wash off. This leaves a hard glue stencil, with openings in the areas that were formerly occupied by the tusche.

The tusche-glue stencil is generally employed by serigraphers, since it allows the use of drybrush and other textural effects. The No. 2 litho pencil can also be used for this purpose. The edges of the printed image are too rough to meet commercial standards, and delicate detail is often difficult to achieve. Sharper image edges may be obtained by sizing the screen with a starch-and-water solution before applying the tusche.

The Hand-Cut Stencil.   The hand-cut stencil is made from a layer of film laminated to the surface of a transparent backing sheet. An advantage of this type of stencil is that the design may be cut while it is laid directly over the artwork; there is no need to trace or transfer the design onto the screen. The backing sheet holds the free-standing areas in position until the stencil can be transferred to the screen.

The stencil is placed over the artwork, and the design is cut on the stencil with a knife. There are several types of swiveling knives, parallel-blade knives, and cutting compasses manufactured to facilitate this operation. Care must be taken that the knife does not cut through the paper backing; only the laminated layer is cut. When the design has been cut, the film in the printing areas is removed, leaving all the nonprinting areas held together with the backing sheet. The stencil is cut in positive form.

When the stencil has been cut and the printing areas peeled away, it is placed, face up, on the underside of the stretched fabric. The upper side of the screen is rubbed with a rag soaked in thinner. The thinner softens the film sufficiently to cause it to adhere to the screen. When the film is properly attached, the backing sheet is peeled off and the screen is ready for printing.

The hand-cut stencil produces an image with a clean, sharp edge. Glue may be used in conjunction with the hand-cut stencil in order to obtain soft edges in desired areas. It is painted directly onto the screen after the stencil has been attached.

A well-cut stencil is good for several thousand impressions. It may be retained for reprinting, or may be cleaned with a solvent in order that the silk may be reused for a new stencil.

The Water-Soluble Hand-Cut Stencil.   A highly transparent water-soluble stencil material is used for hand-cut screens. Instead of a thinner, water is used to adhere the stencil material to the silk.

The Photographic Stencil.   In the photographic stencil method, the stencil is produced with an emulsion that is sensitive to light. There are three methods of producing the photographic stencil: the *indirect* transfer method, the *direct* method, and the *direct/indirect* image method. The transfer method employs a sensitized transfer sheet that must be attached to the screen after it has been exposed. There are two types of transfer film: one type is sensitized by the operator, the other is presensitized by the manufacturer.

The steps for the preparation of a transfer film stencil are as follows:

1. A photographic film positive is made from the original art.
2. The transfer film is sensitized. This process varies with different types of film. It involves coating the film with an applicable light-sensitive solution by immersing it in a tray or applying it with a brush. Presensitized film eliminates this step.
3. The positive is contact-printed onto the sensitized film. A frontwards-reading image is produced on the film emulsion.
4. The film is developed by immersion in hot water. The printing areas, represented by the unhardened gelatin, will wash away. Presensitized transfer films are developed with chemical developing solutions.
5. The transfer film stencil is fastened to the screen. The stencil is underneath the screen, and the excess moisture is blotted up with sheets of newsprint. The blotting process causes the emulsion to adhere to the fibers of the screen.
6. After the adhesion of the stencil, the backing sheet is removed.

In the direct method, a coat of the sensitized emulsion is put directly on the screen. As in the other photochemical processes, the action of light causes the emulsion to harden. It is necessary to harden the nonprinting areas so that they will block the passage of ink through the screen. As a result, a *film positive*, photographed from the original design, is employed for photographic stencils. This positive is contact-printed onto the emulsion.

When the nonprinting areas have been hardened by the light action, the soft emulsion remaining over the printing areas is washed off. This leaves bare screen in the printing areas of the design.

The direct/indirect method combines the techniques of both processes. Unsensitized film material is placed *under* the screen. A two-part emulsion (liquid

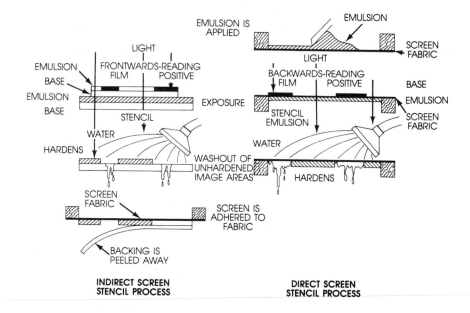

INDIRECT SCREEN STENCIL PROCESS

DIRECT SCREEN STENCIL PROCESS

emulsion and sensitizer) is mixed and becomes light-sensitive. The emulsion is squeegeed onto the screen from the top. When dry, the film sheet is peeled off and regular direct exposure methods are then used. The advantage of this process is the uniform thickness of the emulsion.

Five different kinds of positives can be used to expose indirect or direct photo screens:

1. A frontwards-reading film positive.
2. Diffusion transfer film positives (see page 120).
3. Rub-down type or images on clear acetate.
4. Ink drawings on acetate (preferably treated acetate).
5. Hand-cut Rubylith or Amberlith.

Although the method is free from the artistic limitations of the conventional stencil, designs created specifically for silk screen are best handled in a flat-color poster technique.

Halftones with Silk Screen

Creditable halftones for silk screen may be produced in the following way, providing the halftone screen is coarse enough to be compatible with the material being printed.

As previously mentioned, it is necessary to produce a film positive (in this case, a screened one) in order to make a transfer film stencil.

1. A halftone film negative is made, using a 65-line halftone screen. The negative is then contact-printed to make a film positive.

2. Using any convenient size of halftone screen, the printer makes a reduced negative that will fit an available enlarger. The halftone negative is then enlarged onto high-contrast film to make a desired-size film positive.

3. Using the halftone screen, the printer then makes a same-size halftone negative from the copy. Using a back-lighted camera copyboard, the printer enlarges the negative to produce a desired-size halftone positive on high-contrast film.

4. A 100-line diffusion transfer (see page 120) halftone screen is used to make an *opaque* positive the size of the original art. The positive is camera-enlarged, using either a diffusion transfer (with a transparent sheet) or high-contrast film to make a film negative. A film positive is then contact-printed from it.

PRINTING

The screen frame is hinged to the printing surface—either a flat table or some supporting device designed to hold a three-dimensional object in the proper printing position. The object to be printed will be placed in the printing position by hand. If this object is paper, corner guides are employed to make certain that it will be inserted in proper register with the stencil.

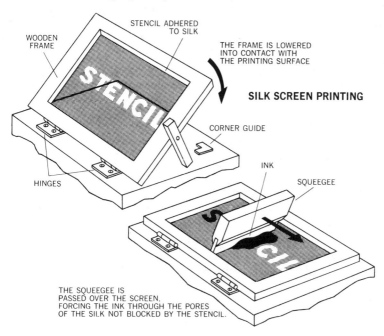

The hinged screen is brought into contact with the paper. The ink or paint is poured into a corner of the tray formed by the frame with the screen on its underside. The ink need not be replenished after each impression, but is used until the supply is almost exhausted.

The paint is scraped across the screen with the rubber squeegee. The squeegee should be wider than the design, so that one "pass" will be sufficient to force the ink through the pores of the screen.

The screen is lifted and the printed piece is removed. Most screen frames are equipped with some device that will hold them up while the next sheet is being inserted.

In multicolor printing there must be a separate screen for each color. There is no limit on the number of screens—thus, the number of colors—that may be printed. Accurate registration, both in the screens and in the positioning of the paper, must be maintained.

As previously mentioned, silk screen may be used to print on almost any surface. It may also use any color, in any of a great variety of inks and paints. Colors may be opaque, transparent, glossy, or matte. Water-base paints, lacquers, enamels, fluorescent paints, plastic colors, and textile colors are all readily used with the silk-screen process. Silk-screen printing produces a heavy layer of ink. This heaviness is responsible for the hand-painted appearance of screen prints. This heaviness contributes to the coarseness of attempted halftone reproduction and poses considerable drying problems, but some of these have been overcome by mechanical printing developments.

Except in the case of small type, or other intricate detail, most stencils are hand-cut. The experienced cutter can cut anything the artist can draw, usually with a higher degree of precision. As a result, it is generally wasted effort to preseparate silk-screen art unless photographic screens are to be used. The stencil cutter will probably cut and register separations with greater accuracy than can be expected of the average mechanical artist.

Automatic Printing Equipment

It is possible to go into the silk-screen printing business with less capital outlay than for any other area of the graphic arts. All one needs are screen frames, a printing surface, and an adequate arrangement for drying the prints—plus, of course, silk, stencil material, and the necessary inks. As a result, many screen shops are small operations, even though the quality of their work may be excellent. One of the advantages of the process is that it may be economically used for extremely short runs. Small shops are ideal for this purpose.

The versatility of the process, with its ability to print on almost any surface, has brought it into widespread use. No longer is silk-screen used solely to print signs and displays. Bottles, glasses, souvenir ash trays, cans, metal drums, and numerous other containers are printed with silk screen. Printed electrical circuits are silk-screened. The metal signs used in the cockpits of aircraft and spacecraft are silk-screened. Decalcomanias, wallpaper, and textiles are printed with the process.

Such popularity has necessitated automated production. Three types of automatic equipment are available for the silk-screen process: (1) The rotary screen, where the stencil is attached to a cylinder which has a fixed squeegee and ink in its center. As the cylinder revolves, the material to be printed is brought together with it at the point where the squeegee is attached. This system makes web printing feasible, permitting high-speed printing. (2) Automatically fed, air-dried presses for printing flat objects. (3) Automatic drying equipment. Larger silk-screen shops are equipped to perform die-cutting. This is usually accomplished with a steel-cutting die mounted in a small platen letterpress. Equipment for applying flock (finely cut cloth fibers) and tinsel may also be employed.

A Summary of the Silk-Screen Process

Silk-screen printing is a stencil medium in which a woven screen is used to hold the elements of the stencil in place. The stencil may be hand-applied to the screen, hand-cut separately and then fastened to the screen, or produced photographically. The printing pigment is forced through the mesh of the screen onto the printing surface.

Silk screen, known as serigraphy, enjoys considerable popularity as a fine art medium.

Screen cutters apply considerable personal skill to their craft. Their judgment and accuracy with regard to color separation and registration is probably more reliable than that of the average artist.

The process can print any number of impressions, in any color, in a wide variety of pigments. It can print on a great variety of three-dimensional objects. However, it is not able to compete with the long runs of letterpress and lithography.

As a line medium, the process is unexcelled. Halftone and process-color work, although possible to some degree, have not attained a quality comparable to that of other printing processes.

Due to the simplicity of the printing equipment, and the fact that once the stencil has been produced there is little preparation of the printing equipment, silk screen is an ideal medium for printing in small quantities.

CHAPTER 8
GRAPHIC
COMPUTERS

In order to make a sensible examination of the sometimes awesome world of computers, one must first organize computers into categories in accordance with the tasks they perform: *Personal computers* store and chart personal records and activities, assist children in their studies, and play games. *Word processors* replace typewriters in the production of correspondence and individual documents. *Data processors* input, store, and retrieve information concerning the conduct of almost every conceivable business or governmental function. *Image processing* systems generate and combine type and graphic images that are to be multiply reproduced. *Digital pre-press* systems process graphic images and separate color in order to produce press-ready printing plates. *Desktop publishing*, a relative newcomer, attempts, by employing sophisticated versions of the personal computer, to emulate the quality of the professional printer. This chapter will concern itself with only the last three.

Additionally, since it contains hardware capable of drawing a graphic image, *computer-aided design* will be discussed, as well as *computer graphics*—images generated for output, for the most part, on film or videotape.

When the first edition of this handbook went to press in 1966, there were traditionally only *four* systems for automated typesetting, each utilizing cast metal type. The manufacturers of these systems were also beginning to manufacture phototypesetters—machines that provided master negative images in order to produce type photographically. Today, in what manufacturers consider five generations later, type is set with a laser. The machines that now do this are called *imagesetters*, rather than typesetters. Obviously, with proper input, they are also capable of processing the graphic image.

Except for the experts, confusion about computers must occur to almost anyone who looks at any publication devoted to them. Many deal with this confusion by ignoring the matter completely, while others attribute demonic characteristics to computerdom as a whole. A worthwhile, well informed graphic designer cannot afford to do either.

Much of the confusion stems from the fact that in this country and abroad, a multitude of firms are producing both computer hardware and software. The desire to be at the forefront of this new technology, especially in the area of desktop publishing, has produced frantic competition, making programs and systems obsolete almost as fast as they can be written about. Computer programs have been designed to perform almost every conceivable function, from personal budget keeping to the training of airline pilots, and the development of pertinent hardware has kept pace.

To allay some of the perplexity, this volume will consider programs and systems for the most part in generic terms, only referring to a corporate or trade name in the case of a product that is widely accepted as a standard for the industry.

Familiar Computer Terminology

The Image Components

Bit. The smallest unit of information that can be accepted by a computer. Stands for *BI*nary digi*T*.

Byte. Eight bits. The amount of memory needed to store one character.

Pixel. A tiny square which becomes a component of the digital image. Stands for picture element—*PIX EL*ement. A bit map is an image that is represented by bits that have been converted to pixels.

Memory. The amount of information that can be stored by a computer. Measured in bytes or megabytes.

K. 1024 units of a computer's storage capacity.

RAM. Random-Access Memory. The chip is accessible to the user in order to store and retrieve information. Also known as *direct access*.

ROM. Read-Only Memory. The memory can supply data, but the user cannot alter it.

The Computer Itself

Hardware. The principal components of a computer system.

Software. Information, stored on disks, which instructs the hardware how to function. This information is known as a *program*.

Disk. A circular piece of plastic upon which information can be magnetically encoded. A *floppy disk* (or soft disk) is a thin, removable plastic disk which is used to insert a program into a system or to store work. A *hard disk* is one that is permanently mounted within a computer. Able to handle much more information than a soft disk, it substantially increases the capability of the computer. The *CD* is a compact computer disk, similar to those used by the entertainment industry. It is possible to store an entire encyclopedia on one. A *disk drive* is a device that rotates the disk during encoding or decoding; a hard disk is driven by an *internal drive*, while a floppy disk is driven by an *external drive*. If a computer has no hard disk, an external drive is required.

Peripherals. Additional devices used to make up a complete computer system.

Cathode Ray Tube (CRT). Also known as a VDT (Visual Display Terminal), it is the screen that displays the images being generated by the computer.

Menu. The list of functions displayed on the computer's screen, delineating those it is capable of performing.

Cursor. A flashing symbol used to select commands for the computer and to locate and define the area of the work in which the computer is to function. The cursor is used to select commands from the menu.

The Image

Raster Image. A raster image is one that is generated and outputted by a line-for-line scan, most often with a laser. This is an image with an extremely high resolution.

Raster Image Processor (RIP). The current demand is for system-output, which includes not only the text, but the illustrations—halftone and line—and other elements such as tints, reverses, rules, etc. The raster image processor is a device which assembles such images in order to output them in raster form. Such a device is mandatory for driving an electronic printer or a laser platemaker.

Vector Image. A vector image is one that is generated by a continuous beam, resulting in a point-to-point image as opposed to the line-for-line raster image.

Resolution. The clarity of the graphic image, as determined by the number of pixels per inch.

Aliasing. The stairstep edges of a computer-generated line or shape caused by the necessarily staggered rows of pixels.

Anti-aliasing. The assignment of middle-value pixels along a staggered edge in order to minimize the stairstep effect.

Image Transmission

Optical Character Recognition (OCR). A device that scans printed characters and digitally converts them for input to a typesetting system.

Facsimile (FAX) Machine. A system by which a page may be electronically scanned and thus transmitted as a visual image over a distance.

Modem. A device whereby electronic impulses (such as digitized typography) may be transmitted over the telephone.

COMPUTERS

There are two basic types of computer: *analog* and *digital*. The type used in the graphic applications described in this chapter is digital.

Analog computers process data in continuous form, thus they can be used to perform such functions as monitoring, recording, and, if necessary, correcting the operation of a piece of machinery.

HOW A COMPUTER OPERATES

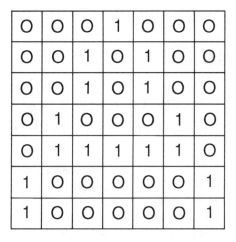

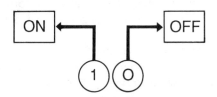

THE COMPUTER IS LITERALLY AN "ON–OFF" SWITCH.
EITHER AN ELECTRICAL CURRENT IS ALLOWED TO FLOW
THROUGH A CIRCUIT, OR IT IS NOT.

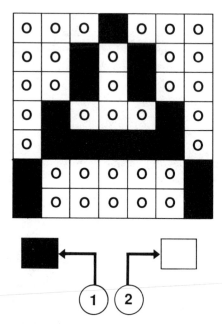

IF THE PIXELS FORM AN IMAGE ... IN THIS CASE THE
LETTER "A" ... THE IMAGE IS BOTH STORED IN THE
COMPUTER'S MEMORY AND DISPLAYED UPON ITS SCREEN.
THE CURRENT THAT IS ALLOWED TO PASS CREATES PIXELS.

Digital computers process data as tiny increments known as *bits*. Information is fed to the computer with a *binary* (two-digit) code represented by either a "1" or a "0." The circuitry of the computer, activated by the coded input, is capable of sending an electric current in either of two directions. Thus, in effect, it is either a bit or it isn't. The bits that have been accepted by the computer are transformed on a *bit map* into *pixels* (square dots), which combine to form either the images viewed on the computer's screen or the images produced by the computer's printing device.

There are three categories of computer systems: the microcomputer, the minicomputer, and the mainframe computer. The *microcomputer* is the personal computer (PC) and is the one used in desktop publishing. It is a single workstation unit. A *minicomputer* is faster and contains a larger memory. Such a system may have several workstations and is used for such functions as typesetting, graphic assembly, and drafting. *Mainframe* computers are the largest and most powerful computers, containing a central processing unit to which the workstations are interfaced. These are the ultrasophisticated systems used to produce color graphics for print or for television.

INPUT DEVICES

Input—any command that is given to the computer—is accomplished at the workstation. Input is accomplished with a variety of devices which function in three ways:

Pointing. The operator uses a device which will point to, and thus identify, the part of the graphic image which is to be acted upon. It may also be used to define the extremities of a line that the computer is to draw, or the location and desired alteration of a geometric shape.

Positioning. The operator uses a device which will move (drag) objects or portions of them to different locations on the computer's screen.

Selection. The input device is used to select and activate a command from the menu offered by the computer.

Input devices function in the following manner:

Keyboards.   Most computers are equipped with a keyboard—an alphanumeric keyboard arranged in Qwerty, which is the customary arrangement. This is used for giving verbal or coded commands to the computer, as well as for introducing words for word processing. Most keyboards can be used to create a number of shortcut commands which will bypass the need to select a command from the menu with a cursor. A *program function keyboard* is a supplementary keyboard which is used to control special functions of the system.

Digitizers.   A digitizer is an input device that electronically transmits to the computer the precise location of any point within a specified area. This area, or tablet—literally an electronic drawing board—is underlaid with a grid of wire lines defining the horizontal and vertical coordinates of the tablet's surface. The resolution of the digitizer is governed by the fineness of the grid, as it is with the halftone screen in printing. Activation of the digitizer above any coordinate transmits its location to the computer. Thus, an image may be drawn with an input of successive coordinates by a digitizer. A drawn image is known as *graphic data*. In order for such information to be stored in a computer, it must be converted to binary form, known as *digital data*. This conversion process is known as *digitizing*.

Cursor. A cursor is a tiny movable symbol that appears on the system's screen to indicate the point being located by the digitizer. A digitizer operates in one of two modes: In the *point mode*, a single pair of coordinates are defined as the digitizing device touches upon it, thus defining one point at a time. The *stream mode* continuously updates the coordinates as it passes over them, thus providing the capacity to draw or trace. There are several types of digitizer-activating devices:

Puck. A puck (also known as a cursor) is a small device with a crosshair locating viewer. When moved over the digitizer tablet, it is capable of locating precise points and transferring them to the computer. As such, it is an ideal device for digitizing graphic data by tracing it.

Stylus. The stylus is an electronic pen which is literally an on-off switch. Touched to the digitizer, it is used for selecting functions of the computer, drawing, and the positioning of objects. A stylus may also be utilized for digitizing the surface coordinates of a three-dimensional object.

Light Pen. The light pen, similar in appearance to the stylus, is used for selecting or positioning objects on the computer's screen. Not to be confused with the stylus, the light pen functions *only* when held to the computer screen.

Mouse. The mouse is a small input device used for selecting and positioning objects. It may be used to generate graphic images, provided the operator is capable of coordinating his or her hand movements with those of the cursor on the screen, but since the mouse is opaque and has no crosshair viewer, it is impossible to locate precise points on the digitizer in order to trace graphic data. Used on any flat surface, but preferably on a rubberized pad, a ball within the mouse rotates in the direction of its movement, activating coor-

ANTI-ALIASING

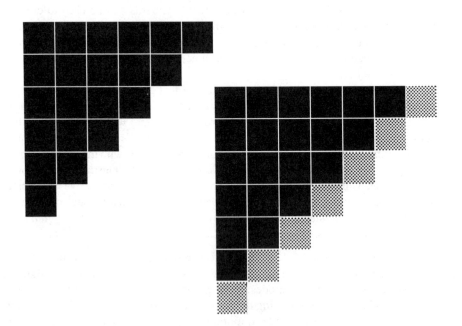

Aliasing is the ragged, so-called "ladder-effect" caused by square pixels in low resolution. Anti-aliasing is an attempt to minimize this by introducing toned pixels at the edges of the solid ones in order to soften them.

dinate-measuring wheels, which convey the mouse's location to the cursor on the screen. The cursor is then used to select the desired function. More sophisticated mice employ optical technology and have no moving parts. As such, they must be operated over a special digitizing pad.

Thumbwheels, Trackballs, and Joysticks. These devices are used primarily as controllers for animated graphics and games. *Thumbwheels*, which are rotated like knobs, move the cursor on either a horizontal or a vertical axis. Manipulated in pairs, they can move the cursor in any direction. A *trackball* functions like an upside-down mouse, in which the ball is rotated with the palm of the hand. Proper coordination can also move the cursor in any direction. A *joystick*, its name derived from the motion of the control stick of a vintage aircraft, is literally a handle, capable of producing movement in any direction. It is generally equipped with a button at the top of the handle, which stops motion when released.

SCANNERS

A scanner is an electronic device which translates an existing drawing or photograph into digital information. Ranging from a simple device that can be attached to a dot-printer to an ultrasophisticated system that can separate color, the scanner introduces graphic images into the computer so that they may be worked upon. Once the graphic image has been stored in the computer's memory, it may be called up and revised in almost any conceivable manner. Line or form may be added or altered; color may be changed; images may be separated, combined, or have portions removed.

Image combination is a particularly efficient function of digital imagery. Traditionally, it has been necessary to either mask or cut out the underlying image (with transparencies) or to laboriously combine photoprints in order to superimpose one image over another. Digitally, this poses no problem, because the pixels of the superimposed image *replace* the pixels of the underlying one. Removal is equally as facile as far as the computer is concerned, but the operator must possess the skill to generate the replacement image to fill the vacated area of the original image.

Since the video camera is also a device which digitizes images, input to a sophisticated computer system need not be restricted to still imagery.

PRINTERS

The Impact Printer

The impact printer is a printer in which a preformed image slug is struck by a hammer, impacting the image through an ink ribbon, thus printing a solid character on the paper. Although they print one character at a time, impact printers, with their characters arranged in a circle as in the daisy wheel, or on an elliptical revolving chain as in the chain printer, are considerably faster than

THE IMPACT PRINTER

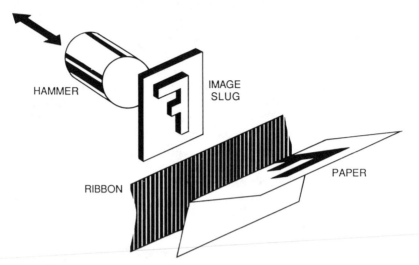

HAMMER

IMAGE SLUG

RIBBON

PAPER

THE DOT-MATRIX PRINTER

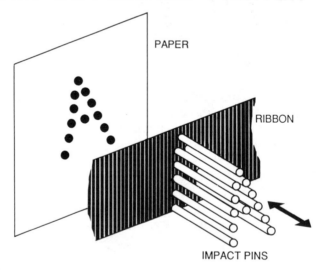

PAPER

RIBBON

IMPACT PINS

typewriters because there is no wait for the rise and fall of a letter key. The output of a chain printer may be as fast as 2,000 lines per minute.

Drum printers print one line at a time. Almost as fast as a chain printer, the drum has a complete column of characters for each position on the line. The characters rotate into proper sequence, and, in this case, the hammer presses the paper against the ribbon and the character image.

Impact printers are used for the high-speed output of data or information.

The Dot-Matrix Printer

Also known as a wire-matrix printer, the dot-matrix printer is one that deposits the image on the paper in the form of dots, rather than with a solid-image slug. The mechanism consists of a set of tiny pins arranged in a rectangular format, which, when electronically activated into patterns, are pressed against the ribbon and thus onto the

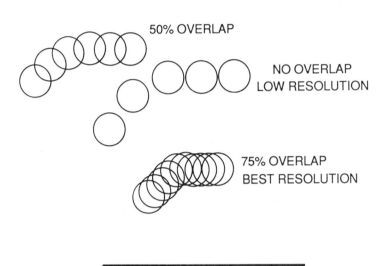

50% OVERLAP

NO OVERLAP
LOW RESOLUTION

75% OVERLAP
BEST RESOLUTION

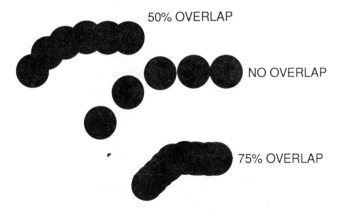

50% OVERLAP

NO OVERLAP

75% OVERLAP

THE OVERLAPPING DOT MATRIX

Overlapping the dot produced by the dot-matrix printer can substantially enhance the resolution of the image. This is accomplished by staggering the rows of pins on the printer head, making multiple passes of the head, or both.

paper. This patterned image allows for the printing of graphic images as well as type characters. The printer produces a low-resolution image, but one that may be enhanced by altering the pin format in order to overlap the dot pattern. These printers are used primarily for imaging the output of personal computers.

The Plotter

The plotter is a computer-activated device which can produce a line drawing on paper or on film. Usually employed for CAD (Computer-Aided Drafting), the

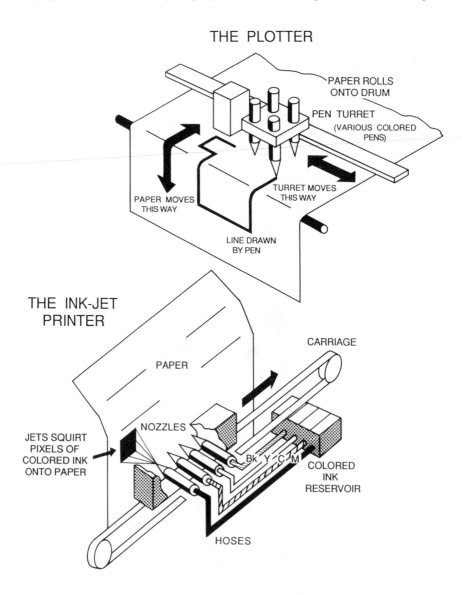

THE PLOTTER

PAPER ROLLS ONTO DRUM

PEN TURRET
(VARIOUS COLORED PENS)

PAPER MOVES THIS WAY

TURRET MOVES THIS WAY

LINE DRAWN BY PEN

THE INK-JET PRINTER

CARRIAGE

PAPER

JETS SQUIRT PIXELS OF COLORED INK ONTO PAPER

NOZZLES

Bk Y C M

COLORED INK RESERVOIR

HOSES

plotter consists of a pen turret which moves from side to side over paper or film which is being moved back and forth by rollers. The combination of the two movements can draw a line in any direction, and since the pens are actual ones, the image consists of a solid line rather than a digitized one. Lettering drawn by the plotter appears as the single-stroke letters of a conventional drafting. There are several colored pens in the turret, making the system capable of drawing several colors of line.

Slower than a printer, the plotter is used for design, drafting, architectural rendering, mapping—almost any application where excellent linear quality is desired.

The Ink-Jet Printer

The ink-jet printer is used for printing images generated by colorgraphic computers. Images are formed by colored pixels, which the eye perceives as full-color as in process printing. Colored ink is stored in a sectioned reservoir, which in turn is fed to four nozzles which move horizontally across the paper, spraying either magenta, cyan, yellow, or black onto the paper a dot at a time. Four-color ink-jet printers are slow.

In the case of a black ink-jet printer used for printing typecharacters, electrically charged ink is sprayed through a computer-controlled grid, which arranges the droplets into letter forms.

The Laser Printer

The laser printer utilizes a laser beam, electrical charges, and powdered toner to deposit an image on paper.

The Apple Macintosh® microcomputer uses PostScript® language to send page descriptions to its LaserWriter®. *PostScript*, a registered trademark of Adobe Systems, Inc., is a page-descriptive language that instructs a laser printer how to reproduce a page containing text and/or graphic images. Without such a language as PostScript, text and graphics would require complicated procedures to output them. PostScript interprets the contents of a page and instructs the laser printer to print exactly what has been created, whether it is an element of a type character, a line drawing, or a halftone.

The laser printer consists of a rotating, negatively charged, light-sensitive drum. A computer-activated laser scans the drum, neutralizing the negative charge in the dots which will form the image, leaving the surrounding (white) areas still negatively charged. The powdered toner is also negatively charged. As such, it will be repelled by the white areas, yet will adhere to the neutralized dots. This is not unlike the oil/water repelling principle of lithography. The paper becomes positively charged as it enters the printer. The toner, now on the drum and negatively charged, is attracted to the paper. The paper then passes between two heated rollers which fuse the dots permanently to the paper.

Laser printers are used for good-resolution desktop publishing and for high-resolution imagery in imagesetting systems.

THE LASER PRINTER

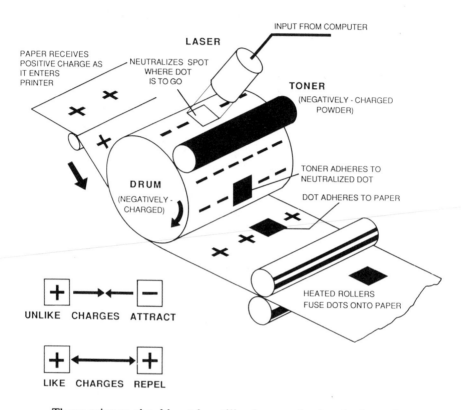

INPUT FROM COMPUTER

LASER

PAPER RECEIVES
POSITIVE CHARGE AS
IT ENTERS
PRINTER

NEUTRALIZES SPOT
WHERE DOT
IS TO GO

TONER
(NEGATIVELY - CHARGED
POWDER)

TONER ADHERES TO
NEUTRALIZED DOT

DRUM
(NEGATIVELY -
CHARGED)

DOT ADHERES TO PAPER

HEATED ROLLERS
FUSE DOTS ONTO PAPER

UNLIKE   CHARGES   ATTRACT

LIKE   CHARGES   REPEL

These printers should not be utilized as production devices; they are too slow. Output from the computer should be to a compatible laser printer or to a Linotronic® 300 imagesetter. Their output should be considered as camera-ready art and submitted to an offset lithographer for plating and printing.

COMPUTER-AIDED DESIGN/DRAFTING (CAD/D)
AND COMPUTER-AIDED MANUFACTURING (CAM)

CAD is an acronym for "Computer-Aided Design," often with an additional "D" added to designate "Drafting" as well. It is the process of utilizing the digital computer to accomplish design or drafting. CAD finds widespread use in design for mechanical technology, architecture, aerospace, civil engineering, electronics, as well as any attendant mechanical drafting required by them. Variations of CAD systems are applied to a wide variety of cartographic (map-making) functions.

WIRE-FRAME MODELS

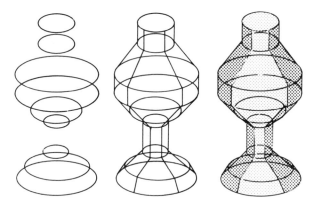

A SURFACE MODEL MAY BE CREATED BY CONNECTING SURFACE ELEMENTS WITH LINE SEGMENTS. THE MODEL MAY THEN BE GIVEN FORM BY ASSIGNING VALUE OR TEXTURAL PATTERNS TO THE SURFACE SEGMENTS.

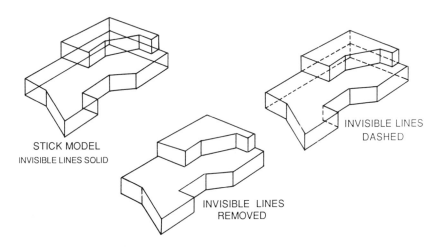

STICK MODEL
INVISIBLE LINES SOLID

INVISIBLE LINES DASHED

INVISIBLE LINES REMOVED

METHODS OF
WIRE-FRAME REPRESENTATION

Functional capabilities of the CAD system include:

Geometric Modeling. The designer constructs a geometric model on the CAD terminal, either as a wire-frame model (shapes representing cross-sections of the object drawn to look dimensional by adding interconnected line segments) or as a solid model (models built up from blocks of basic solid shapes known as primitives). These visual representations are then stored by

SOLID MODELLING

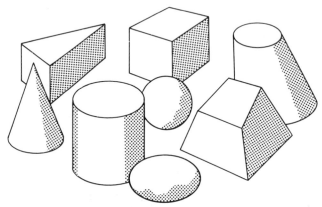

TYPICAL MENU OF THREE-DIMENSIONAL SHAPES WHICH CAN
BE COMBINED TO FORM SOLID MODELS
(PRIMITIVES)

the computer as digitized information, which may be recalled at any time to the workstation for further refinement.

Analysis. Once the object has been modeled, most CAD systems are capable of analyzing its physical properties and its structural characteristics. Such output data, which may be substantial, may often be translated into graphic form in order to facilitate its evaluation.

Kinematics. Kinematics[1] is a science that deals with the aspects of motion. The kinematic equations which define motion are often incredibly complicated; the use of articulated cardboard models or traditional graphic methods for such calculation is tedious. Capable of animating the intended motion of the design, the CAD kinematic program can eliminate much of this complexity.

Drafting. Upwards of 90% of all mechanical drafting is now done by CAD. Any conventional drafting technique formerly performed at the drawing board can now be accomplished with CAD. Drawings are plotted on a screen monitor or a digitizing board and then plotted on paper. Standard symbols and part drawings, utilized for various types of drafting, may be created and stored for protracted use.

Thus, the computers which can generate wire-frame or solid models, as well as those capable of describing motion (although probably originally designed to

---

[1]From *kinematics*, the words *cinematograph* (the motion-picture camera) and *kinescope* (the cathode-ray tube) are derived.

perform CAD functions) when interfaced with memory systems capable of retaining large quantities of data, are the ones that form the basis of the computer graphics that are being produced for the advertising and the entertainment industries. Such systems are also capable of fulfilling the increasing demand for animated business graphics.

DESKTOP PUBLISHING

This technology enables a person with a personal computer to design and produce graphic material—images and type—that bears a reasonable resemblance to professionally produced material.

Desktop publishing requires a personal computer (PC), software for word processing and type generation, software to generate the graphic image, software to assemble these elements into page formats, and a printer.

Computer manufacturers either produce their own systems for word processing and graphic imaging or manufacture hardware that will accommodate the software of other manufacturers.

The Aldus Corporation of Seattle and Adobe Systems of California, respectively, manufacture PageMaker® and PostScript®; software that is used for page layout and which is capable of driving a laser printer. PageMaker is a program for desktop publishing, which is the production of sophisticated page layout and mechanical art on a personal computer. Using Apple Macintosh™ hardware, PageMaker has the capacity to arrange type and graphics, outputting them to a LaserWriter™, or with PostScript language to a Linotronic® Imagesetter.

PageMaker can edit and format up to a 16-page document at a time, positioning text and graphics while simultaneously displaying results that reasonably represent the finished output.

Some features of the PageMaker 2.0 are:

Using the Macintosh mouse as an input device, graphics created on MacPaint or MacDraw can be cropped or proportionally reduced and inserted into a page layout. Text may be wrapped around a graphic. Rules, rectangles, and ovals may also be drawn with the mouse.

Thirteen type fonts are provided, and additional fonts are available. Reverse type may be created. Automatic page numbering is available.

Automatic kerning adjusts the space between letters that tend to overlap (see page 144).

A hyphenation dictionary, which will break words in their proper intersyllabic spaces at the end of a line as prompted by an 110,000-word dictionary, that has been built into the system (see page 151).

Desktop publishing systems require a printer:

A *dot-matrix printer* forms characters and graphic images with patterns of dots. It is categorized as an impact printer, because it physically strikes a ribbon against paper. A *laser printer*, known as a non-impact printer because nothing strikes the paper, utilizes a concentrated beam of light to expose the image onto the paper.

The laser printer produces images with a much higher resolution than those of a dot-matrix printer, but it is substantially more expensive and, since it requires toner rather than a ribbon, it is also more costly to maintain. These systems produce their output on plain paper.

A DESKTOP PUBLISHING SYSTEM

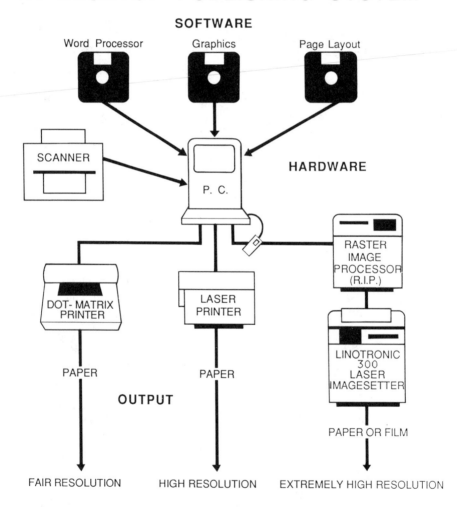

A laser imagesetter, such as the Linotronic 100 or 300, can be interfaced with an Apple Macintosh system in order to produce raster images of incredibly high resolution. The output of such a system can be either positive or negative paper positives, or positive or negative plate-ready film.

None of these printers should be utilized for a printing run. The dot-matrix printer does not have a high enough resolution; laser printers are too slow. System output should be printed out once, either as paper or film, and submitted as art to an offset lithographer.

GRAPHIC SYSTEMS

Image Input

The most significant device in the development of modern graphic arts technology is the laser. The laser affords the capability for uninhibited image input, because of the extremely high resolution with which it scans copy, and because of the uncomplicated versatility of its output. It may produce images generated by its own scan, or those generated by digital output. The impulses may be transmitted long-distance, and output can be on paper, film, or printing plate. The advantage of laser-scanned images is that they can be immediately deposited upon these output surfaces without the intervention of any photographic-negative process; laser-scanned images are processed instantly and directly onto the paper, film, or plate.

The resolution of images need not be a problem because, while an entire telecast image is resolved into 575 lines, cathode-ray tubes and laser scanners are available with resolutions of 600-900 lines per *inch*. Thus, any graphic image—drawn or photographed—can be scanned, color-separated, altered or retouched, transmitted or stored, and produced in any desired visual medium in any desired quantity—all of this in extremely high resolution and with incredible speed.

Image Generation

In addition to accepting the input of preproduced images, sophisticated systems are capable of generating images of their own. In other words, art and design can be created by the system, in accordance with the commands of its operator.

There is no graphic image that cannot be defined by delineating the coordinates of its contours, provided enough coordinates are used to ensure adequate resolution.

Since full-color images can be created by video imagery, there is no single hue that cannot be generated by the proper electronic command.

If the coordinates of the images are located, the system can connect them with lines. Once these have been established, altering the proportions of the coordinates—literally upon command—can distort the image in a variety of ways, causing it to fatten, squeeze, shrink, rotate, whatever.

ADVANTAGES OF A GRAPHIC SYSTEM

In conventional preparation, the following steps are required:

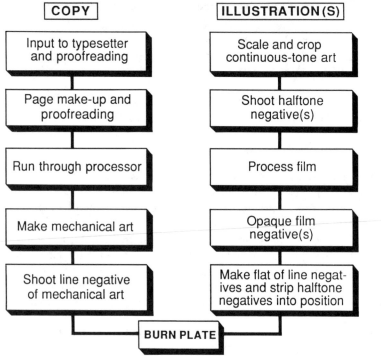

COPY / ILLUSTRATION(S)

COPY	ILLUSTRATION(S)
Input to typesetter and proofreading	Scale and crop continuous-tone art
Page make-up and proofreading	Shoot halftone negative(s)
Run through processor	Process film
Make mechanical art	Opaque film negative(s)
Shoot line negative of mechanical art	Make flat of line negatives and strip halftone negatives into position

BURN PLATE

With a graphic system, only the following steps are necessary:

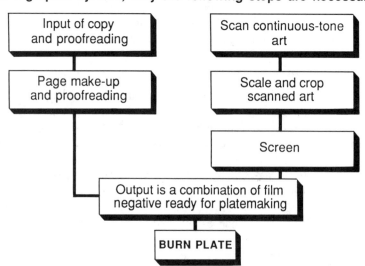

Input of copy and proofreading	Scan continuous-tone art
Page make-up and proofreading	Scale and crop scanned art
	Screen
Output is a combination of film negative ready for platemaking	

BURN PLATE

The stated purpose of the graphic system is to expand the dimensions of the creative person's imagination. Properly used, it can eliminate the drudgeries of visualization, of animation, and of mechanical preparation, leaving the artist with greater freedom and fewer encumbrances.

A typical graphic system consists of: A *keyboard*, for operator-controlled input commands for typesetting, color, stored formats, symbols and logos, design forms, etc. Either an *electronic stylus and tablet* or a *puck* with which the operator draws input. A *CRT monitor*, sometimes two—one for displaying the artwork in progress and one (often called the "menu") that displays the key to the system's stored functions.

System storage carries, digitally encoded, all of the system's predetermined patterns, shapes, type fonts, and color capabilities. *Peripheral storage* is the system's storage for individualized imagery. Additionally, any imagery that is scanned into the system is stored here. Capacity can range from on-line computer disks (hard disks), which may store thousands of images, to floppy (soft) disks, which may store as few as twenty.

Thus, the operator can generate images, shapes, colors, and typography, arrange these elements into new formats, combine them with stored formats, or superimpose them upon images that are either stored, scanned, or ongoing video input. Such systems are used most effectively in the production of television graphics, sport programs, and, of course, commercials. Full-length motion pictures have been produced, combining both live characters and animation. Applications are rapidly being developed for animated charts and graphs, drafting, and technical illustration. Both the military and the airlines extensively utilize the output of graphic systems for pilot training.

Output may be generated on paper as art or copy, generated on videotape, generated on film—a frame at a time—as a motion picture, or laser-scanned onto a plate for print production.

Image Assembly Systems

The image assembly system enables page assembly by either optics, electronics, or a combination of both; thus eliminating the necessity for mechanical art or stripping. These systems can enlarge, reduce, and position any of the elements of the layout—type, line art, halftones, and color art—according to the discretion of the operator and can produce completely composed film output, ready for platemaking.

Capabilities of the Systems

Electronic, computerized systems have the ability to accept pictorial input: art, photography, video, or film. They can also:

Generate a digitized tonal image of high resolution.

Store the image.

GRAPHIC SYSTEMS

There are two types of graphic systems:

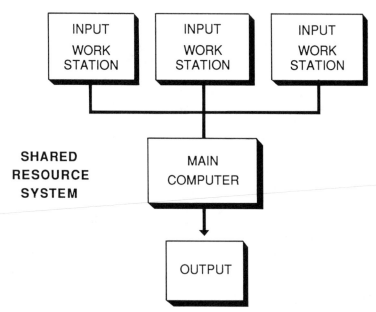

In this type of system, if the main computer is down, the entire system is down.

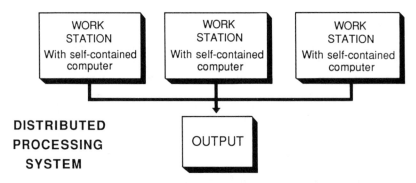

In this type of system, if one workstation (a microcomputer) is down, the rest of the system remains operational.

Crop it.

Reduce or enlarge it, in or out of original proportion.

Position it on a flat, in a desired format.

Separate its colors.

Alter its hues.

Convert the pictorial image into a graphic design.

Transmit it to another location.

Output the image(s) onto paper prints, transparent film, videotape, film, or printing plates.

The systems have the ability to accept processed words: from disk, tape, or by direct entry. They can also:

Using digitally stored typeface characters, compose them into type of a prescribed size, style, and order.

Reduce, enlarge, or distort characters.

Arrange them in a desired, often graphically enhanced format.

Color them.

Position them on a flat.

Superimpose them on a pictorial image.

Output them appropriately.

Drawings and designs can be generated by the systems themselves, combining preprogrammed capability with input from the operator. It is possible to:

Scan and accept existing drawings and designs.

Draw with a stylus or a puck.

Combine and manipulate preprogrammed input with operator input.

Create any conceivable geometric figure.

Distort the figures.

Color them—adding, subtracting, altering.

Arrange them in a format, or in a graphic environment.

Graphically enhance them by:
Multiplying the images.
Defocusing or blurring the edges.
Creating visual effects—strokes, washes, textures—that simulate conventional art techniques.
Enlarge or reduce desired detail.
Images can be corrected, retouched, stored, recalled for alteration or reevaluation, and transmitted to appropriate output devices.

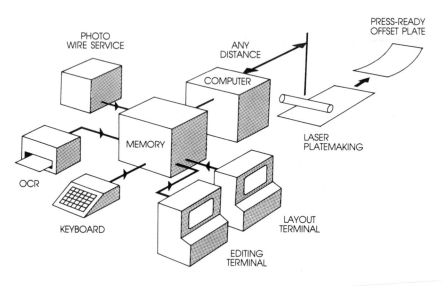

A TYPICAL NEWSPAPER LASER PRINTING SYSTEM

Considerations for System Acquisition

The following factors may be considered when making decisions concerning the acquisition of such image-generating systems:

Cost. Will the cost of the system be offset by the saving of time and by the efficiency of the system?

Capability. Does it supplement, expand, or reduce the organization's creativity? How does it affect the quality, economy, and speed of production of finished art, typography, copy transmission, platemaking, and printing? Can/will personnel make use of it to the highest degree?

Suitability. Is the system adaptable to the style and quality of work expected from the organization, or must work be designed to conform to the idiosyncracies of the system?

Capacity. Is the system capable of storing all the information that will be required of it?

Reliability. Is the system dependable, or will it be plagued with breakdowns?

Prestige. It is possible that mere proprietorship of technological hardware by a graphic-design producing firm may confer greater prestige than will be attributed to any design produced by it.

THE LINOTYPE® GRAPHIC SYSTEM

The Linotype Graphic System is designed to produce platemaker-ready offset negatives for black-and-white printing. The system translates both continuous-tone and line art into digital data, which can be immediately displayed and manipulated on a high-resolution monitor.

The system is capable of producing fine-line halftone screens of up to 300 lines per inch. Halftones may be customized by using a variety of dot shapes.

The system combines four processes of traditional preparation: layout, camera, typesetting, and stripping. Linotype typesetters, as well as other popular systems can drive the Linotype Graphic System. Color prints, black-and-white photos, line art, and transparencies are all accepted by the system's scanner, and it has a large capacity for storing these images, if necessary. At the system's visual workstation, art may be scaled and cropped to any desired proportion. Continuous-tone art may be retouched. Its tonal contrast may be enhanced; it may be posterized; portions of the image may be accented or dramatized; continuous-tone art may be converted to line art. Separate elements may be readily combined into collage or montage form, without resorting to the traditional technique of cutting and pasting. All of this may be readily combined with appropriate type and line art.

The output of the system may take the form of frontwards-reading plastic plates, frontwards- or backwards-reading paper negatives, film negatives or film positives, and frontwards-reading paper positives, as well as paper litho plates. Additionally, the Linotype Laser Printer may be employed for plain-paper proofing purposes.

The system has its own self-contained processing unit and does not require traditional darkroom procedure.

THE SCITEX® SYSTEM

The Scitex Response System is a computer-based image assembly and page make-up system. The system is also able to clone, retouch, and alter images.

It records and stores images in digital form, enabling the production of four-color film separations in less time and with greater versatility than traditional techniques.

The system accepts line art in the form of illustration or text (type), digitized line art or type, and continuous-tone art in both color and black and white. These input images must first be "scanned" into the system's memory. This can be done with any four-color scanner calibrated to work with the system. At this stage, both line and continuous-tone images are translated into the digital mode.

The difference between line scanning and continuous-tone scanning lies in the resolution of the image. The system produces a very high-resolution line scan, resulting in an extremely crisp image.

The Response System scans all four colors in a single pass. This enables immediate viewing on a screen where its color components and its proportions may be altered in any manner imaginable. At this stage, color percentages may be checked and altered, as well as the size of the picture. Obviously, such a system can produce an infinite number of color variations of any given original.

THE COMPLETE
COMPUTER-GRAPHICS SYSTEM

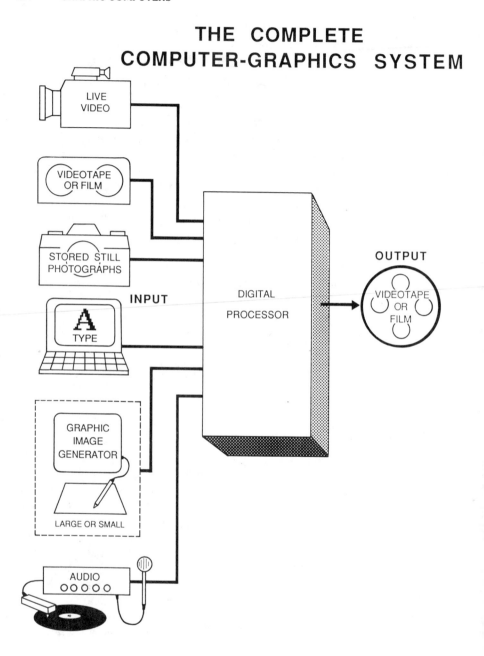

After its initial use, an image may be stored for later use, without any loss of quality or resolution.

Once the input has been scanned and checked, the Response System may be used to arrange and, if necessary, modify, all of the text and art page by page. At this stage, the line and the continuous-tone input have been merged.

Thus, the Response System electronically replaces the manual operations formerly done on the drawing board or on the stripping table. Procedures like masking (eliminating background in order to superimpose another image) can be accomplished with a much higher degree of accuracy with the System than by hand.

Color retouching is the next stage in the process. Electronic retouching enables the changing of any part(s) of the image in terms of its color or its size, whether text or illustration. Enlargements will still retain sharp definition—an image may be blown up to 48-sheet billboard size without significant loss of resolution. An image may also be copied and placed elsewhere. Images may be rescaled and recropped before final electronic assembly.

These steps completed, the pages may be made up. The elements are arranged, pictures are placed in the masked areas—the counterpart of paste-up or stripping has been accomplished electronically.

The system's output is four-color film separations. These can be of different types, depending upon the printer's requirements:

Dot sizes can be changed.

Screen angles can be changed.

The output can be printed as negative or positive film.

For newspapers, the system can compensate for poor dot resolution.

A special selection of dot shapes is available for gravure.

In addition, the Response System's shape library contains a wide variety of shapes—borders, rules, corners, bursts and other similar forms—which formerly required execution by the mechanical artist.

CHAPTER 9
REPROGRAPHY

Copy duplicating runs the gamut from the electrostatic duplication of a single sheet to fast-copy systems that use automated offset lithography and have a production capacity of over 600,000 copies per month. These systems have given rise to an "instant printing" industry, one in which the customer may purchase economical offset reproduction produced on a while-you-wait basis.

Duplicating systems, for the most part, have the ability to reproduce copy or artwork specifically designed for their utilization or to directly copy and mass-reproduce art, copy, documents, etc. Aware of this ability to copy in volume, no organization or its agent should indulge in mass duplication of existing material without carefully considering the legal implications.

Duplicating equipment is expensive and may be either purchased or leased. Its selection should be made in terms of reliability, desired output, and cost per unit of reproduction. Acquisition of duplicating equipment should be made in terms of *need*, not *want*.

Copy duplicating systems may be classified in the following categories:

Convenience Copiers. Convenience copiers are machines designed to produce a modest number of copies of an original. These machines have capacity of up to 20,000 copies per month. Push-button operated, they utilize plain or coated paper.

Copy Duplicators. These machines are designed for a higher monthly volume—from 20,000 copies upward. Also push-button operated, they utilize plain or coated paper and often come equipped with automatic collating devices.

Color Copiers. Long awaited, there are now color copiers on the market that will accurately reproduce the full range of color. Colors may be fine-tuned to suit individual preferences for intensity and contrast, and there is considerable latitude for enlargement or reduction. Additionally, these machines will copy 35mm color slides and are capable of producing transparencies for overhead projection. The machines can copy full-color photographs, or they can make single-color copies in a variety of different colors.

Duplicators. These systems include spirit, mimeo, and offset duplicators, all of which utilize plain paper and are more cost-effective for longer runs than are copiers. They require preparation of a master and take some degree of skill in their operation.

Fast-Copy Systems. Utilizing automated offset lithography, these systems have proved successful with high-volume duplication—100,000 copies monthly. Their operation requires the services of a highly skilled operator.

Electronic Printing Systems. These are systems in which (in addition to their high-speed xerographic output) digitized typefaces and standardized or customized business formats can be stored in their computer memories, ready for instant use. The printers normally associated with personal-computer output are not suitable for this. Dot-etch printers do not provide a high enough resolution, and laser printers are too slow.

Blueprinting and Diazo Printing. Time-honored for the reproduction of plans and drawings, these processes require the preparation of an original on translucent material; modern originals are produced by a plotter activated by a CAD system (see pages 90–91). The advantage of these processes is the size of the original that may be duplicated.

CONVENIENCE COPIERS
AND COPY DUPLICATORS

Both of these machines are electrostatic copiers. As such, they utilize the principles of static electricity, employing photosensitive materials that may be electrically charged in the form of a desired image and then caused to attract powders or ink-like solutions known as "toners." There are two types of machine: those that print on plain paper and those that require presensitized paper.

In a plain paper copier, the image of the document is optically transferred to an electrically charged selenium-covered drum. The charge disappears in the background area but is retained in the image area. The developer powder (toner)

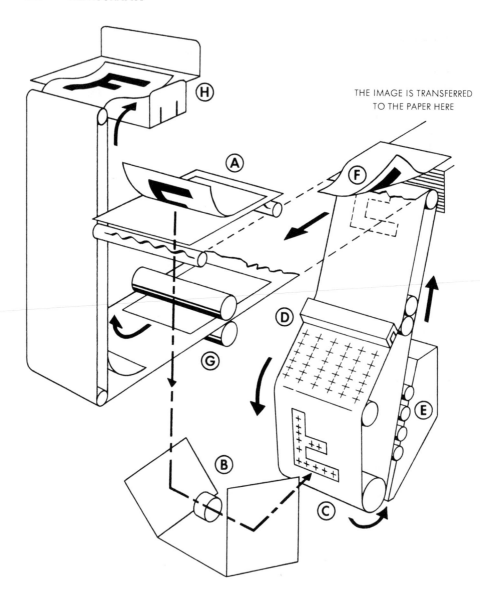

THE IMAGE IS TRANSFERRED
TO THE PAPER HERE

THE PHOTOCOPY MACHINE

THE IMAGE PLACED ON COPYBOARD "A" IS REFLECTED THROUGH LENS SYSTEM "B" ONTO
CHARGED SELENIUM-COATED BELT "C". THE BELT HAS BEEN POSITIVELY CHARGED AT "D". THE
REFLECTED LIGHT REMOVES THE CHARGE, EXCEPT IN THE IMAGE AREA. TONER IS BRUSHED ONTO
THE CHARGED IMAGE AT "E", AND THE BELT COMES IN CONTACT AND TRANSFERS THE TONER TO
THE PAPER AT "F". AT THE FUSER "G" HEAT AND PRESSURE FUSE THE TONER IMAGE TO THE PAPER,
WHICH IS THEN TRANSPORTED TO THE RECEIVING TRAY "H". THE WORD "XEROGRAPHY" HAS
BECOME THE GENERIC NAME FOR THIS PROCESS.

adheres to the charged image on the drum, and the powder is next transferred from the drum to the paper by an electric charge. Heat then fuses the powder to the paper.

In machines that require coated paper, light is reflected from the document onto the paper, which can serve as a photoconductor, due to the chemistry of its coating. Thus, the coated paper substitutes for the drum. Charged particles of toner are brushed or sprayed onto the charged image (which has been deposited on the coated paper) and are permanently fused to the paper with heat.

These systems are designed for the casual user. The operator need only place the document in the holder, set the machine to produce the proper tonality and the desired number of copies, and activate the machine. The emerging copies are either collated by the machine, or collected by the operator for collation by hand.

DUPLICATORS

The Spirit Duplicator. Universally known as the "ditto machine," the spirit duplicator utilizes a master sheet to produce the image. This carbon-coated sheet is written, typed, or drawn upon. The dye from this sheet is pressure-transferred to the master, which is then placed on the cylinder of the machine. An alcohol(spirit)-based fluid dissolves a thin layer of dye from the master, which is then brought into contact with, and transferred to, the paper.

Spirit masters can be made on a thermal copier, which can copy from existing material, provided there are no halftones involved. The thermal unit may also be used to laminate.

The spirit duplicator does not require a trained operator. It utilizes plain paper in a variety of colors; by combining them, multicolor work may be produced.

The Mimeograph. The mimeograph uses a wax-covered stencil. Typing or drawing on it with a stylus pushes aside the wax but does not perforate the stencil. The stencil is wrapped around the ink-filled cylinder of the machine. The padded surface of the cylinder absorbs the ink and forces it through the impressed areas of the stencil, thus depositing it on the paper, which has been brought in contact with it.

The mimeograph utilizes somewhat coarser-grained plain paper. The stencil will stand up to a longer run than the ditto master.

The Offset Duplicator. The offset duplicator is, literally, a small offset lithographic press. The paper capacity may run up to 14" × 20", but utilization of 8 ½" × 11" or 11" × 14" is widespread. These presses accommodate *paper masters* (plates), which may be typed, written, drawn upon, or exposed by a laser activated from either an adjacent or a remote location. Also accommodated are *presensitized* plates of aluminum, paper, or plastic, which will accept a photomechanical line or halftone image produced with a conventional negative, or *direct-image* plates (such as diffusion-transfer plates) that are produced directly from the copy, without the intervention of a film negative. In the direct-image plate, the light-sensitive coating of the plate performs the function of the film negative; thus the image is photographed by the plate itself.

Offset duplicators will print on plain paper ranging from onionskin to light cardboard at speeds of several thousand per hour. Both colored ink and colored paper may be used.

FAST-COPY SYSTEMS

Fast-copy systems consist of a small offset press (an offset duplicator) with an electrostatic plate (or master) maker. The original copy is inserted into a master-making station that uses a flatbed electrostatic imager for producing masters for long or short runs.

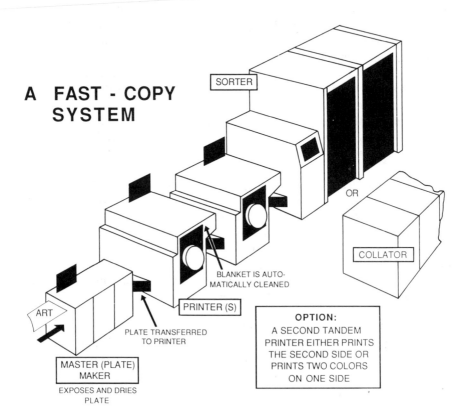

A FAST - COPY SYSTEM

SORTER

OR

COLLATOR

BLANKET IS AUTO-
MATICALLY CLEANED

PRINTER (S)

ART

PLATE TRANSFERRED
TO PRINTER

OPTION:
A SECOND TANDEM
PRINTER EITHER PRINTS
THE SECOND SIDE OR
PRINTS TWO COLORS
ON ONE SIDE

MASTER (PLATE)
MAKER

EXPOSES AND DRIES
PLATE

The image master is passed through a converting and drying station and is either placed on the press cylinder or held in reserve in the loading station. This feature permits the operator to process a batch of masters at maximum speed and then hold them while devoting attention to the printing/sorting operation.

The machine may then be programmed to convey the master from the loading station and attach it to the press cylinder, etch the master, reproduce the desired number of copies, eject the master, and wash the blanket. A tandem offset for two-sided printing and an on-line collator may be added to the system.

In this system, the elapsed time from the imaging of the master to the first printed copy is a matter of seconds. This type of machine fills the "instant printing" needs of the casual consumer. The production capacity of fast-copy systems is well in excess of 100,000 copies monthly. The unit cost is a few mills per impression, and a noticeable degree of quality can be achieved. Obviously such a system has well-defined advantages for those who would continue to employ a photocopier as a printing press.

ELECTRONIC PRINTING SYSTEMS

The latest electronic printing systems combine computer, laser, and xerographic technologies. The keyboarded input is abetted by computer-stored information, generated with a laser, and printed by xerography.

In addition to printing and collating at speeds of up to two pages per second, they can also set type from digitally stored type fonts, business forms—standard or customized—logos, and charts. Data pertaining to the compilation of such documents may also be stored in the computer's memory. All of this may be imaged upon demand.

Designed for continuous operation, these systems are capable of printing on a large variety of paper types and weights.

These systems are ideal for the maximum in-house productivity of catalogs, manuals, directories, proposals, and similar material. They may be activated by computer software capable of generating layout and page assembly. In addition, should the system require more sophisticated input than can be generated in-house—such as type fonts or specialized formatting—it may be interfaced by telephone line (modem) with distant input consoles.

BLUEPRINTING

Blueprinting is a contact-printing reversal process, one in which the values of the image are the reverse of the original. The original drawing must be done on translucent material capable of blocking ultraviolet light. The exposed paper reacts to the ultraviolet light, is developed, and turns blue.

A slow process, it is, however, ideal for the reproduction of large draftings because it is not confined to the size limitations of most duplicating equipment. Blueprints are also used as proofs for lithography; they are printed directly from the litho negatives. If a two-color job is involved, the negative for *each* color is contact-printed onto a single sheet of blueprint paper. The image of the second color negative is developed for less time, resulting in a lighter shade of blue. Thus, all of the copy will appear on the blueprint, and the colors will each be defined in a separate shade of blue.

DIAZO PRINTING

Diazo printing has taken over most of the older blueprinting techniques. It requires copy preparation on translucent material, but it prints directly—not in reverse. Ultraviolet light exposes the chemicals coated on the printing paper and prevents them from accepting dye. In the image area, there is no light action. This leaves the image lines free to form the dye, which is activated by chemicals transported by an alkali solution or ammonia fumes.

The process is fast and inexpensive, and it reproduces actual size. As with the blueprint process, it has the capacity to reproduce large drawings.

CHAPTER 10
IMAGE-PROCESSING
SYSTEMS

Image processing is photographically enlarging or reducing an image, maintaining or reversing its values, and depositing an image on paper or film so that it can be used either for mechanical art or for some other aspect of graphic arts production.

As equipment for image processing becomes more compact, individual art-producing organizations are showing a willingness to invest in such hardware, thus permitting this vital function to occur "in-house," rather than as a service performed by an outside supplier. Thus, it is not unusual for an art-producing firm to expect a beginner to be able to rapidly learn to operate its image-processing equipment.

PHOTOSTATS

The photostat is one of the most useful items employed by the advertising artist, serving a multitude of functions in the preparation of both preliminary and finished art. Photostats enable the artist to enlarge and reduce line art at will and provide a means of reversing the values of original art. They can be used as copies of continuous-tone art that—though not suitable for reproduction—may be used to indicate the appearance, cropping, and positioning of a halftone on either comprehensive or mechanical art. They can be used to make duplicate copies of line art for future use; they may be colored by hand or dyed for displays and exhibits. They represent an inexpensive method of clear duplication when a small number of copies is required.

The photostat machine is a copying camera that uses paper negatives. The machine photographs the subject matter through a lens that has a prism mounted in front of it. The prism prevents the lens from recording a backwards-reading image, producing, instead, a frontwards-reading image on sensitized paper contained within the machine. This image is in negative form. The paper negative is developed and dried. Traditionally, in order to obtain a positive image, a *second* photostat must be made from the paper negative; the negative is reshot as if it were the original art. This second shot, or *positive*—also paper—returns the values to those of the original subject matter. However, the use of direct-positive paper will produce a positive print directly from original positive copy, and a reverse print can be produced directly from original reverse copy.

The machine will enlarge up to twice the size of the original, or reduce to half the size in one shot. In order to make a further enlargement or reduction, the negative is enlarged or reduced to the maximum amount, and the positive is further enlarged or reduced to the desired size. Thus, if a negative is reduced to half the size of the original, and the positive is reduced to half the size of the negative, the result will be one-fourth the size of the original. Greater reduction requires additional shots.

Photostat paper is blue-sensitive: blue will photograph as white and red will photograph as black. In order to correct this tendency, a yellow filter must be employed. Its use should be specified by the person ordering the photostats,

THE PHOTOSTAT MACHINE

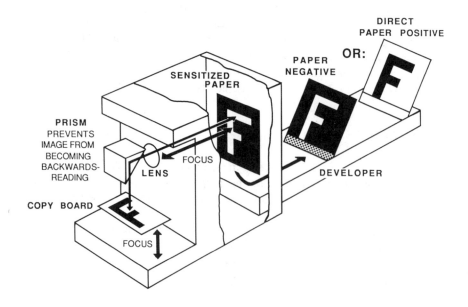

should the filter be required. Photostat paper comes in either matte or glossy finish. The paper is of the high-contrast type designed to record near-white areas as white and dark gray areas as black. Glossy paper gives the maximum contrast and should be specified when one is ordering copies of *line art* for reproduction. Good quality glossy photostats provide a sharp, perfect duplication of original line art. Matte paper is more sensitive to tonal values, but lacks the sharpness of a photographic print. Matte photostats are used to provide visual indications of drawings and photographs on comprehensive layouts and to delineate cropping and positioning on the mechanical art.

If required, a photostat may be "flopped"—photographed in order to produce a backwards-reading image.

Photostats should be carefully ordered to make certain there is no misunderstanding on the part of the operator. The following items should be clearly indicated on the artwork:

1. *Whether the print is to be positive or negative.* To the photostat operator, a negative means one shot of the original; a positive, two shots. If the photostatter is supplied with a negative photostat as original art, the first shot made from it will result in a positive image. If the specifier has requested a "positive," the photostatter has no way of being certain whether the specifier wants a positive image or a duplicate of the original negative. In order to avoid confusion, many specifiers prefer to order an "opposite" (one shot) or a "duplicate" (two shots). Others order "first prints" or "second prints."

2. *The type of paper desired.* Glossy paper is specified for line copy that is to be used for reproduction; matte paper is ordered for photostats used for the identification or positioning of halftone copy.

3. *The size(s) desired.* Size indication should be accomplished by marking lines at the horizontal or vertical extremities of the copy, and indicating the size within a double-headed arrow that touches each line. The lines should be accurately placed, since the operator uses them rather than the actual copy as a guide when reducing or enlarging. If the photostat is to be made the same size as the original, it should be marked "S. S."

The size indicator on the photostat machine is marked in percentages of enlargement or reduction, with 100 percent representing the original size. If the specifier has a proportional calculator, it may be convenient to indicate enlargements or reductions in terms of percentages of the original.

Do not write photostating instructions in blue pencil. If a number of photostats is ordered, the fastest means of checking them for proper size is to measure between the lines that appear on the actual photostat and compare the result with the size indication that has been written there. If marked in blue pencil, the instructions will not appear on the print, and considerable time will be wasted locating and comparing it with the original.

The exact appearance of a photostatic enlargement or reduction may be determined in advance with the Lacey-Luci; or if there is none available, the

PHOTOSTATS MAY BE USED TO:

ENLARGE

REDUCE

FLOP

REVERSE

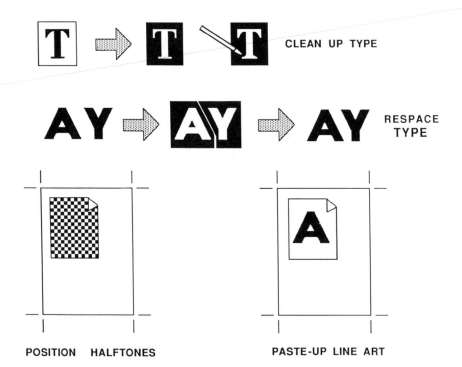

CLEAN UP TYPE

RESPACE TYPE

POSITION   HALFTONES   PASTE-UP LINE ART

area may be calculated with the diagonal-line method. This should always be done in order to eliminate the possibility of incorrect size indication.

4. *The number of prints desired.* The job may require several prints, either the same size or in varying sizes.

5. *The job number.* The specifier's job number should accompany all photostat orders. This facilitates identification for billing purposes. The typographer

or the platemaker may attach a proof to the bill, but the photostatter has no visual evidence of the work performed.

The following procedures may prove helpful in the efficient utilization of the photostatic process:

All photostats should be checked for the correct size and sharpness of focus immediately upon receipt from the photostatter. The messenger should be detained until this has been done in order to return any that may prove incorrect.

PHOTOSTAT ECONOMY

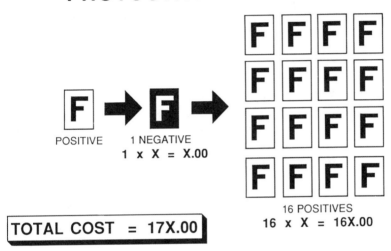

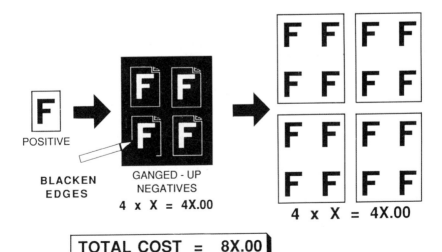

The cost of the photostat is based on the size of the paper required not on the subject matter. Material to be photostated in the same focus should be closely grouped together so that it may be accommodated on a minimal-sized sheet of paper. If the subject matter is very small, extra material—logotypes, trademarks, constantly used items—may be mounted around it, and so long as they do not exceed the minimum paper size, they will be included at no extra charge.

Glossy paper costs slightly more than matte paper. It is poor economy to order glossy photostats when matte photostats will suffice.

Time is an important factor. Whenever possible, photostats should be ordered far enough in advance to be on hand when the mechanical art is begun. Rush orders involving overtime charges should be avoided by proper job planning. Often, after the mechanical is in progress, it is found that an element does not fit properly and must be photostated to the desired size. If there is any error in sizing at this stage, it may delay delivery of the job. Thus, if there is any doubt about the size, it is often practical to order two or three photostats to slightly different sizes. One of them should certainly fit properly.

Original art—line drawings, logotypes, lettering, etc.—is the property of the client and should be returned. Photostat negatives of all such material should be kept on file. This eliminates the need for requesting original art from the client each time such material is needed. Clients will tend to favor an art source that is known to have an ample photostat file of their advertising material. If a negative photostat is available, only one shot is required to make a positive image. This results in a considerable saving.

Material that is continually used for a particular account—logotypes, trade-marks, slogans, address lines, etc.—should be ganged up on a master cardboard. If several positive and negative logotypes of various sizes are ganged up on a board and a photostatic copy is occasionally ordered, there will always be a constant supply of such material on hand in a wide variety of sizes. This makes it unnecessary to send out to the photostatter every time such material is required.

It is easier to clean up enlarged type or hand lettering when it is in negative form, since the cleanup can be accomplished with black ink. If time permits, a negative photostat may be ordered, cleaned up by hand, and a positive photostat made from the cleaned-up negative. When appearing in reverse, the serifs and thin strokes of the type or hand lettering may tend to fill in. A negative photostat affords the opportunity to appraise this possibility and strengthen the offending lines with white paint before submission to the platemaker.

A minor paste-up assembly—the repositioning of elements of a line draw-ing, or the respacing of large lettering or type are good examples—can be accomplished in negative form and recopied as a positive. The positive will show no evidence of the alteration. When this is done—when any negative photostats are cut apart—the pieces should be mounted on black paper and the white cut-edges blackened so that these cut lines will not show on the positive.

Photostats are generally billed to the client at cost, plus a 15 percent service charge. It is possible for a skillful production person or an artist to effect consid-

PHOTOSTATS MAY BE USED TO:

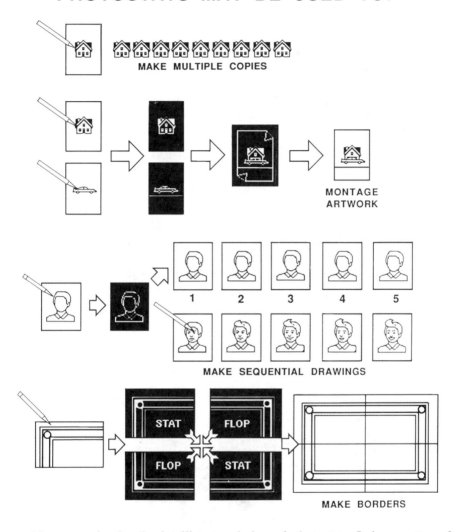

MAKE MULTIPLE COPIES

MONTAGE
ARTWORK

MAKE SEQUENTIAL DRAWINGS

MAKE BORDERS

erable economies by the intelligent ordering of photostats. It is a matter of discretion whether or not to pass this saving along to the client.

DIFFUSION TRANSFER

Many rapid processing systems, because of their versatility, are replacing the traditional photostat. Manufactured by a number of firms, these systems utilize the diffusion transfer process.

Diffusion transfer, in its simplest form, is used to produce good-quality opaque or transparent *positives* from positive originals. These may be used for copy preparation—enlargement or reduction of copy, to clean up dirty original copy, to convert line color-art to black and white, to introduce screen tints to copy, and to make screened halftone prints (Veloxes). The process may also be used for proofing—in black and white, multicolor or four-color process, and for litho platemaking.

The transfer utilizes a light-sensitive image sheet and a chemically sensitized receiver sheet, which may be opaque or transparent. The image is produced in the following way:

1. The negative sheet is camera-exposed—either as line copy or through a contact screen.
2. The negative and the receiver sheet are contacted and passed through a single-bath activating solution.
3. The negative image acts as a chemical mask, producing reversed values that are transferred (as a positive image) onto the receiver sheet. Transfer occurs in a few seconds, then the sheets are separated, resulting in either an opaque or a transparent positive, depending on the type of receiver sheet used.

The single-bath positive transfer can be used to produce either paper or metal litho plates.

The positive transfer may be used to make an opaque halftone positive for producing a halftone silk-screen stencil (see page 76).

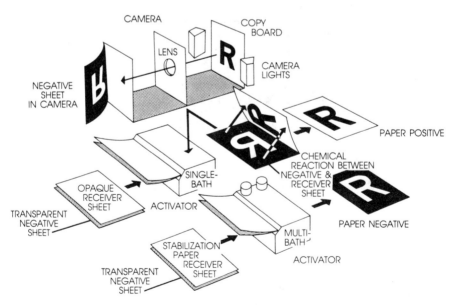

DIFFUSION TRANSFER

Stabilization paper or film, which incorporates the developer within the emulsion (see page 159), is used with multibath activators to produce both paper and film negatives in line and in halftone.

Color receiver sheets can be exposed and processed in a variety of standard hues and used as transparent multicolor or process proofs.

Diffusion transfers will not produce an opaque paper image from a positive color transparency, such as would be used to indicate position on mechanical art. For this purpose, a photostat must be made. Flopped images cannot be produced with diffusion transfer. They, too, must be made by the photostatic process.

The previously discussed requisites for good photostatic production apply to diffusion transfer as well.

CHAPTER 11
THE REPRODUCTION OF COLOR

Definitions

Color. Color is a visual response—both physical and psychological—to the wavelengths of visible light. *Color* is the inclusive term for this phenomenon and is so used in this chapter.

Spectrum. The spectrum is that area of visible radiant energy whose wavelengths fall between 3,800 and 8,000 Angstrom units. Varying wavelengths within this range evoke different color sensations. When white light is passed through a prism, it is decomposed into a band of its varying component hues. The sequence in which these hues occur is commonly known as the *color spectrum.*

Hue. The descriptive name given to a spectrally pure color in order to distinguish it from the remainder of the color spectrum. Hue is the first characteristic of color that the eye detects.

Hue is the spectral characteristic to which most persons refer when they say "color." Thus red is not a *color,* it is a *hue*—the common name of a specific visual sensation falling within a specified wavelength.

In this chapter, the word *hue* is used when reference is made to a specific color.

Value. Value is the lightness or darkness of a hue, noted in terms of the light it is capable of reflecting.

The Value Scale. The value scale is a series of ten recognizably graduated tones ranging from black to white. Value is noted by comparing a given hue to this scale. In the Munsell system of color notation, value "10" represents white and value "0" represents black. Conversely, the platemaker uses a percentage scale in which 100 percent represents black (or a solid hue) and 0 percent represents white. In this book, values are represented in terms of platemakers' percentages.

Primary Hues. Primary hues are the basic components of color that, when combined, produce the remaining hues of the spectrum. The hues that are considered primary vary with the way color is produced.

Physical or Light Primary Hues. These are the primary hues of the physicist, who produces color by means of light. When light is decomposed by prismatic analysis, the resulting primary hues are red, green, and blue—with wavelengths of 650, 550, and 460 millimicrons, respectively.

Pigment Mixture Primary Hues. These are the primary hues of the artist, who produces color with pigment. When pigments are mixed and deposited on a white background, the three primary hues are considered to be red, yellow, and blue—or, more specifically, crimson lake, gamboge, and Prussian blue.

Physical Secondary Hues. These are hues produced by any combination of two of the physical primary hues. The secondary hue magenta (pinkish-red) is a combination of red and blue; yellow, a combination of green and red, and cyan (cyanine blue), a combination of blue and green.

These secondary hues more closely resemble the primary hues of the artist than the primary hues of the physicist; therefore they are the ones used by the color printer. In color printing, these secondary hues are known as *process colors.*

Although these hues represent primary hues so far as the printer is concerned, they will still be considered *secondary hues* in this chapter, in order to maintain a consistency of terminology in the discussion of both physical and printed color.

Complementary Hues. Complementary hues are hues that differ most radically from each other. The complement of a primary hue is the resulting secondary combination of the two remaining primary hues. To the artist or printer, who deals with pigment and considers red, yellow, and blue to be primary hues (though they are actually the secondaries magenta, yellow, and cyan), the complement of red is the combination of yellow and blue—green. To the physicist or the photographer who deals with light and uses the physical primaries red, green, and blue, the complement of red is the combination of blue and green, or the secondary hue cyan. The mixture of a hue and its complement will produce either white, black, or value of gray, depending on the method by which it is combined.

Additive Color Mixing. Additive color mixing consists of adding, by the superimposition of light rays in equal proportions, the three physical primary hues in order to produce white light. In the additive process, utilized by the physicist, the primary hues are red, blue, and green, the secondary hues are magenta, yellow, and cyan. Combined, the three additive primaries will produce white light. The complement of any additive primary hue is the secondary hue composed of the two remaining primaries:

HUE	COMPLEMENT
Red	Green and Blue, or *Cyan*
Green	Red and Blue, or *Magenta*
Blue	Green and Red, or *Yellow*

Subtractive Color Mixing. Subtractive color mixing produces a visual sensation by subtracting light from the whiteness of the paper. For example, magenta, when placed on the paper surface, *subtracts* cyan and yellow from the reflected light, allowing the eye to perceive only the sensation of magenta. In the subtractive process utilized by the artist, printer, and the modern color photographer, the primaries of the subtractive process are the *secondary* hues of the additive process—magenta, yellow, and cyan. Any two of these will combine to form one of the additive primaries. The combination of all three will produce black. The complement of any secondary hue is the primary hue composed of the two remaining secondaries:

HUE	COMPLEMENT
Magenta	Yellow and Cyan, or *Green*
Yellow	Magenta and Cyan, or *Blue*
Cyan	Yellow and Magenta, or *Red*

Transmission Copy. Copy that is viewed by light passing *through* it, for example, the positive color-film transparency.

Reflection Copy. Copy that is viewed by light that is *reflected* from the copy, for example, the color photographic print, the painting, the printed image.

Color Separation. The separation of a color image into its component primary hues in order that it may be reproduced by either the additive or subtractive process.

Register. The accuracy with which separated colors are superimposed over each other when reproduced—either photographically or photomechanically. Colors that are accurately superimposed are said to be in perfect register.

Pin Register. A system for maintaining accuracy of registration. Holes, located in identical positions on copy, film, plates, or presses, are placed on similarly positioned metal pins, ensuring that each separation will be positioned in exact register with its counterparts.

Filter. A piece of colored glass, which, when placed over the lens of the camera, will remove unwanted color from the image recorded by the film.

Panchromatic. Sensitive to all colors. Panchromatic film records all colors with equal sensitivity and is thus able to differentiate between colors that would appear to be similar on other types of black-and-white film.

Screen Tint. A value reduction of a solid color, produced by reducing it to a uniform dot pattern (the smaller the dot, the lighter the value). A screen tint differs from a halftone in that there is no tonal variation. Screen tints are measured in percentages of the solid tone.

Moiré. Derived from the textural pattern characteristic of watered silk, the term "moiré screen" denotes the result of two photomechanical screen patterns which have been improperly superimposed. The resulting wavy effect is considered objectionable in both screen tints and halftones, since it produces an irregular tonal appearance.

MULTICOLOR PRINTING

The first thing that should be understood, in order to develop a knowledge of color printing, is that a printing plate can be printed in *any color suitable for inking*. With modern printing inks, it is possible to ink a plate in almost any conceivable color. It is not essential that a plate printed in black must continue to be printed in black. The plate can be washed, then printed in red or any other hue. It is the ink that controls the color, not the plate.

When one-color is printed, the only problem encountered is the mixing of the desired hue of ink. When two solid colors appear simultaneously in the same design, a different situation occurs. It is impossible to ink a plate in more than one color. Since both colors cannot be printed by the *same plate,* there must be an individual plate for each of them. The parts of the image that are to be printed in the first color—and *only* those parts of the image—must appear on the first plate; those that are to be printed in the second color—and *only* those—must appear on the second plate. The division of the two colors—the process by which the proper part of the image becomes incorporated in the proper plate—is known as *separation.*

The simplest type line-color separation is the instance where neither of the colors in the design touch or overlap each other. This type of separation is accomplished photographically. Two identical film negatives are made from the original art. On the first negative, everything that is *not* to print in the first color is opaqued out by hand. On the second negative, the parts of the design that were *not opaqued* on the first negative are in turn obliterated. Thus, the design has been separated into its two components, the nonopaqued parts representing an individ-

COLOR KEY FOR THE ILLUSTRATIONS ON PAGES 127, 131, 132, and 207

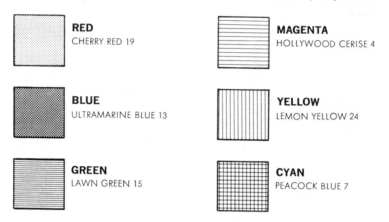

RED
CHERRY RED 19

MAGENTA
HOLLYWOOD CERISE 4

BLUE
ULTRAMARINE BLUE 13

YELLOW
LEMON YELLOW 24

GREEN
LAWN GREEN 15

CYAN
PEACOCK BLUE 7

THE FOLLOWING ILLUSTRATIONS CAN BE CLARIFIED CONSIDERABLY BY COLOR-CODING THEM ACCORDING TO THIS KEY WITH VENUS "PARADISE" COLORED PENCILS OR SIMILARLY-HUED FELT-TIP MARKERS.

ual negative for each plate. It is important to understand that *the negatives are not colored;* they are black—identical in appearance to any other film negative. It is merely that the component color areas of the design have been disassembled on negative photographic film.

A plate is made from each negative in the normal manner of the printing process. Obviously both plates cannot impress the paper simultaneously. The color press must have a separate plate cylinder for each plate, and the feeding mechanism must be so arranged that the paper comes in contact with each plate in perfect register. Each plate can be inked in any color that is desired. It is important to note that in printing terminology, *black* is considered a color. A black-and-red impression is as much a two-color job as a red-and-green impression.

It is possible to use a one-color press by printing the first color on all the sheets, mounting a second plate, and running all the sheets through the press again. In the case of long runs, this is an extremely inefficient method.

A more complex situation arises when the colors in the design overlap each other. If the art is prepared in two colors, one superimposed over a background of another, the colors will appear superimposed on the negative, and it will be impossible to separate them by hand-opaquing. If the colors are too close in value, the second color may not even be apparent on the negative; it may prove impossible to differentiate it from the background. When this is the case, the colors must be separated photographically by using a transparent color *filter* placed over the lens of the camera. This is known as camera separation. In order to separate a color photographically, a filter of the complementary hue is used. For example, to filter the *red* from a design, a *green* filter is used. The resulting negative will contain all the elements of the design necessary for the production of the red plate.

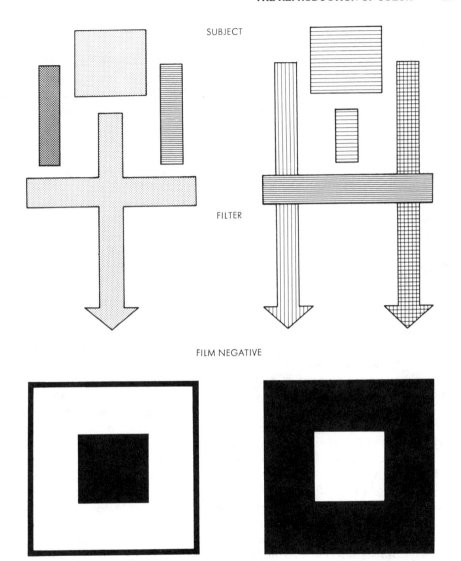

SUBJECT

FILTER

FILM NEGATIVE

FILTER SEPARATION

EACH FILTER PASSES ITS OWN HUE. IN "A", THE EXPOSED AREA IN THE CENTER OF THE
NEGATIVE REPRESENTS A POSITIVE IMAGE OF THE RED IN THE ORIGINAL SUBJECT. IN "B", THE
THE GREEN FILTER PASSES CYAN AND YELLOW (GREEN) AND BLOCKS MAGENTA. THUS, THE
UNEXPOSED AREA IN THE CENTER OF THE NEGATIVE REPRESENTS A NEGATIVE IMAGE
OF THE MAGENTA IN THE ORIGINAL SUBJECT.

The alternative to this process is *preseparation* by the artist. The artist produces the design by placing all portions of the art that involve the second color on a transparent overlay, registered accurately in position on top of the "key" art. The key art contains all the first color. The key art and the overlay are photographed separately and the resulting negatives are used to produce the plates. No opaquing or filtration is required. Accurate registration of the colors necessitates a high degree of skill on the part of the artist, but the cost of camera separation is eliminated.

If continuous-tone art is drawn in two colors by the artist, it is normally filter-separated with the camera. There are special art processes for the preseparation of continuous-tone art, should it be desirable. These methods will be discussed in another chapter.

When printing in a single color, the printer is capable of mixing ink to produce any desired hue. Often a one-color job will contain both solid and screened areas of the color. Obviously, the nature of the tonal areas will be governed by the hue used to print the solid areas. It is the job of the artist to anticipate this effect.

When printing in more than one color, one achieves variation by screening, surprinting, or both. *The variations that may be produced are limited by the nature of the hues with which the plates are inked.* Since artists are not hampered by such limitations, they must learn by experience to compensate for the limitations of the photomechanical processes, rather than expecting them to be capable of reproducing anything they may choose to create.

When two colors overlap, a third color results. In areas where blue and yellow overlap, a green hue will result. But if the inks are opaque, and the blue is particularly strong, the overprinting will not produce a true green; the blue will bear a greenish tint. When one *surprints* solid color, solid blue on top of yellow, or vice versa, the second color underneath must be *dropped out* of its plate in order to prevent discoloration of the surprint. This is not necessary when black is used, because black will surprint any other color. Dropping out behind fine-line detail is a problem of such critical registration that it is best handled by the camera. Specific instructions to drop out an underlying color should be given to the platemaker.

The tendency for two overlapping colors to form a third can be used to great advantage. If the solid colors are opened up by means of a dot formation (screen) and the screen angles turned to prevent superimposition of the dots, the resulting overlap will mix optically and form a third color of equal clarity and intensity. In this manner, screen patterns of two colors can be combined to form a third color—three colors for the price of two. If the percentages of the screen patterns are knowledgeably varied, an infinite number of combinations can be obtained. For example: an 80 percent (almost solid) screen of yellow and an 80 percent screen of blue combine to form a solid green. A 50 percent yellow and a 50 percent blue produce a green of a similar but lighter hue. However, an 80 percent yellow and a 50 percent blue will produce a *yellow-green,* while an 80 percent blue and a 50 percent yellow will form a *blue-green.* The possibilities are endless.

In this method of printing there is no necessity for a third color plate; therefore, there is no charge. The extra color can be obtained for the cost of stripping the screen patterns into the proper areas of the two negatives.

Similar results may be obtained by overprinting solid areas of *transparent* ink. The production techniques of these methods will be discussed later.

FULL-COLOR PRINTING

It does not require much imagination to conjure up the infinite range of hues and values suggested by the term "full-color." If one were to develop a press to print each of these colors, its size would be incomprehensible. But when the variations that can be obtained by the combination of various screen tints are considered, duplicating "full-color" with a minimum number of impressions becomes feasible.

The artist uses three *primary* hues—red, yellow, and blue—which can be combined in varying percentages to form every other hue. Mixed on paper, red-yellow, red-blue, and blue-yellow combinations form, respectively, the *secondary* hues orange, violet, and green. The three primaries, mixed in strength, form brown. Each secondary hue, mixed with its adjacent primary forms the intermediate or *tertiary* hues red-orange, yellow-orange, yellow-green, blue-green, blue-violet, and red- violet, respectively. In this manner, the three primary hues, mixed in appropriate percentages, can be combined to produce all the hues of the spectrum. The mixture of any two complementary hues will produce black.

It has already been noted that a printed color, when screened, will mix optically with another color that is superimposed over it. It follows logically that if three primary colors can be screened to the proper component percentages and superimposed, the full color range of the spectrum can be produced. This method of printing, using three plates, each inked with one of the three primary hues, is known as *three-color process printing.* A fourth plate, *black,* is generally added to produce strength of detail and neutral values of gray. The black ink can also be employed to print the accompanying typography. This process of printing full-color with the three primaries and black is known as *four-color process printing.* This is the most prevalent method of full-color printing, whether in letterpress, lithography, or gravure.

It is important to realize that every color wheel is an arbitrary affair. The traditional red, yellow, and blue primaries of the artist provide much latitude of interpretation. In the development of process printing, it was necessary to scientifically determine *which* red, yellow, and blue would most effectively combine in *printing* full color, as well as to provide standard inks that would be consistently used by the industry.

Spectrum red and spectrum blue do not provide the answer. Spectrum red, overprinting yellow, will still produce red. Spectrum blue and yellow are complementary and will combine to produce black. Red and blue are spectrally exclusive colors, and their overprint will produce black. The primary hues of the artists are not the same as those utilized in process printing.

The artist must become aware of the scientific aspects of color in order to understand color printing. To the physicist, who is concerned with color in terms of light rays, the primary hues of the spectrum are red, green, and blue. The physicist finds that when beams of red, green, and blue light are added together in a darkened room, the result is white light. This method of color combination is known as the additive process.

The Additive Color Process

The additive color process depends on the fact that the addition of light rays of the three primaries—red, green, and blue—will produce white. It takes equal parts of all three to produce white. If lesser combinations occur, intermediate hues will result. In this manner, the combination of red and green light produces *yellow;* red and blue produces a pinkish-red known as *magenta;* and blue and green produces a blue-green called *cyan* (cyanine blue). In the additive process, then, red, green, and blue are the primaries, and *yellow, magenta, and cyan* are the *secondary* hues.

The secondary hue, magenta, composed of red and blue, is the complement of green; yellow, composed of green and red, is the complement of blue; cyan, composed of green and blue, is the complement of red.

The physicist and the artist/printer are dealing with two different aspects of color. The physicist is concerned with *light;* the artist/printer, with *pigment.* The physicist *adds* color, proceeding from black (no light) to white. The artist/printer *subtracts* from the white of the paper, superimposing color upon color until black (no light) is finally achieved, indicating that all the light the paper is capable of reflecting has been *subtracted.*

The process of mixing pigment on paper (assuming for the purposes of this explanation that the paper is white) is an example of the *subtractive process.*

The Subtractive Color Process

Subtractive color processes depend on the *subtraction* of unwanted colors from light in order to reproduce, to the eye, the colors of the original subject matter. When white light reaches the eye, no color is perceived. It is not until some of the color is subtracted from the totality of light that the eye perceives color. It perceives the color that has *not* been subtracted.

White paper is a reflective surface, a source of *reflected* white light. The very nature of its manufacture was designed to make it so. When this surface has been altered by the addition of color it no longer reflects white light—some of the color has been subtracted. This subtraction is accomplished in the following way:

In order to subtract colors from light, one must move in the opposite direction from the additive process, proceeding from white *through the secondaries* to produce the primaries that are their complements. The three secondary hues

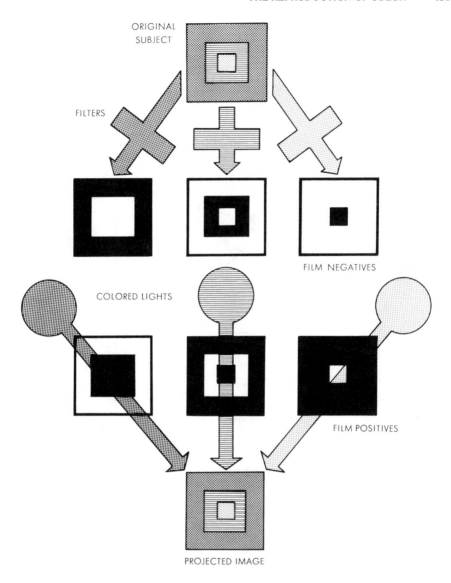

ORIGINAL SUBJECT

FILTERS

FILM NEGATIVES

COLORED LIGHTS

FILM POSITIVES

PROJECTED IMAGE

ADDITIVE SEPARATION

THE ADDITIVE HUES OF THE ORIGINAL SUBJECT ARE SEPARATED BY FILTERS OF THEIR OWN HUE. THE RESULTING FILM NEGATIVES ARE CONVERTED INTO FILM POSITIVES AND ARE PROJECTED, IN REGISTER, WITH COLORED LIGHTS OF THEIR OWN HUE. THE RESULTING IMAGE IS A DUPLICATE OF THE ORIGINAL SUBJECT.

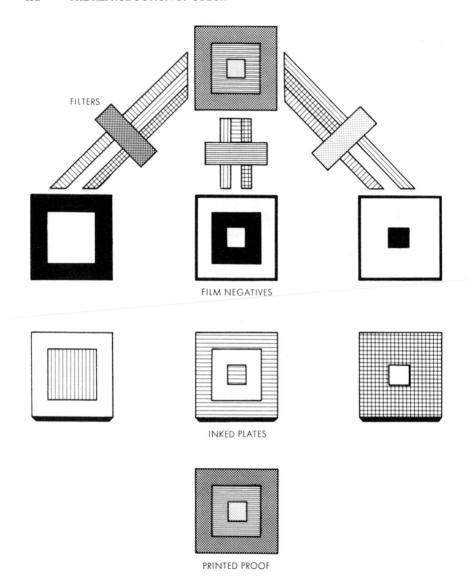

FILTERS

FILM NEGATIVES

INKED PLATES

PRINTED PROOF

SUBTRACTIVE SEPARATION FOR
FOUR-COLOR PROCESS PRINTING

THREE FILM NEGATIVES, REPRESENTING THE SECONDARY HUES YELLOW, MAGENTA AND CYAN,
ARE SEPARATED FROM THE ORIGINAL WITH COMPLEMENTARY-HUED FILTERS—BLUE, GREEN,
AND RED. PLATES ARE MADE FROM EACH NEGATIVE, AND ARE INKED WITH THE SECONDARY
HUES. PRINTED IN REGISTER, THEY COMBINE TO DUPLICATE THE HUES OF THE ORIGINAL.

are as has been noted, magenta, yellow, and cyan. If magenta ink is printed on the paper, it subtracts or eliminates the other two secondaries—yellow and cyan—from the white, allowing only the color sensation of magenta to reach the eye. If magenta and cyan are superimposed, they subtract the yellow. Since the subtracted yellow is composed of green and red, the remaining complementary primary, *blue*, is the only hue remaining for the eye to perceive.

The primary hue, blue, composed of magenta and cyan, is the complement of yellow; red, composed of magenta and yellow, is the complement of cyan; green, composed of cyan and yellow, is the complement of magenta.

In this manner, the physical secondary hues, magenta, yellow, and cyan, can be combined to produce the physical primaries red, green, and blue. Magenta, yellow, and cyan have become the standard hues used throughout the industry for color-process printing. Because these are somewhat close to the artist's primary hues of red, yellow, and blue, it is often erroneously stated that process printing is accomplished with the primary hues red, yellow, and blue.

To summarize, one-color printing requires merely the inking of the plate in the desired color. Two-color printing requires a printing plate for each color, and the art must be separated into its components by camera separation or by preseparation. Any number of colors can be printed in this manner, so long as there is a plate for each color and a cylinder in the press to accommodate each plate. Or it may be done, if time permits, by running the sheets through the press several times, changing plates and reinking at each pass. *Multicolor* printing is distinguished from full-color (process) printing in that there is no attempt to reproduce the full range of the spectrum. The inks need not be process colors, but can be mixed to the individual requirements of the job. Multicolor art may be camera separated or preseparated. *Process printing* is the printing of a full-color impression utilizing three or four plates, inked in the three process hues, plus black. Process inks are the physical *secondary* hues, magenta, yellow, and cyan. Full-color art for process printing must be camera-separated.

COLOR SEPARATION

Color separation involves the extraction of the component hues of a full-color image in order that each of these hues can be recorded on photographic emulsion—an emulsion capable of ultimately producing a positive image—either by the additive or the subtractive process. Separation requires the extraction of not only the solid areas of a hue, but also the percentages of the hue that are found in other hues. As a result a separation negative will carry a great variety of tonal areas, some of which will print in the hue itself, and others which will be contributing factors of different hues.

This extraction or separation is accomplished by photographing through a filter, making a separate exposure through a different filter for each component hue. Colored light, rather than white light, is being reflected from the subject. The filter *subtracts* all the light reflected by a particular hue, thus extracting it from the totality.

An additive image is produced by a combination of the physical primaries—red, green, and blue. To produce an additive transparency, each primary hue must be recorded as an exposed area (black) on the film negative so that when a positive is made, the hue will be represented as a *transparent* area through which light of the same hue may be projected. Three hues of light, superimposed and passing through the separated positive, *add* to form a full-color image.

In order to filter for the additive primaries, filters of the desired hue are used. This red is separated with a red filter. The filter *subtracts* the green and blue from the reflected light. Only red light passes through the filter, exposing the corresponding areas of the negative as desired.

COLOR OF LIGHT	ADD	PRODUCES SENSATION OF:	
Red	—	Red	
Green	—	Green	Primaries
Blue	—	Blue	
Red	Blue	Magenta	
Green	Red	Yellow	Secondaries
Blue	Green	Cyan	
—	Red, green, & blue	White	

COLOR OF INK	SUBTRACTS	PRODUCES SENSATION OF:	
Magenta	Yellow & cyan	Magenta	
Yellow	Magenta & cyan	Yellow	Secondaries
Cyan	Magenta & yellow	Cyan	
Magenta & cyan	Yellow	Blue*	
Magenta & yellow	Cyan	Red	Primaries
Cyan & yellow	Magenta	Green	
Magenta, yellow, & cyan	All light	Black	

Modern color transparencies, color prints, and process printing plates are a result of the subtractive process. As such, the image is produced with a combination of the physical *secondaries*—cyan, magenta, and yellow. In this case, each secondary hue of the subject must produce an *unexposed* area on the negative. In the photographic process, this area will be positively reversed and replaced with

*This color is described as violet in many sources.

COLOR SEPARATION

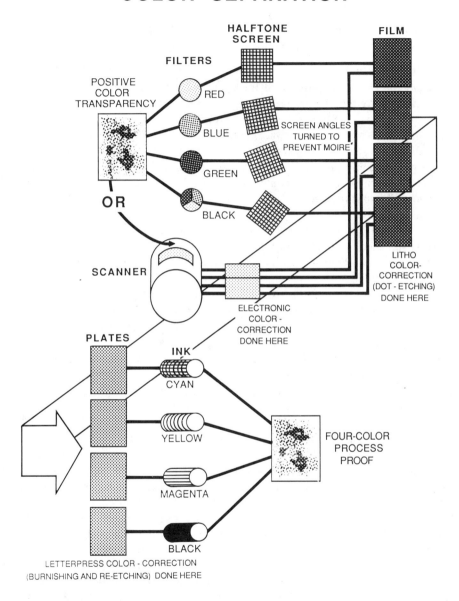

a dye. In process printing, it will produce a printing area on the plate which will be inked with the appropriate hue.

A *secondary hue* is separated from the original image by *filtration through its complement*. The complement of any secondary color is the primary color that is the combination of the remaining two secondaries.

FILTER	SUBTRACTS FROM COPY	SEPARATES FROM COPY
Green	Cyan & Yellow	Magenta
Blue	Magenta & Cyan	Yellow
Red	Magenta & Yellow	Cyan

The green filter is a combination of cyan and yellow. Magenta light, reflecting from the copy, combines with the cyan and the yellow and is completely subtracted. *No light* passes from the purer magenta areas, and only *partial light*—gray—passes from the partial percentages found in the other hues. The reflected magenta light is represented by *unexposed* areas of the film negative.

Black is a separation used solely in process printing and has no counterpart in the photographic process. It is separated either with an amber filter, which subtracts the primaries but allows certain gray values to pass, or by a split-filter exposure. The split filter separates black by a varied exposure through all three of the primary filters.

In order to print the three- or four-color process, the negative separations must be screened and halftone printing plates produced from them. A screen of less than 110 lines per inch is seldom used, except in the case of newspapers which run color. Halftone separations are produced by the direct or the indirect method.

Direct method separation exposures are made directly through the halftone screen, using high-contrast film. Halftone negatives are produced in one step. Plates are made directly from the screened negatives. Screen positives for deep-etch lithography are made by contact-printing the negatives.

In the *indirect method*, halftone negatives or positives are made from intermediate continuous-tone separations. Retouching can be accomplished on the continuous-tone images with either retouching pencils or dye. The indirect method provides a greater degree of tone and color control.

Screen Angles. When color is reproduced photographically, the image is produced by the superimposition of *transparent* dyed layers. In the photographic print, the combined layers of the transparent emulsion subtract from the white of the paper in order to form a full-color image. In printing, the component hues are deposited on paper as dots of ink. The ideal situation would consist of dots of perfectly transparent ink, superimposed exactly over each other. Some dots, however, due to their pattern and size, print partially either on top of or alongside the dots of the first-printed hue. Printer's ink is necessarily more opaque than photographic dye; as a result, some of the lighter dots will be obliterated by the darker ones. This conflict of dot pattern produces an undesirable effect known as moiré. This effect can be readily examined by superimposing two identical sheets of dot-patterned Zip-A-Tone and rotating the top sheet.

The moiré pattern is minimized by changing the screen angle at which each separation is made, forming a mosaic pattern of the dots, which, when viewed at any distance, creates the effect of continuous-tone color. The ideal condition is achieved when the screen angles of the separation are 30 degrees from each other. Thus, in three-color process, the cyan screen is shot at 45 degrees, the magenta at 75 degrees, and the yellow at 105 degrees. In four-color process, it is impossible to include four 30-degree intervals within the 90-degree range of the cross-ruled screen. Therefore, the yellow—the weakest hue—is shot at a 15-degree interval, between either the black and magenta or the magenta and cyan. A typical screen-angle variation for four-color process would be black—45 degrees, magenta—75 degrees, yellow—90 degrees, and cyan—105 degrees.

Often, in order to avoid a moiré pattern, a different screen ruling may be used for the yellow separation. For example, if a 133-line screen is used for magenta, cyan, and black, a 155-line screen will be used for the yellow.

Color Correction

There is a loss of color fidelity in photomechanical reproduction due to the inability of the filter to compensate for ink and printing deficiencies and because the photographic negative does not record the exact ratios of the color densities of the original subject. Consequently, considerable effort is expended by the platemaker in an attempt to "correct" the color—to bring it to a point where it most closely duplicates the color of the original.

Color correction has been traditionally accomplished by the handwork of etchers, either by etching and burnishing on the letterpress plate or by dot-etching on the litho-film positive. Color areas are corrected by dot-alteration in the same manner as the black-and-white halftone.

Suppose, for example, that a red area on a color proof does not match the hue or the value of the original copy. This red area is composed of dots that appear on the magenta and the yellow plates, plus, in all probability, as light dot patterns on the cyan and black plates. If the printed red appears too orange, the yellow dots must be reduced in size or the magenta dots enlarged. If the red appears purplish, the cyan dots must be reduced and perhaps the yellow and the magenta dots enlarged. If the value of the red is too light, the black dots may require enlarging; if too dark, reduction may be necessary. It is the skill of the etcher in visually determining *how much on which plates or negatives* must be corrected that makes the etcher a valued craftsperson.

Although handwork has always been the basis for color correction, photo-graphic masking techniques are currently eliminating a good deal of such work. A *mask* is a photographic image that, when superimposed on another photographic image, will improve its reproduction characteristics. A mask may be negative or positive, and may be employed to alter either a negative or a positive image. Simply stated, the continuous-tone mask is a device for holding back unwanted colors so that the wanted color may be recorded in its proper density. A mask is made by exposing a continuous-tone original film to panchromatic masking film through a special filter.

Masking is an integral part of color separation; the filter goes over the lens, and the mask goes in front of the film. Used in indirect color separation, masks reduce the work of the dot-etcher. They compress the density range of the original, compensate for the deficiencies in process inks, and enhance the detail of the result.

Color Scanning

Electronic color scanning is modern technology's attempt to compensate for the inherent deficiencies of filter separation and process printing.

The electronic color scanner can do the same operations that are done with the camera in direct or indirect color separation. The copy is scanned with a narrow beam of light and collected by three photocells employing red, green, and blue filters. These signals are fed into a computer, which analyzes the information and translates it into an appropriate image—either continuous-tone or halftone—which is exposed onto film by projection lamp.

The computer converts the additives of the original copy to the subtractives required for process printing. The black separation is computed from the other three. The output is either continuous-tone or halftone film. Enlarged separations can be made from 35mm transparencies without grain enlargement.

Images may be computer-enhanced by the color scanner. Sharper picture detail can be created by amplifying the shadow areas of the original. Tone-line

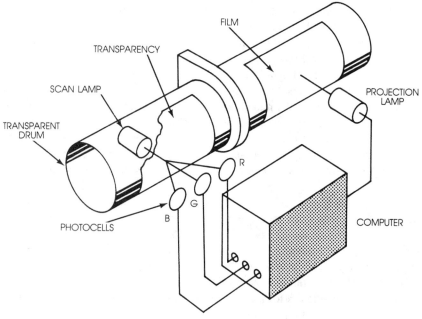

HOW A COLOR SCANNER WORKS

effects and posterizations can be effected by either selective or arbitrary manipulation of the computer. Color correction may be accomplished by either manual manipulation of the signals or by the intervention of computers programmed to compensate for ink, paper, and other printing conditions. Obviously, the result is still dependent upon the skill of the operator.

The electronic scanner can only accept copy that is flexible enough to be wrapped around the scanner cylinder.

Photocomp.   Photocomp(osition) is the montage assembly of positive color transparencies for placement on the color scanner. Rather than "cut and butt" to montage transparencies—a process in which the transparencies are literally cut apart with a razor blade and butted together to form a montage photocomp, by masking and multiple-exposing, produces a one-piece film montage. This is more desirable than cut and butt, which tends to spread apart when it is wrapped around a scanner cylinder, causing an unsightly gap between the montaged pictures (see also page 208). Graphic imaging systems are rendering this technique somewhat obsolete.

The Magenta Contact Screen.   The magenta contact screen consists of cross-lines ruled in magenta rather than black, enabling the opacity of color to be manipulated with the use of filters. It cannot be used in direct separation, as its use will interfere with the separation filters. Use of the magenta screen improves the sharpness of highlight detail and simplifies contrast control.

The Gray Contact Screen.   The gray contact screen, due to its neutral gray color, may be used for direct separation in order to effect some degree of color correction by strengthening dot formation. Filters cannot be used for contrast control; instead, this is effected by standard procedures, such as controlled flash exposure.

The Densitometer.   The densitometer is an electronic device used to measure tonal values accurately. It is especially useful in color separation and correction. *Transmission densitometers* are used to examine negatives and transparent copy; *reflection densitometers* are used to measure opaque copy.

A visual densitometer employs human judgment to visually compare copy densities to a scale of known densities, as observed through its viewer.

Copy for Process Printing

Process printing was an accomplished fact even before a commercially practical method of color photography was perfected. Full-color illustration, executed by hand, could be filter-separated into its three component hues. From these, halftone plates could be made. The first reproduction of color art was made from black-and-white photographs that had been tinted by hand. The development

TYPES OF COPY

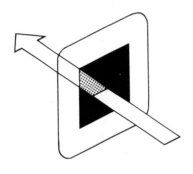
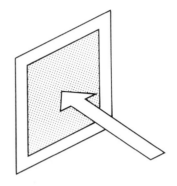

TRANSMISSION COPY   **REFLECTION COPY**
COPY THAT ONE   COPY THAT ONE
SEES THROUGH   LOOKS AT

of a practical color photographic film was the final link in the chain of processes that contribute to printing as we know it today.

There are two types of copy from which platemaking negatives are made—*transmission copy* and *reflection copy*. Transmission copy is photographed with light passing *through* the copy, for example, the color transparency. Reflection copy is photographed with the light that is *reflected* from the copy, copy such as artwork and the photographic print—black and white or color. One looks *through* transmission copy and *at* reflection copy. Both transmission copy and reflection copy are submitted to the platemaker in positive form.

Printing in Color

Process color is printed either dry or wet. In dry printing, each color is allowed to dry before receiving the next impression. This is accomplished in the press by having a separate impression cylinder for each plate cylinder. Thus, the ink is given a short interval in which to dry before proceeding to the following pair of cylinders. The ultimate result in color printing is accomplished in this way. In dry printing, the platemaker makes heavy-printing magenta, cyan, and yellow plates, and a light-accentuating black plate.

Wet printing better meets today's requirements for high-speed press runs. Colors are printed wet—impressions of each color follow so rapidly that there is no appreciable drying time between them. This is accomplished by arranging the plate cylinders around a single large impression cylinder. This allows for a much faster press run, but does not equal the quality of dry printing. In wet printing the plate must use as little ink as possible, avoiding excessive overprinting that would make the colors bleed. In order to accomplish this, black is substituted for the magenta, cyan, and yellow in the darker areas of the subject, thus creating a dark value with less ink. Wet printing almost necessitates the use of four-color process.

Accurate register of the succeeding impressions is a critical factor in both methods.

Progressive Proofs. Progressive proofs, known as "progs," are color proofs submitted by the platemaker or engraver for the client's approval prior to the actual press run. They are made from the separation plates and show the impression of each plate and the resulting effect of each successive color as it is applied. Progressive proofs are pulled on the type of paper that will ultimately be used; publications supply samples of their particular paper for this purpose.

Hollywood progs are sets of progressive proofs showing every possible four-color process combination.

CHAPTER 12
TYPOGRAPHIC
PRODUCTION

Until recently, typographic composition had been the exclusive domain of the typographer. It was the job of the artist or the production specialist to specify and order the type from the typographers, and their concerns were for the sharpness of the type characters, the ability to produce spacing to a critical degree, and the speed with which the job could be accomplished. The advent of the laser typesetting machine was a quantum leap in the attainment of these typographic goals, but technology did not rest upon this accomplishment. Today, with small typesetting machines or personal computers, typography can be composed and proofed by almost anyone who can type, and with this capability has come concern that the world will become inundated with inept typography.[1] Indeed, there is a multitude of contemporary systems capable of producing wider variations in the quality of typographic output than ever before.

Thus, not only is the knowledge of the methodology and the specification of typography essential for the modern artist, it should also be coupled with an eye toward the appropriateness and the aesthetic appearance of the typography itself.

[1] This concern has led the Typographer's International Association to develop the "Q" (Quality) Mark. Licensed to producers and users of photocomposition, it is hoped that the mark will differentiate between genuine photocomposition and its lesser imitators.

TYPOGRAPHIC MEASUREMENT

The unit of measurement for all type, regardless of the manner of its production, is the point, which measures .013837 in., or approximately 1/72 in.

The Units of Type Measurement

Point = 1/72 in. (.0138 in.)
Pica = 12 points, 1/6 in.
Em = a square of the type size
Agate = 5 1/2 points, 1/14 in.

Definitions

The Point. The point is used for the measurement of type height, leading (line-spacing), and the thickness of rules (straight lines).

The Pica. A pica is equal to 12 points and is used for measuring line width (measure), margin width, depth of columns, paragraphs, etc. The *nonpareil* is half a pica or 6 points.

The Cicero. A Cicero is a European unit of type measurement of 0.178 in., roughly equaling a pica. This measuring unit sometimes appears in American computerized page-assembly programs.

The Em. The em is a square of a type size—the exact size depending on the size of the type in question. For example, an 8-point em is 8 points × 8 points, i.e., 8 points square. An en is one-half an em, divided vertically. Thus, an 8-point en would measure 4 points × 8 points.

The em is used to measure spaces, indentions, column sizes, and pages and can be utilized in an area method of type estimation or cost determination. Prices are frequently quoted at a certain figure per thousand ems.

The Agate. The agate is 5 1/2 points or 1/14 inch and is used as a unit of measurement of newspaper column depths.

The Unit. Units are vertical subdivisions of the em. Unit size varies from one type size to another, as does the em. It is the measurement of the *width* of the character, including a small amount on each side. Type characters are usually designed on a 54-unit em system.

Units are used by photo and digital typesetting systems (rather than picas) to measure when a line of type is ready to be justified. Thus, type can be set with normal, loose, or tight letterspacing, and letters can be *kerned* (tucked over or under an adjoining letter).

Set-Width. Set-width is the width of a character, including minimal letterspacing on each side, measured in units.

The Characteristics of Type

Typeface. The classification of a particular type style based on the characteristics of its design; often named after its designer. A typeface may be distorted and still remain within the boundaries of its classification. Thus, the width of the character may be expanded or condensed. The weight—the thickness of the strokes—may be thinned or thickened. Some typical adjectives employed to describe such variations are:

WIDTH	THICKNESS
Condensed	Light
Medium condensed	Medium
Extra condensed	Demibold
Wide	Bold
Extended	Extra bold
Expanded	Black
Open	Ultrabold

Serif. The cross-stroke at the terminals of the letter. The majority of typefaces may be classified as either *serif* or *sans*(without)-*serif* faces.

Kern. The part of the typeface that extends beyond the body—usually occurring in the letters "f" and "j." Italic and script faces require a larger number of kerned letters than Roman and Gothic faces (see page 159).

X-Height. The height of the body of the letter form. Typefaces may appear larger or smaller, depending on the X-height (see page 158).

Gothic. An American colloquialism for any upright, sans-serif typeface.

Roman. A general term used to describe any upright, serif typeface—though not necessarily Roman in its derivation. The term "roman" is applied to all upright typefaces when they are being differentiated from "italic" faces.

Italic. Any slanting typeface; used to distinguish words for importance, emphasis, etc.; also used to differentiate between picture captions and body copy.

Body Type. Typefaces, mostly roman, used for paragraphs and running text, usually in sizes of 14 points or smaller.

Display Type. Typefaces used for headlines and other attention-getting elements, as distinguished from body type. Display type commonly comes in sizes of 14 to 72 points; however, sizes up to 144 points are available.

Pi Characters. Special characters not included in a normal font; scientific and mathematical characters, foreign accents, Greek letters, etc.

The Spacing of Type

Letterspacing. The spacing between the letters. This spacing may be increased in order to avoid a crowded appearance and afford better legibility.

Word Spacing. The spacing between the words, which may be increased or decreased in order to lengthen or shorten a line.

Line Leading. The spacing between the lines.

Minus Spacing. Back-letterspacing on a phototypesetting machine in order to kern letters.

Reverse Linespacing. In some phototypesetting machines, the paper or film may be moved backwards, in order to set a second or third column alongside the first.

Set Solid. Type that has been set without any line leading.

Justification. The process of setting type so that the lines of type will be equal in width (measure) and so that both the left- and right-hand margins will be vertically aligned. This is accomplished by varying the spaces between the words.

Flush Left. Type that has been set so that the left-hand margin aligns vertically and the right-hand margin is allowed to terminate "ragged right," this format has gained in popularity in recent years.

Flush Right. Type that has been set so that the right-hand margin is vertically aligned and the left-hand margin has an irregular alignment. This practice has its artistic applications, but it is often difficult to read.

Flush Left and Right. Justified.

Runaround. Composition wherein a portion of the text has been indented (left or right) to accommodate the insertion of an illustration.

HAND-SET (FOUNDRY) COMPOSITION

Hand-setting was the original method of setting movable type as developed by Gutenberg. It is known as foundry type, because it is cast by and purchased from a type foundry in sets or *fonts*.

The individualized characters are hand-picked from a compartmentalized drawer or *case* and are inserted, one at a time, into a metal composing stick which can be set to a desired line measure. Spacing material, both for words and for lines (see page 147) is at hand in the case; the nomenclature of hand-set typespacing materials persisting even into laser typography. Capable of the discriminate spacing required for headlines, foundry type was combined with machine-set body copy in letterpress forms or furnished as type proofs for pasting on mechanical art. It was still used into the 1960s for headlines, but it has been mostly superseded by photolettering.

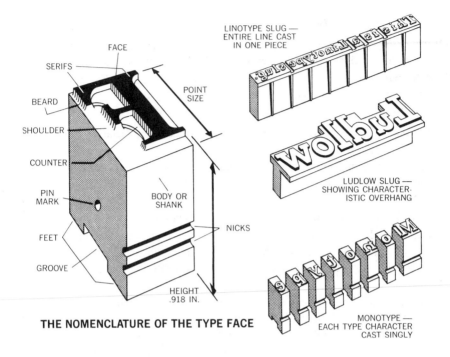

THE NOMENCLATURE OF THE TYPE FACE

METAL TYPE COMPOSITION (HOT TYPE)

Hot type is type that has been set in a mold, or matrix—type that in one stage of its production has existed as molten metal. In addition to foundry type there are (or more accurately, were) three basic hot typesetting machines: the Linotype and the Intertype, the Monotype, and the Ludlow Typograph.

The Linotype

The Linotype was a keyboard-operated machine, invented by Ottmar Mergenthaler in 1886. As the name implies, it cast (molded) one line of type at a time. When a letter-key was depressed, a brass matrix, contained in a magazine atop the machine, was dropped to an assembling elevator which delivered it to the matrix line. Words were formed by the matrices. The spaces between the words were prepared for justification by the insertion of wedge-shaped *space bands*. The machine was preset by its operator to cast lines to a desired pica measure. When the line was nearly full, a justifying lever was activated, forcing the space bands in further, expanding them, which increased the spaces equally until the line was full. Hot metal was then forced into the matrices, and a line of cast-metal type was ejected from the machine.

The Intertype was a keyboard-operated machine, which, from a production standpoint, was similar to the Linotype.

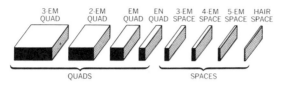

WORD SPACING MATERIALS

LINE SPACING MATERIALS

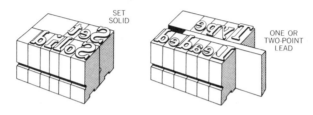

HOW LINE SPACING IS INSERTED

The Monotype

The Monotype was a dual-unit, automatic typecasting machine, invented by Tolbert Lanston in 1887. A machine that cast single type-characters rather than lines of type, it came into commercial use around 1900. It was a two-unit machine in which the "keyboard" unit produced punched paper tape. The machine measured the actual accumulation of character codes on the tape and calculated the necessary justifying and spacing information when the line was almost full. The completed tape was then inserted *backwards* into the "caster" unit. Thus, the instructions for spacing were received *before* the actual casting of the individual characters commenced.[2]

The critical spacing capability of the Monotype made it ideal for setting tabular matter, catalogs, timetables, and other complex typography.

The Ludlow Typograph

The Ludlow was a semiautomatic machine that combined hand and machine setting. Brass Ludlow matrices were stored in compact cases, requiring less room than a comparable selection of foundry type. The matrices were hand-inserted into

---

[2]This concept of inserting separately encoded copy into a typesetter prevails today. Efficient because the encoding can predetermine information about size, style, spacing, and format and thus program the typesetter before it starts to set type, modern typesetters are activated with magnetic tape or computer disks.

This block of copy has just been set solid in 9-point News Gothic. The shoulders of the face provide normal spacing between the lines.

This block of copy has just been set in 9-point News Gothic, leaded one point. A one-point lead has been inserted between each line.

This block of copy has just been set in 9-point News Gothic, leaded two points. A two-point lead has been inserted between each line.

These characters have no letterspacing.

These characters have been letterspaced two points.

LINE SPACING AND LETTERSPACING

a composing stick, which was then inserted into a machine that cast large faces on a 12-point body mold. The resulting T-shaped overhang, found on all sizes larger than 12 points, was characteristic of the Ludlow slug. In printing, this overhang was blocked up with spacing material.

Ludlow matrices and spacing material were easier to handle than foundry type, making the machine ideal for the setting of display lines of 14 points or larger. It was a completely impractical method for the composition of body type in any quantity, although a few lines of type could be set in less time than it took to set up an automatic machine. Ludlow type was also practical when the same line had to be set many times.

Output

The output of the hot-type machine is either the metal type itself, which is used for letterpress printing, or paper proofs which are pasted on mechanical art. The *proof press* is a small but precise printing press designed to print an impression of type that can be examined for errors or defects. Hand-inked and fed, it is not intended for long printing runs.

There are several types of hot-type proof:

Galley Proofs. Type for running (page-to-page) text is initially set in long (9" × 22") trays (galleys) without regard for page separation. A galley proof is a proof pulled from such type, often on newsprint, which is used for proofreading purposes.

Page Proofs. Proofs of text after it has been arranged into separate pages. Sometimes the illustrations appear on page proofs. If not, space is provided for them.

Rough Proofs. Proofs that are pulled without regard for perfection. They show all elements in press position and are used for the purpose of proofreading and press positioning.

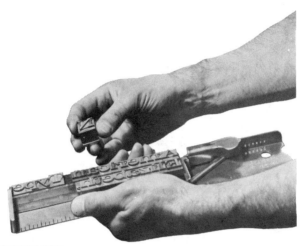

HAND-SETTING FOUNDRY TYPE
IN THE COMPOSING STICK

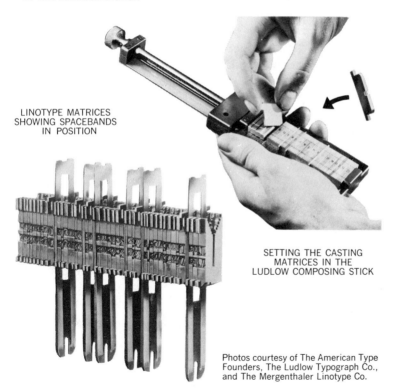

LINOTYPE MATRICES
SHOWING SPACEBANDS
IN POSITION

SETTING THE CASTING
MATRICES IN THE
LUDLOW COMPOSING STICK

Photos courtesy of The American Type
Founders, The Ludlow Typograph Co.,
and The Mergenthaler Linotype Co.

METHODS OF HOT TYPE COMPOSITION

Reproduction Proofs. Clean, perfect proofs that are pulled on coated stock and used for paste-up on the mechanical art. These are commonly known as "repros."

Glassine Proofs. Proofs that are pulled on semitransparent glassine. These are used for placement over the layout or the mechanical art in order to check the "fit" of the copy.

PHOTOTYPESETTING (COLD TYPE)

Cold type is so named because there is no molten metal involved in its production; its output is a result of photography or laser imagery, and the image is produced on either film or paper. Since typewriters also produce type on paper—without recourse to hot metal—they, too, are classified as "cold" composing machines.

There are four generations of phototypesetting machines:

First Generation. These are modifications of hot-type systems in which a photographic negative of a character form is mechanically brought before a lens system and projected photographically onto film or paper.

Second Generation. The character-form negative is scanned electronically and converted into a dot-mosaic or a raster-line image and projected—by a lens—onto film or paper.

Third Generation. The character forms are stored digitally, rather than photographically. They are scanned electronically and projected by a lens system onto film or paper.

Fourth Generation. The character forms are stored digitally. A computer-controlled laser raster-scans the letter forms onto output paper, film, or a printing plate.

In each system, there must be a unit that will generate an *input* of letter characters, together with information concerning the desired type style, size, and format.

There must be a *typesetter,* which will select the desired characters from an optical or a digital font and arrange and space them in accordance with the input information.

There must be *output* of some kind—paper, film, or plate—that can be used for photomechanical reproduction.

Input

The Problem of Justification

A considerable percentage of all type set is set in justified columns (flush left *and* right). Justification is difficult because the rules of hyphenation require the hyphen to be placed between the syllables, precluding its arbitrary insertion at the end of any line that might require one. Thus, justification is generally accomplished by word spacing. Letterspacing cannot be inserted at random to aid in justification; if used at all, it must be equally distributed throughout the line.

Foundry type is justified by eye, and Linotype/Intertype is justified by the expansion of spacebands between the already assembled matrices. Monotype—the hot-type system that produces infinitely more critical spacing—first assembles the character codes as perforated tape. The assembled characters are then measured and the necessary word spacing for justification is determined. The spacing information, followed by the copy, is then fed to the casting unit, which adjusts itself to set columns to the desired measure.

Any typesetting that provides aesthetically pleasing justification may be considered superior. Justification is easier to accomplish if the characters of the copy can be somehow assembled, measured, and distributed into even columns *before* the commencement of the actual typesetting. Computers can be programmed to resolve linebreaks in order to produce justified copy. There are four systems for doing this:

1. *Hyphenless.* Nothing is hyphenated. Lines are justified by manipulating word and letterspacing. The results can be poor.

2. *Discretionary.* The operator hyphenates *every* word of three syllables or more. The computer uses its "discretion" to hyphenate only the necessary words.

3. *Logic.* The computer is programmed with a set of hyphenation rules and all appropriate words are hyphenated. If the rules do not apply to a particular situation, the word will not be hyphenated. Instead, the line will be justified with word or letterspacing.

4. *Exception dictionary.* Some computers have a dictionary of words that are exceptions to the rules. Some dictionaries are more extensive than others.

Because of the extra effort and/or expense involved in justification, the flush-left format—type that is aligned on the left margin without any attempt to do so on the right—has gained popularity in recent years.

Input Devices. Retaining the principle of the original Monotype, many input devices are keyboard-operated consoles that encode the copy by perforating paper tape or encoding either magnetic tape or a floppy disk. Many of these units are equipped with a visual display terminal (VDT), which enables the operator to view the line being encoded. The input unit programs the necessary information for the typesetting unit—copy, point size, spacing, often including hyphenation, line width, and leading—on the tape, which is then used to activate the typesetting unit. In more up-to-date systems, there is no necessity to encode a tape; the type is composed and specified on the VDT and fed directly to the typesetting unit.

Many input devices incorporate a memory. This enables the operator to store and recall portions of the copy in order to edit, revise, or rearrange the copy before it is sent to the typesetting unit. Encoded copy that has not been edited is known as *raw*, while copy that has been encoded, edited, and is ready for the typesetter is known as *clean.*

It is not necessary for the input device to function in proximity to the typesetting unit; it may transput the input over wire for a considerable distance. A *modem* is a device which can be used to transmit typesetter input over the telephone. Wire transmission is preferable to radio, microwave, or satellite transmission, because wire can be rendered static-free.

OCR Systems.   Input may be accomplished with an OCR (Optical Character Recognition) system. The OCR is a high-speed device that can read typewritten, typeset, or in some cases even handwritten, manuscripts and convert them into typesetting machine language. Older OCRs read from typewriters equipped with ball fonts that bear OCR bar codes underneath the normal characters.

OCR produces either paper or magnetic tape or input to a computerized storage device. It is not improbable that in the very near future, input tape may be capable of being encoded by the human voice.

Editing typewriters—often known as revision typewriters—permit fast typing onto magnetic cards or magnetic tapes that can be easily corrected, edited, and even transposed before producing the final clean tape. Tape-merging devices are devices that enable a second corrected tape to override the original tape in selected places, thus producing a single clean tape.

A *teletype* machine may be used to generate input for a typesetter. If the teletype is transmitting raw news from a wire service, it will probably have to be fed into a computer storage unit first, so that it may be edited.

A *line printer* is a high-speed device that produces a printout from either raw or clean tape. The printout may be used for proofreading, additional editing, or filing. *Hard copy* is copy produced by a line printer *before* the typesetter sets it.

Typesetters

First Generation.   The phototypesetting machine is basically a device that produces typography on film or photographic paper by the use of master photographic character negatives rather than casting matrices. Each character negative must be selected, brought into position, possibly enlarged or reduced, and exposed to the film or the paper. The film or paper must be properly shifted to accommodate the spacing requirements of the next character. Thus, the criteria of such machines are the speed of their character assembly and exposure and their ability to provide acceptable spacing.

The way this is accomplished varies from system to system. Systems rely on optics and mechanics rather than electronics, and their photographic character fonts may be stored on photo-disks, drums, or grids. The variety of sizes that may be obtained from a single font varies considerably.

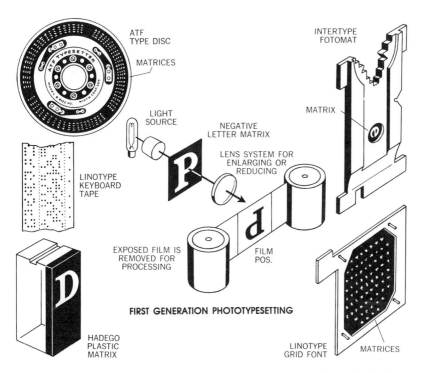

ATF
TYPE DISC

MATRICES

INTERTYPE
FOTOMAT

LIGHT
SOURCE

NEGATIVE
LETTER MATRIX

MATRIX

LINOTYPE
KEYBOARD
TAPE

LENS SYSTEM FOR
ENLARGING OR
REDUCING

EXPOSED FILM IS
REMOVED FOR
PROCESSING

FILM
POS.

FIRST GENERATION PHOTOTYPESETTING

HADEGO
PLASTIC
MATRIX

LINOTYPE
GRID FONT

MATRICES

Input to these machines is by *direct entry*—a keyboard built into the machine. As desktop models, they are ideal for in-office typesetting functions. Unless such a machine has a correcting terminal, there is no way to correct the input, and its speed is determined by the skill of the operator.

Second Generation.   Second-generation typesetters rely more heavily on electronics than their first-generation predecessors. They encompass such electronic functions as optical character recognition, information storage and retrieval, and cathode-ray tube (CRT) imagery.

The photo unit contains the interchangeable type matrices—disks, grids, or drums containing the character negatives. The input is paper or magnetic tape, although some models are activated by the electronic input of a computerized memory system. The input is read by the unit and transmitted to the control circuitry, where it is merged with programmed information—character widths, spacing combinations, etc.—about the typeface in use. Utilizing this combined knowledge (the justified copy and the type characteristics), the control circuitry activates the phototypesetter, bringing the desired character negative and the enlarging/reducing lens into the proper combination for exposure.

The CRT typesetter is an ultra high-speed system that composes type by photographing characters generated on the screen of a cathode-ray tube. Stored on a negative character-grid, the characters are scanned and built up with a series of vertical "raster" lines in such high resolution (number per inch) that the "strokes" are not discernible; the resolution is finer than printing-plate or photographic-paper grain. In a dot-mosaic system, the image is composed of dots rather than raster lines. The raster image forms on the CRT screen from whence it is projected, through a lens system, onto output film.

A CRT typesetter can set lines on each pass of the scan carriage. Setting alternately from left to right and right to left doubles the output of the system.

Digital Typesetting. A digital type font is a computerized set of minutely spaced coordinates for each character, stored on magnetic disks in a typesetter's electronic memory. These coordinates plot the outline shape of the character, which is then filled in by parallel strokes generated on either a CRT screen or by a laser. The greater the number of strokes employed, the sharper the character.

Unlike film masters, the digital character shapes do not physically exist. They are merely stored electronic information, which is called up by an input code to be processed to the output tube or the laser.

Photographic negative masters are made in small point sizes and enlarged, while digital masters are stored in large sizes and reduced, thus minimizing the "staircase effect" caused by the ends of the strokes. The trend is to offer one master

PHOTOTYPESETTER MEASUREMENTS

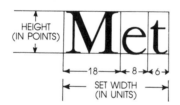

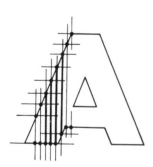

A HIGHLY EXAGGERATED VIEW
SHOWING HOW DIGITIZED INFORMATION
PLOTS THE COORDINATES OF THE EDGES
OF THE LETTER AND FILLS IN THE SPACE
WITH RASTER OR LASER LINES.

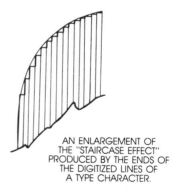

AN ENLARGEMENT OF
THE "STAIRCASE EFFECT"
PRODUCED BY THE ENDS OF
THE DIGITIZED LINES OF
A TYPE CHARACTER.

of each typeface, which may to be utilized to create all other sizes of the face. The initial digitizing of an alphabet—converting it to a grid pattern—is a complex, highly sophisticated operation. Considerable editorial discretion is required of its manufacturer to assure its ability to meet the standards of the market—especially those of good advertising art.

Third Generation. Third-generation typesetters store their character forms digitally in their computers. Copy input is with tape, disk, or OCR. The digital characters thus generated are formed on a CRT, where they are photographed on paper or film by a lens system. Due to a minimum of moving parts, this results in extremely high operating speeds.

Digital-scan machines are extremely expensive. In order to reduce the machine's cost, the digitized fonts of several systems are stored on soft disks, rather than hard ones. Soft ("floppy") disks are thin, flexible, inexpensive magnetic disks that store digitized information and can be easily inserted or removed from the computer. The typographer can be provided—by the manufacturer—with a master font disk, which can be copied onto a less expensive floppy disk by the typographer's machine.

By electronically deflecting the beam of the CRT scan, special typographic effects, such as slanting (not true italic), expansion, or condensation, can be created from the original digitized type design.

Fourth Generation. Fourth-generation typesetters also store their characters digitally, but the characters are generated by a laser, rather than a CRT. "Laser" is an acronym for Light Amplification by Stimulated Emission of Radiation. A laser consists of a tiny, highly concentrated 1.3 mil-wide beam of light. (A mil is $\frac{1}{1000}$th of an inch.) The laser light source, activated by the digitized type characteristics, scans the image onto dry output-paper, film, or a plate with a resolution of about 700 lines per inch. This can be accomplished with as few as four moving parts.

Since the character forms are defined by a scanning beam that deposits them on the output surface a scan-line at a time (rather than by photographing the entire character form as it appears as a complete set of lines displayed on a CRT), the signals activating the output laser can be transmitted to any desired location. All generations of phototypesetters can be activated by input transmitted over a distance; it is the ability of the laser typesetting system to transmit impulses, over a distance, which will produce a printing plate, that makes its potential greater than that of its predecessors.

The Linotronic® Imagesetting System

Called an imagesetting system rather than a typesetter, the Linotronic 100 series is a frontrunning laser typographic system. The Linotronic system accepts input from its own workstation, where the type is keyboarded, composed, and

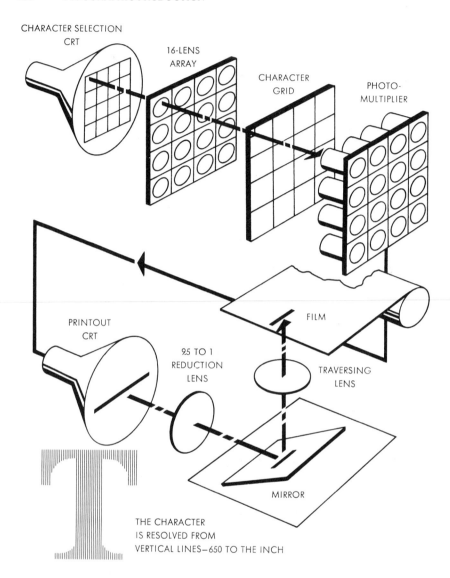

CHARACTER SELECTION CRT

16-LENS ARRAY

CHARACTER GRID

PHOTO-MULTIPLIER

PRINTOUT CRT

9.5 TO 1 REDUCTION LENS

FILM

TRAVERSING LENS

MIRROR

THE CHARACTER IS RESOLVED FROM VERTICAL LINES—650 TO THE INCH

THE LINOTRON 505 CATHODE-RAY TYPESETTER

ACTUATED BY TAPE CODES, THE SELECTION CRT PROJECTS A SCANNING RASTER (STROKE) IN ONE OF 16 POSITIONS. THIS PASSES THROUGH A LENS AND A CHARACTER-NEGATIVE IN ONE OF THE 16 SECTIONS OF THE GRID. A PHOTOMULTIPLIER TRANSMITS IT TO THE PRINT-OUT CRT, WHERE THE CHARACTER IS FORMED, A STROKE AT A TIME. THE IMAGE IS THEN PROJECTED THROUGH A LENS SYSTEM ONTO THE OUTPUT FILM.

THE LINOTRONIC®300 IMAGESETTING SYSTEM

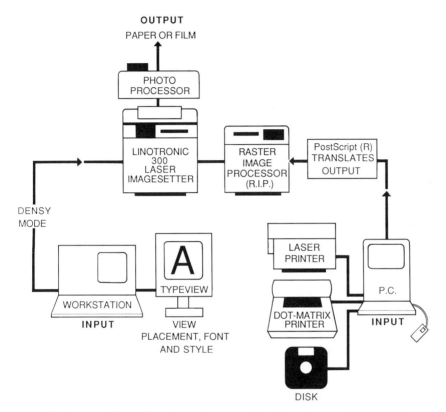

specified on a VDT. The input is transmitted in densy, which is Linotype's language, to the imagesetter where type and stored graphics are processed with a laser. The imagesetter also accepts input from personal computers, sending it through a controller driven by Adobe's PostScript® software in order to produce laser-imaged output of the highest resolution.

Low-cost personal computers such as Apple's Macintosh® may serve as composing workstations, driving the Linotronic 100 or 300 laser imagesetters. Multiple workstations may be networked to the imagesetters. Text, tints and patterns, line art, and halftones may be generated at the workstations as well as a wide range of business applications, which may be produced by the appropriate software. The inclusion of Linotype's imagesetting system provides the user with access to the entire library of Linotype type faces.

Output from this system is paper or film, which must be processed in the darkroom.

STYLES OF SERIFS

BRACKETED   UN-   SQUARE   SANS (WITHOUT)
             BRACKETED   SERIF

PARTS OF THE TYPEFACE

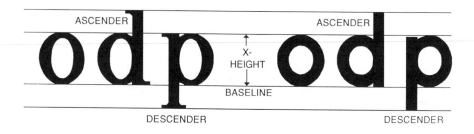

ASCENDER

ASCENDER

X-HEIGHT

BASELINE

DESCENDER   DESCENDER

OUTPUT

When the character forms are exposed by the typesetter to a photographically sensitive surface, the surface must be processed (developed). This may be accomplished in a separate darkroom—as in some older systems—or by a photographic film processor attached directly to the typesetting unit.

The output of the phototypesetter can be:

Paper positives   Film negatives
Paper negatives   Film positives

The output of a laser typesetter is dry (silverless) paper or a laser facsimile plate.

Paper positives are used for mechanical art; they are pasted up according to normal procedures.

Paper negatives are used to produce reverse copy on mechanical art.

Film negatives may be stripped onto a flat and used for letterpress or negative-working offset plates.

Film positives can be used for making *reverse* letterpress plates, *reverse* negative-working offset plates, positive-working offset plates, and deep-etch offset plates.

Rough Proofs.   For proofreading purposes, photographic or digital type is submitted as a paper positive, or *reader,* whether it was produced as positive or negative film. Paper output is copied electrostatically (photocopied). Thus type for reading is submitted as:

Vandykes	Photoprints
Blueprints	Electrostatic prints

Reproduction Proofs.   Sharp, perfect proofs are submitted for pasteup on the mechanical art.

Transparent Proofs.   Proofs on transparent material such as 3-M Color Key or film positive typesetter output may be submitted for checking the "fit" of the copy on the mechanical art.

Photographic Paper.   There are two types of photographic paper used in cold typography: *RC* (resin-coated base) and *S* (stabilization) paper. RC produces flat, durable prints, which are processed in the normal manner—develop, fix, and dry. S has a developing agent. Development takes seconds. A second stabilizing bath sets the image, producing a print dry enough to paste up. Such a print is not permanent and must be hypo-fixed if permanence is desired.

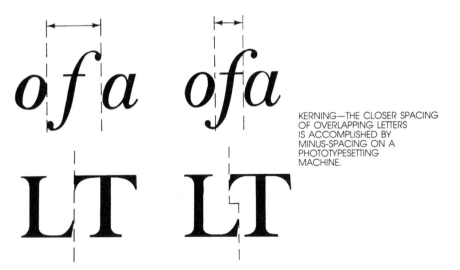

KERNING—THE CLOSER SPACING OF OVERLAPPING LETTERS IS ACCOMPLISHED BY MINUS-SPACING ON A PHOTOTYPESETTING MACHINE.

KERNING

Criteria for Selecting a Typesetting System

What typefaces are available and how well are they designed?

What sizes are available? (Copy set in the same size and style face will vary from manufacturer to manufacturer, in both the type design and the number of characters per pica.)

What is the system's maximum line width?

What is the maximum and minimum line leading?

How many units are there to the em? (This is the system's capacity for critical justification.)

Is the system capable of producing kerned letters? (The ability to kern letters—tuck them under, or over, the overhang of an adjacent letter—is critical to aesthetic letterspacing. On some machines, kerning is controlled by the operator, while in others, kerning information is stored in a computer memory.)

Can typefaces be mixed within a line?

Can type sizes be mixed within a line?

When characters and sizes are mixed, are they bottom-aligned or top-aligned?

Are pi characters (special characters not included in a normal font) available?

What is the width of the output paper or film? Will it produce both positives and negatives?

What type of input is utilized? Direct from keyboard, paper or magnetic tape, disk, OCR, teletype, computer cards?

How does the machine make justification decisions, and will it accept unjustified input?

Photolettering

Photolettering, or film type, should not be confused with phototypesetting. Photolettering is used for display lines and eye-catching headlines, a substitute for hand-lettering rather than typography.

The film-type machine delivers positive or negative lettering in single strips, usually about 35mm, which are pasted on mechanical art. Available fonts consist of fancy scripts, brush letters, outline letters, and unique shadow arrangements; standard typefaces are also available.

Since a skilled film-type operator can connect script-letter strokes more accurately than a typographer, film type represents an excellent source of inexpensive script lettering. Some machines enable the operator to distort letter and word shapes in order to obtain unique effects. This is especially useful when it is necessary for lettering to appear in perspective.

Courtesy of the Visual Graphics Corp., Manufacturer

A CHART SHOWING THE VERSATILITY OF THE PHOTO-TYPOSITOR®

The Typositor.   The Typositor is an extremely versatile photolettering machine used for the composition of display headlines. The machine has over 500 fonts available in all styles and, additionally, will accept any 2-inch negative film reel. Sizes ranging from 9 to 144 points may be set. A modification lens system condenses, expands, backslants, and italicizes—and is capable of bouncing, staggering, and altering proportion. Lettering can be curved, set in an arc, or set in perspective.

The machine is electronically timed and controlled. A viewing system allows the operator to see every letter, space, or distortion; a visible developing chamber develops each letter individually and instantly as it is exposed. The film is developed with concentrated liquids; no darkroom facilities are necessary.

The Typositor produces lettering on paper or film. Film and paper positives are converted to negatives with a reversal apparatus.

Kroy Type.   Kroy type is produced by a typewriter-like machine that uses a photo-negative matrix. Body type emerges as opaque characters on a strip of self-adhesive transparent tape, which may be adhered, in position, to charts, presentations, and so on.

Impact Lettering Machines.   Similar to typewriters, these machines produce type on pressure-sensitive tape. Available in the larger display-type sizes, the font contains relief character images which are struck onto the tape through a carbon ribbon.

Typewriter Composition

The prevalence of offset lithography, especially the use of the paper offset plate that can be typed upon directly, has resulted in considerable use of typewriter composition for work where economy is an important factor. Although an ordinary manual or electric typewriter may be used, these contain no mechanism for proportional letterspacing or for the justification of lines. Common typewriter faces are somewhat less than distinctive. As a result, typewriters that have letterspacing and justifying devices as well as unique and often interchangeable typefaces have come into widespread use. Some of these machines are:

The Vari-typer. The Vari-typer is a type-composing machine designed for office use. Resembling a typewriter, it has a removable type bar that comes in over 600 varieties of typefaces, ranging in size from 6 to 18 points.

The machine is equipped with a differential letterspacing mechanism, which spaces out the characters of the alphabet to their individual width. Thus wider characters like "M" and "W" are set in wider spaces than narrow characters such as "i" and "l." An automatic justification mechanism spaces out each line of the copy to a predetermined width. Line leading is accomplished by means of a special point-calibrated scale.

The Justowriter. The Justowriter is an automatic, tape-operated composing machine consisting of two units: the *recorder* and the *reproducer.* The first unit produces unjustified typewritten copy and punched tape. The tape is fed into the second unit, which justifies the line automatically from information contained on the tape. The units are similar in appearance, each having an electric-typewriter keyboard. The reproducer is capable of reproducing justified lines at the rate of 100 lines per minute. The end result may be a justified paper-page, a galley, or a direct-image plate for offset reproduction.

The IBM Selectric Composer. This system utilizes a Selectric typewriter with its interchangeable "ball" type font. The *SC* system is a single-unit machine that involves double-typing; the *MT* system is a more sophisticated one, activated by encoded magnetic tape. The machine uses electronic logic to compose the copy into the desired format.

The typist operates a Selectric typewriter which records the copy on magnetic tape. Proofreading copy is being produced simultaneously. The tape is placed in the MT reader unit, and the appropriate composing instructions are programmed on the control panel. The Selectric composer—a second typewriter—is set up with the desired type element, and the typesetting is monitored by the operator. Camera-ready copy is composed automatically.

Word-Processing Typewriters. Word-processing typewriters facilitate the production of typed composition in that it is easier to revise, delete, or insert material than with normal corrective procedures. Additionally, they may feature memories and spelling/hyphenation dictionaries. Output from these machines is dot-printer quality; it takes a more sophisticated system to produce type-quality output.

Automatic Electric Typewriters. The automatic typewriter is used to produce multiple letters for direct-mail purposes when it is desirable to have each letter appear as if it had been individually typed rather than reproduced. These typewriters operate from a master tape; several are used simultaneously. The operator produces the master tape—the body of the letter—on a special machine. A letterhead page—or whatever—is inserted into each typewriter, and the address, salutation, or personalized information is input to each machine by an individualized punch-card. The tape then takes over, and each machine automatically types the body of the message from the information stored on the tape. The operator can stop any machine and insert individual information at will.

Instant Lettering

There are several brands of instant lettering, each of which enables the artist to produce display lines and emergency jobs for which there is no time to call a typographer. Additionally, instant lettering finds widespread use in the preparation of comprehensive art and for charts and other presentational material. Instant lettering can be highly effective in the hands of a competent artist.

Transfer Type. Also known as "rub-down" lettering, transfer type consists of a transparent font sheet containing letters that, when rubbed with a pencil or a stylus, will transfer to any smooth surface directly beneath the sheet. This is an effective method only if the artist has an eye for letterspacing and alignment, as each letter must be hand-positioned and rubbed off one at a time. Transfer type is available in over 500 faces, ranging in size from 10 to 188 points.

Adhesive Type. Adhesive type is furnished in transparent, adhesive-backed font sheets. Each letter must be individually cut out, positioned, and burnished in order to make the adhesive adhere. Adhesive type is not as effective as transfer type, since the transparent sheet is still in evidence after the letter has been fixed in place. This type is also available in a wide variety of faces and sizes.

COPY-FITTING

Copy-fitting is the process of determining the exact area that a piece of typewritten copy will fill, or can be made to fill, when set in specific typeface and size.

Copy area must be measured to determine the space it will occupy so that a well-designed layout may be created. After the layout and the copy have been approved for production— often entailing changes from the originally submitted versions—the typography must be specified so that the typographer can compose it in accordance with the layout. The neophyte artist may be content to submit an outline of the desired area, instructing the typographer to "fit this," but the professional artist is concerned with accurate measurement and specification that will produce a predictable result.

In order to copy-fit efficiently, one needs the following items:

1. *Typewritten copy.* Copy to be fitted should always be typewritten, and it is within the province of the copy-fitter to insist that this be done.

2. *Pica rule.* The printer's (and the specifier's) rule is known as the *pica rule.* Inches, picas and nonpareils, agate lines, and often 8- and/or 10-point scales are included.

3. *Line gauge.* A line gauge is a plastic template containing several point-size scales, which are used to measure the depth of type composition. Each type size is measured with its own scale, but if the lines are to be leaded one or two points, a scale of one or two points larger is used to measure the leaded depth (see page 182).

4. *Specimen book.* No typographers stock all the existing typefaces; neither are they generally equipped with all the various composing machinery; therefore, it is often frustrating to attempt to select type from specimens supplied in a textbook. Any typographers who anticipate doing business will gladly supply specimens of the faces they stock. Such specimens are known as *type books.*

Some specimen books contain *single-line specimens.* These are sample lines, printed in a single convenient size, of each face the typographer stocks. Accompanying these specimens is a listing of the available point sizes, together with an indication of the typeface's composing system.

Other, more elaborate, books contain each face printed in a variety of sizes—often, in the case of body type, with various line endings. Many contain copy-fitting charts showing the number of characters that will fit in a desired pica measure. If not, such charts are readily available from most typesetting systems. To attempt to fit or specify type accurately without such material at hand is unwise.

Few type-specimen books contain complete alphabets. Usually the specimen is composed in some sort of sentence; sometimes a portion of the alphabet is included. This is done because typographers are in business to sell type, and wish to discourage the photostatting of alphabets for use in pasting up display lines by hand. A complete alphabet book is an invaluable asset as reference for finished or comprehensive lettering and should be preserved with the utmost care and regard.

In order to determine the size of printed type, it should be compared with either a specimen of known size or a gauge designed specifically for measuring type sizes. Measurement of a printed impression with a *point scale* does not determine the *actual point size,* since a typeface does not occupy the entire area of the body. The face of a 14-point type may measure only 10 points, the rest of the measurement being taken up with shoulder. An 18-point light condensed face can measure more than an 18-point bold of the same family.

5. *Copy-fitting charts.* Copy-fitting charts—an absolute must—show the *average number of characters per pica* for each size and style of typeface (see pages 170–73).

6. *Haberule.* The Haberule is a patented device that affords easy specification of body copy without reference to additional copy-fitting charts. The Haberule consists of a plastic depth-measuring scale, a complete listing of body typefaces, and a set of spiral-bound scales for the determination of pica width. A number of manufacturers of contemporary typesetting machines also provide scales or other devices for measuring their output.

7. *Pocket calculator.* Although copy-fitting requires only simple arithmetic, a pocket calculator will speed the process and eliminate errors.

Fitting Display Type

The fitting of display type is generally a simple matter, because such copy is seldom so lengthy that an accurate character count cannot be easily made. A comparative count of a specimen of the desired type will determine the space the copy will occupy in that particular face and size. This measurement can be transferred to or from the layout with a ruler or dividers. (It should be kept in mind that capital letters occupy more space than lower-case letters.)

Body copy is generally indicated on the layout by a series of ruled lines. Headlines, however, are generally lettered out, since it is desirable to give the client an indication of how the headline will actually appear. Therefore, when lettering the headline on the layout, the artist should provide an accurate representation of the particular typeface and size that will eventually be ordered. For layout purposes—if the specimen contains most of the alphabet—the desired lettering can be traced. In order to prepare a tight comprehensive layout, either transfer or adhesive lettering may be used. If the layout lettering has been done accurately, it is a simple matter for the type specifier, or the mechanical artist, to locate the matching face and size in a specimen book and specify accordingly.

The type specifier and the mechanical artist should become accustomed to checking headline fit in the event that the layout artist has miscalculated.

Headlines are not always set in a single line. A headline may consist of several lines—flush left or right, centered, or justified. When a headline sentence is broken into several lines by the artist, care should be taken that the breakup does not alter the meaning of the sentence in any way. Headline width is a critical factor, since it may have been designed to fit within a certain limited area, to run the extreme width of an advertisement, or to align with an illustration or accompanying body copy. Therefore, it is often necessary to have the headline attain an *exact* measure. A precise fit may be obtained by any one of the following methods:

1. Select a size that will come to slightly less than the desired measure, and instruct the typographer to space the line(s) to the desired measure. This can be accomplished by letterspacing, word spacing, or both. It should be borne in mind that typographers can only *increase* the normal length of a line, they cannot *decrease* it.

2. Select a type size that will come to slightly less than the desired measure; cut the proof apart and word space the line(s) on the mechanical art.

3. Set the line in any convenient size and photostatically enlarge or reduce it to fit.

4. Order photolettering to size.

Fitting Body Type

The purpose of accurate copy-fitting is to predetermine, as closely as possible, the actual area the copy will occupy in order to produce a layout or to order typography that will fit the layout. This fit is determined by count and measurement and by the clarity of instructions that are given to the typographer.

The typographer sets type to a specified size and measure. Once these have been established, the amount of copy will govern the number of lines, and no degree of wishful thinking will cause the lines to shrink. For example, 630 characters, set solid in 8-point Times Roman to a 20-pica measure, will run 10 lines deep or 6.6 picas. They cannot be set in fewer lines or made to occupy less depth so long as the type size and measure are maintained. By leading 2 points, 18 points can be gained—increasing the total depth to 8.1 picas—but there will be 10 lines of copy. If the depth must be decreased, a wider measure or a smaller or narrower size must be used. If the depth must be increased beyond the 2-point leading, a narrower measure or a larger or wider size must be employed. It is the ability to manipulate size, measure, and leading that constitutes good copy-fitting.

The Character-Count Method.   The character-count method is the most accurate and widely used means of copy- fitting.

Copy area is determined by counting the number of characters in the typewritten copy, ascertaining the number of characters of a particular typeface and size that will fit in a desired measure, and dividing the total number of characters by this figure in order to determine the required number of lines. Once the characters have been counted, it is a simple matter to refer to a chart showing the number of characters per pica measure of a particular typeface. Thus, the method that provides the fastest, most accurate character count is obviously the most efficient.

46 CHARACTERS

−11

|← ——— *66 CHARACTERS* ————— →|

There are a certain number of characters in this typewritten copy.
The object is to count them. Not just the letters, but each punctuation
and space as well. If some of the typing has been ~~xxxxxxxxx~~ crossed
out, this also must be taken into account. The characters could be
counted individually, but obviously this would result in a considerable
waste of time. The number of words could be counted, but "is", "and"
and "considerable" are all words. The result would be an inaccurate
average, especially if this copy were to contain a lot of words like
"polyethylene" and "photomechanical". The character count is the most
accurate method and is the one used by the professional. *−10*

Once the characters have been counted, the next step is to determine
how many characters of a particular type face will fit into a desired
width (measure). Obviously, it is possible to fit more 8-point characters than 10-point characters into a line. The size is determined
by the amount of legibility that is required - the larger the type, the
easier it is to read. *+21*

Type faces of a similar size do not necessarily have the same character
width. A 30-pica measure will, for example, accommodate 78 characters
of 10-point Baskerville, while the same measure will hold 83 characters
of 10-point Times Roman. Therefore, it is necessary to refer to the
chart of the specific type face that is desired. *−18*

21 LINES

$$\begin{array}{r} 66 \\ 20 \\ \hline 1320 \\ + \ 21 \ (SHORT\ LINE) \\ \hline 1341 \\ + \ 46 \ \left(\begin{array}{c}CHARS.\ TO\ RIGHT \\ OF\ LINE\end{array}\right) \\ \hline 1387 \\ - \ 39 \ (11 + 10 + 18) \\ \hline 1348 \ \ TOTAL\ CHARACTER \\ COUNT \end{array}$$

COUNTING CHARACTERS IN TYPEWRITTEN COPY

Each typewriter character occupies the same width.[3] Thus if the left-hand margin has been kept flush, the total character count of any typed line will be equal to any other line of the same measure. If a vertical pencil rule is drawn through the last character in the shortest line of the copy, all the lines to the left of the rule will contain an equal character count. If this is not true due to proportional letterspacing, the number of characters per line should be considered as an average per-line count rather than a precise one. The characters to the right of the line can be easily counted and added to the total of those on the left. The pencil rule should not be drawn through a short line at the end of a paragraph, or any other abnormally short line.

Steps in the character-count method of copy-fitting are:

1. Draw a vertical pencil rule through the shortest line of the typed copy.

2. Count the number of *characters* in the line. A character consists of *every* letter, space, and punctuation mark. Do not forget to include the character that falls on the line. Depending upon the typewriter, this total will represent either the *exact* number of characters in each line or the *average* number of characters in each line.

3. Multiply this count by the total number of lines. Do not include the short, end-of-paragraph lines in this total.

4. Count the characters to the *right* of the pencil rule and in the short lines (if any) at the ends of the paragraphs. *Subtract* any characters that have been crossed out or otherwise deleted.

5. *Add* this figure to the multiplied total. This gives the *total character count.*

6. Select an appropriate typeface—10-point Times Roman, for example, which measures 2.6 characters per pica. (This information was determined from the copy-fitting chart on pages 170–71.)

7. Measure the layout width in picas. In this instance, assume that the layout area measures 24 picas.

8. Refer to the chart on pages 171–72. The chart shows that a 24-pica measure will accommodate 65 characters of a typeface with a 2.6 count.

9. *Divide* the per-line character count obtained from the chart into the total character count obtained in step 5. This gives the total number of *type lines* required to set the copy in the particular face. Each fraction of a line must be counted as a line.

$$
\begin{array}{r}
20.7 \text{ or } 21 \; \textit{lines} \\
65 \overline{)\; 1348.0} \\
\underline{130} \\
480 \\
\underline{455}
\end{array}
$$

[3]Most American manually operated typewriters employ one of two sizes: Pica (12-point), which has 10 characters to the inch, or Elite (10-point), which has 12 characters to the inch. Character-counting scales are available for these sizes. Electric typewriters and newer imports often have distinctive type, as well as proportional letterspacing, which must be individually measured when encountered.

10. *Multiply* the total number of lines by the *point size* of the type. This gives the depth of the required area in points when the type is set solid.

21 × 10 = *210 points*

11. *Divide* this figure by 12 in order to determine the *depth in picas.*

```
      17.5 picas
12 ) 210.0
     12
     ---
     90
     84
     ---
     60
     60
     ---
```

Or measure the depth with a line gauge.

12. *If the copy is short of the layout area,* lead out the lines. Add the *point total* that is added between the lines to the total depth. Obviously, if a paragraph is 10 lines deep and 9 points short of the desired depth, a 1-point lead between each line will cause the type to fill the area. More than 2-point line leading is seldom desirable in normal body copy. If leading is impractical, try a larger size or an expanded face in order to fill the space.

13. If the copy exceeds the layout area, try a smaller size or a condensed face. In either case, if the depth is a critical factor, a different measure may be tried—provided the width is not critical as well.

14. If all steps prove impractical, and the fitting of the copy into the area becomes a complete impossibility, request the client to cut or add to the copy. This should only be done as a last resort.

It is often necessary to calculate copy depth when the type size and measure have been predetermined. Suppose it is mandatory to set copy in 10-point Times Roman to an 18-pica measure. Referral to the chart shows that an 18-pica measure can accommodate 47 characters. The 47 characters are counted off on a typewritten copy line, and a vertical rule is drawn through this point. The number of *lines* to the left of the rule are counted. The *characters* to the right of the rule can be physically counted or estimated and converted to lines by dividing by 47. This line count is added to the total. The total number of lines, multiplied by the point size of the type, *plus the point size of the intended leading* gives the total point depth of the copy, which can be readily converted to picas.

It is often necessary to set copy to a predetermined depth. On such occasions it is desirable to ascertain the width that the copy will occupy in order to make

COPY FITTING CHART
POINT SIZE

	6	7	8	9	10	11	12	14	18
Baskerville with Italic			3.1	2.9	2.6	2.4	2.3		
Beton Extra Bold with Oblique			2.1		1.8		1.5	1.3	
Beton Wide with Extra Bold			2.1	2.8	1.8		1.5		
Bodoni with Italic			3.1		2.6		2.3		
Bodoni Bold with Italic	3.5		2.8	2.5	2.4		2.2	2.0	
Bodoni Book with Italic	3.9		3.2	2.9	2.7		2.4		
Bodoni Ultra with Italic			2.3		2.0		1.7	1.4	
Bookman with Italic	3.5		3.0	2.8	2.5		2.2		
Caledonia with Italic			3.0	2.8	2.5	2.4	2.2		
Century with Italic	3.4		2.8	2.6	2.4		2.1	1.8	1.5
Century Bold Italic									1.4
Century Bold Condensed									1.8
Century with Bold	3.4		2.8		2.4		2.1	1.8	1.5
Cheltenham Bold			3.9		3.5		3.2	2.8	1.5
Cheltenham Bold Condensed								2.2	1.8
Cheltenham Condensed with Bold					2.8				
Folio with Bold					2.3				
Franklin Gothic			3.9		3.5		3.2	2.8	1.5
Franklin Gothic Condensed								2.2	1.8
Futura Medium with Oblique	4.2		3.5	3.1	2.8		2.4	2.1	
Futura Demi Bold with Oblique	4.0		3.4	3.0	2.6		2.3	2.0	
Futura Bold with Oblique	3.6		3.1	2.6	2.4		2.0	1.7	
Futura Extra Bold with Oblique				•	1.8		1.7	1.6	
Futura Medium Condensed	4.5		3.7		3.1		2.7	2.4	2.0
Futura Bold Condensed			4.5		3.7		3.1	2.7	
Futura Extra Bold Cond. with Oblique							2.6	2.4	1.9

Typeface								
Garamond with Italic	3.7		3.2	3.0	2.8	2.6	2.5	2.3
Garamond Bold with Italic		3.2	2.9	2.7	2.5		2.3	1.7
Helvetica with Italic	3.6	3.2	2.8	2.4	2.1		1.9	1.7
Helvetica with Medium	3.6		2.8	2.4	2.1	2.0	1.9	1.7
Helvetica Medium with Italic	3.6		2.8		2.1		1.9	
Helvetica Light with Italic				2.6				
Melior with Semi Bold			2.8	2.6	2.5		2.2	1.7
Melior with Italic					2.5			1.7
Memphis Light with Bold	3.3		3.2	2.8	2.5		2.1	1.8
Memphis Medium with Italic			3.1	3.2	2.5		2.0	1.8
Metro with Bold	3.4		3.1	2.8	2.4		2.1	2.5
News Gothic with Bold	3.4		3.0	2.8	2.5		2.1	
News Gothic Condensed with Alt. No. 2	3.8		3.4	3.2	3.1		2.7	
Optima with Italic	3.7		3.0	2.8	2.5		2.1	
Optima with Semi Bold			3.0	2.8	2.5		1.7	
Remington Typewriter with Underscore			2.4		2.0			
Spartan Black								1.4
Spartan Black Condensed with Oblique					2.8		2.5	2.4
Spartan Heavy with Oblique	3.6		3.3	2.9	2.5		2.2	2.0
Spartan Medium with Oblique	3.6		3.5	3.2	2.8		2.4	2.2
Textype with Bold				2.6	2.6			
Textype with Italic				2.6	2.6			
Times Roman with Bold	3.6	3.3	3.0	2.8	2.6		2.3	1.9
Times Roman with Italic	3.3	3.2	3.0	2.8	2.6	2.5	2.3	1.3
Trade Gothic with Bold			3.0	2.7	2.5		1.6	
Trade Gothic Extended with Bold				2.0	1.8			
Trade Gothic Extra Condensed with Bold		4.0			3.1			
Trade Gothic Condensed with Bold	3.8	3.6	3.5	3.3	3.1	2.2	2.8	2.4
Trade Gothic Light with Italic	3.3	3.0	2.8	2.5	2.4		2.1	1.8
Vogue with Bold			3.2		2.5			2.0

Courtesy of Johnson-Kenro Typographers, Inc.

COPY FITTING CHART

PICA WIDTH OF LINE

PER PICA	4	5	6	7	8	9	10	11	12	13	14	15	16	17	18	19	20	21	22	23	24	25	26	27	28	29	30	31	32	33	34
1.0	4.0	5.0	6.0	7.0	8.0	9.0	10	11	12	13	14	15	16	17	18	19	20	21	22	23	24	25	26	27	28	29	30	31	32	33	34
1.1	4.4	5.5	6.6	7.7	8.8	9.9	11	12	13	14	15	17	18	19	20	21	22	23	24	25	26	28	29	30	31	32	33	34	35	36	37
1.2	4.8	6.0	7.2	8.4	9.6	11	12	13	14	16	17	18	19	20	22	23	24	25	26	28	29	30	31	32	34	35	36	37	38	40	41
1.3	5.2	6.5	7.8	9.1	10	12	13	14	16	17	18	20	21	22	23	25	26	27	29	30	31	33	34	35	36	38	39	40	42	43	44
1.4	5.6	7.0	8.4	9.8	11	13	14	15	17	18	20	21	22	24	25	27	28	29	31	32	34	35	36	38	39	41	42	43	45	46	48
1.5	6.0	7.5	9.0	11	12	14	15	17	18	20	21	23	24	26	27	29	30	32	33	35	36	38	39	41	42	44	45	47	48	50	51
1.6	6.4	8.0	9.6	11	13	14	16	18	19	21	22	24	26	27	29	30	32	34	35	37	38	40	42	43	45	46	48	50	51	53	54
1.7	6.8	8.5	10	12	14	15	17	19	20	22	24	26	27	29	31	32	34	36	37	39	41	43	44	46	48	49	51	53	54	56	58
1.8	7.2	9.0	11	13	14	16	18	20	22	23	25	27	29	31	32	34	36	38	40	41	43	45	47	49	50	52	54	56	58	59	61
1.9	7.6	9.5	11	13	15	17	19	21	23	25	27	29	30	32	34	36	38	40	42	44	46	48	49	51	53	55	57	59	61	63	65
2.0	8.0	10	12	14	16	18	20	22	24	26	28	30	32	34	36	38	40	42	44	46	48	50	52	54	56	58	60	62	64	66	68
2.1	8.4	11	13	15	17	19	21	23	25	27	29	32	34	36	38	40	42	44	46	48	50	53	55	57	59	61	63	65	67	69	71
2.2	8.8	11	13	15	18	20	22	24	26	29	31	33	35	37	40	42	44	46	48	51	53	55	57	59	62	64	66	68	70	73	75
2.3	9.2	12	14	16	18	21	23	25	28	30	32	35	37	39	41	44	46	48	51	53	55	58	60	62	64	67	69	71	74	76	78
2.4	9.6	12	14	17	19	22	24	26	29	31	34	36	38	41	43	46	48	50	53	55	58	60	62	65	67	70	72	74	77	79	82
2.5	10	13	15	18	20	23	25	28	30	33	35	38	40	43	45	48	50	53	55	58	60	63	65	68	70	73	75	78	80	83	85
2.6	10	13	16	18	21	23	26	29	31	34	36	39	42	44	47	49	52	55	57	60	62	65	68	70	73	75	78	81	83	86	88
2.7	11	14	16	19	22	24	27	30	32	35	38	41	43	46	49	51	54	57	59	62	65	68	70	73	76	78	81	84	86	89	92
2.8	11	14	17	20	22	25	28	31	34	36	39	42	45	48	50	53	56	59	62	64	67	70	73	76	78	81	84	87	90	92	95
2.9	12	15	17	20	23	26	29	32	35	38	41	44	46	49	52	55	58	61	64	67	70	73	75	78	81	84	87	90	93	96	99
3.0	12	15	18	21	24	27	30	33	36	39	42	45	48	51	54	57	60	63	66	69	72	75	78	81	84	87	90	93	96	99	102
3.1	12	16	19	22	25	28	31	34	37	40	43	47	50	53	56	59	62	65	68	71	74	78	81	84	87	90	93	96	99	102	105
3.2	13	16	19	22	26	29	32	35	38	42	45	48	51	54	58	61	64	67	70	74	77	80	83	86	90	93	96	99	102	106	109

CHARACTERS	13	17	20	23	26	30	33	36	40	43	46	50	53	56	59	63	66	69	73	76	79	83	86	89	92	96	99	102	106	109	112
3.3	13	17	20	23	26	30	33	36	40	43	46	50	53	56	59	63	66	69	73	76	79	83	86	89	92	96	99	102	106	109	112
3.4	14	17	20	24	27	31	34	37	41	44	48	51	54	58	61	65	68	71	75	78	82	85	88	92	95	99	102	105	109	112	116
3.5	14	18	21	25	28	32	35	39	42	46	49	53	56	60	63	67	70	74	77	81	84	88	91	95	98	102	105	109	112	116	119
3.6	14	18	22	25	29	32	36	40	43	47	50	54	58	61	65	68	72	76	79	83	86	90	94	97	101	104	108	112	115	119	122
3.7	15	19	22	26	30	33	37	41	44	48	52	56	59	63	67	70	74	78	81	85	89	93	96	100	104	107	111	115	118	122	126
3.8	15	19	23	27	30	34	38	42	46	49	53	57	61	65	68	72	76	80	84	87	91	95	99	103	106	110	114	118	122	125	129
3.9	16	20	23	27	31	35	39	43	47	51	55	59	62	66	70	74	78	82	86	90	94	98	101	105	109	113	117	121	125	129	133
4.0	16	20	24	28	32	36	40	44	48	52	56	60	64	68	72	76	80	84	88	92	96	100	104	108	112	116	120	124	128	132	136
4.1	16	21	25	29	33	37	41	45	49	53	57	62	66	70	74	78	82	86	90	94	98	101	107	111	115	119	123	127	131	135	139
4.2	17	21	25	29	34	38	42	46	50	55	59	63	67	71	76	80	84	88	92	97	101	105	109	113	118	122	126	130	134	139	143
4.3	17	22	26	30	34	39	43	47	52	56	60	65	69	73	77	82	86	90	95	99	103	108	112	114	120	125	129	133	138	142	146
4.4	18	22	26	31	35	40	44	48	53	57	62	66	70	75	79	84	88	92	97	101	106	110	114	117	123	128	132	136	141	145	150
4.5	18	23	27	32	36	41	45	50	54	59	63	68	72	77	81	86	90	95	99	104	108	113	117	120	126	131	135	140	144	149	153
4.6	18	23	28	32	37	41	46	51	55	60	64	69	74	78	83	87	92	96	101	106	110	115	120	122	129	133	138	143	147	152	156
4.7	19	24	28	33	38	42	47	52	56	61	66	71	75	80	85	89	94	99	103	108	113	118	122	125	132	136	141	146	150	155	160
4.8	19	24	29	34	39	43	48	53	58	62	67	72	77	82	86	91	96	101	106	110	115	120	125	127	134	139	144	149	154	158	163
4.9	20	25	29	34	39	44	49	54	59	64	69	74	78	83	88	93	98	103	108	113	118	123	127	132	137	142	147	152	157	162	167
5.0	20	25	30	35	40	45	50	55	60	65	70	75	80	85	90	95	100	105	110	115	120	125	130	135	140	145	150	155	160	165	170

1. Find characters per pica number below selected face and size. (Refer to chart on pages 170-71.)

2. Locate number in vertical column of bold figures at left of table.

3. Follow across to find number of characters in desired pica width.

4. Divide number of characters in pica width into total number of characters in copy to determine number of lines of type.

Courtesy of Johnson-Kenro Typographers, Inc.

sure that, when set to this specified depth, the copy will be neither too narrow nor too wide. This is done in the following manner:

1. Count the characters in the copy.
2. Measure the desired copy depth in points, or measure in picas and convert to points.
3. *Divide* the depth (in points) by the point size of the selected type. If the lines are to be leaded, add the line leading (in points) to the type size before dividing into the depth. The resulting figure gives the number of lines that will fit into the depth.
4. *Divide* the number of lines into the total number of characters. This gives the number of characters *per line*.
5. Locate this figure on the type chart. This will give the pica width of the copy.
6. If the copy is too narrow, try an expanded face or a larger size. Do not expect the typographer to overjustify, as this will produce word spacing that is awkward and difficult to read.
7. If the copy is too wide, try a condensed face or a smaller size.

How to Produce a Dummy Booklet

Often, the layout artist is provided with a sheaf of typewritten copy and a number of photographs the client wants to have incorporated into a booklet. Before the actual designing of the pages can begin, the artist must make a dummy that will determine the number of pages the material will require and the distribution of the text and the illustrations throughout the booklet.

Steps in the production of such a dummy booklet are:

1. Count the typewritten characters on a page of the copy.
2. Multiply this by the number of pages. This gives the total character count.
3. Determine the required page size for the booklet. Allow for margins.
4. Select a style and size of type, determine its per-pica character count, and multiply it by the pica width of the page. This determines the characters per line.
5. Measure the depth with a line gauge. Do not forget to include the desired line leading. For example: if it is to be a 10-point face with a 2-point lead, use the 12-point scale.
6. Multiply the characters per line by the number of lines. This determines the number of type characters that will fit into a *full page* of the chosen size.
7. Divide this figure into the total character count. This gives the total number of booklet pages the copy will require.

For example: suppose there are 8 pages of typewritten copy. The type page averages 60 characters wide and 30 lines deep. Thus, there are 14,400 characters in the copy.

60	1800
× 30 lines	× 8 pages
1800	14400
typewritten chars/page	total characters in typewritten copy

The booklet size is to be 4" × 5", and an 18 × 24-pica area is established within it to provide pleasing margins. 10-point Times Roman with a 1-point lead is selected; its characters-per-pica count is 2.6. An 18-pica line will hold 47 characters. A 24-pica depth (measured with the 11-point scale) will accommodate 26 lines. Therefore:

47	
× 26	11.7 pages
282	1222) 14400
94	total chars.
1222	
typeset chars/page	or, *12 full pages* of typeset copy

Next, examine the photos. Decide (the nature of each photo will determine the choice) whether each photo deserves a full page, half page (either a vertical or a horizontal half), or a quarter page. Even though a photo may be treated later as a silhouette, consider now only the appropriate page-fraction it will occupy.

For example, there are 21 photos. It is decided that three are worthy of full-page treatment, four are suitable for vertical half-pages, and six require horizontal half-pages. The remaining eight are allocated a quarter-page each.

Sketch this in the following manner:

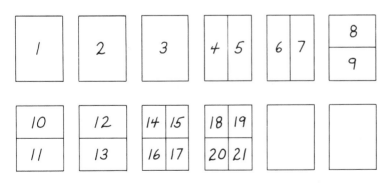

This determines that the photographs will require 10 full pages. 10 pages of photos plus 12 pages of type equals 22 pages. In order to saddle-stitch the booklet, total pages must equal a multiple of four. To do this, it is not advisable to tamper with the copy, especially if it has been approved; it is better to change the size allocations of the photos. The page total can be brought down to 20 by selectively reducing the sizes of 6 photos:

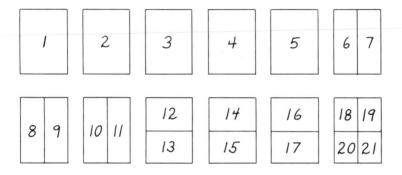

Or the page total can be increased to 24 pages by enlarging the size of 6 photos:

If the 20-page format is decided upon, add 12 boxes—representing the 12 full-pages of typeset copy—to the 8 boxes that indicate the various photo sizes. This represents the entire contents of the booklet reduced to page-size units or fractions thereof.

Draw 20 blank boxes and distribute the photos and copy throughout them as desired, remembering that a half-page photo is to be accompanied by a half page of copy (a vertical half contains as much type as a horizontal half), a ¼-page photo by ¾ page of copy, two ¼-page photos with ½ page of copy, and three ¼-page photos with ¼ page of copy.

As the copy and photos are removed for redistribution into the page boxes, check them off. When finished, the page boxes should be full and the copy/photo boxes all checked off.

This page dummy represents the distribution of the contents throughout the booklet: in short, "what goes where." If photos end up bunched together or there is too much continuous copy, another quick dummy can be made and the elements readily redistributed. Once this has been established, the artist can proceed to the layout stage, the actual aesthetic treatment of the pages.

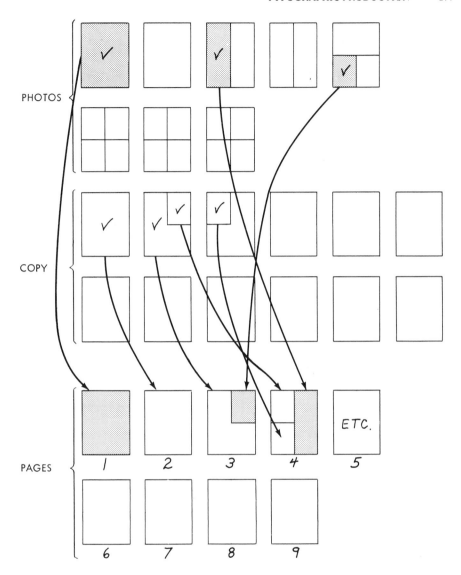

How to Locate Specific Points in the Copy

The copy may carry references—in word or key number—to a particular photo or illustration. It is often necessary to determine whether this reference occurs in proximity to the photo, thus to determine the precise location of the reference point in the typeset copy.

This may be done in the following manner:

1. Divide the typewritten copy into ¼-page units. In this copy, ¼ page would be ¼ × 30, or 7 ½ lines, or 450 characters.

2. Determine the typeset depth of the characters by dividing the typeset characters per line (47) into the 450. This equals 9.5. Thus, 9 ½ lines of typeset copy is equal to 7 ½ lines (¼ page) of typewritten copy. The total number of lines in the typeset copy is 26.

3. Drop the half-lines for the sake of convenience. Make a unit-measurer for 7 lines of typewritten copy and for 9 lines of the 12-point $\left(\dfrac{10}{12}\right)$ typeset copy.

This can be done by setting a divider, with a pica rule, or by simply making tick marks on the edge of a piece of paper. Measure the typewritten copy against the typeset copy:

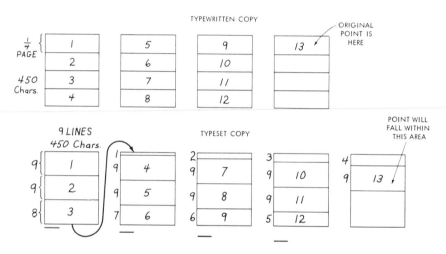

If the point ends up precariously close to the top or bottom of a typeset unit, it may be necessary to add in the half-lines that have been previously dropped for convenience. If using ¼-page units does not provide an accurate enough location of the point, use ⅛-page units instead.

Conversely, it may be necessary to determine where a point in the typeset copy occurs in the typewritten copy:

Divide the typeset copy into ¼-page units (6 or 6 ½ lines). These units will contain 305 characters. 305 characters will equal 10 lines (305 divided by 30) of typewritten copy. Make a 6-line unit-measure for the typeset copy and a 10-line unit measure for the typewritten copy. Work backwards from the typeset copy to the typewritten copy.

How to Locate and Insert
Paragraph Heads in a Layout

It may be desirable to provide isolated paragraph headings in order to break the monotony of lengthy text. These heads may be set in a different type style or in a larger or bolder face than the text, and they will require additional leading above and below the line (except for the first one, which requires no leading above it).

For example, it is decided to set the one-line paragraph heads in a 10-pt. boldface. This will require a 20-pt. leading above the line and a 10-pt. leading below it:

20-pt. leading   {

10-pt. type   {   PARAGRAPH HEAD }   40 pts.

10-pt. leading   {

Therefore, it is necessary to open up a 40-pt. hole wherever a paragraph heading is to occur. This may be done as follows:

1. Locate the paragraph heads in the typewritten copy,[4] using ¼-page units in the same way specific points in the typewritten copy are located.

2. Determine the typeset unit that will be equal in number of characters to the ¼-page typewritten unit.

3. Position the first paragraph head on the first line of the layout, allowing a 20-pt. (or 1.6 pica) hole (the line plus the leading underneath). Then, using the typeset unit, locate the second paragraph head, open up a 40-pt. (3.3 pica) hole; locate the third, and so on. As the copy is opened up for each hole, it will push the remaining type ahead of it, so that the opened-up copy will require more pages than were originally allocated for it.

4. Once the holes have been opened up, it is a simple matter to comp-letter, Greek, or type-indicate the headings in the proper point-size.

The Runaround.   It is relatively easy to master the specification technique for a block of body copy. However, when confronted with the runaround and the necessity of manipulating the text to accommodate illustrative matter, the task may appear to be hopelessly confusing. This need not be so if the copy is broken down into its simple rectangular components.

It is seldom that copy completely encircles an illustration; the copy may be interrupted in order to accommodate it. The illustration occupies the entire column or page width, aligning with both the left and right margins. In this instance, the specifier need only determine the copy depth above and below the illustration that will allow its insertion and still maintain the overall size and format of the column or page.

The illustration may be inserted flush with one margin (right or left) and protrude into the copy to any desired width. The copy, set to the measure of the remaining width, runs alongside the illustration and resumes its normal measure beneath it. An illustration inserted in this manner can be located at any point—top,

---

[4]The heads may not have been isolated in the typing. They may be typed on the same line as the beginning of the paragraph text. They may be capitalized or underscored, and they certainly will have been typed in the same size typewriter face.

HOW TO SPECIFY A RUNAROUND

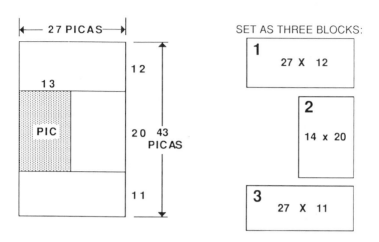

bottom, or middle—of the page. There may be more than one illustration on a page.

The empty space that is to accommodate the illustration should be considered a large indention, from either the left or right margin. If the copy is specified as blocks—located above, alongside, or below the illustration—the necessary calculation becomes a simple matter.

Take, for example, a page that carries an overall copy area of 27 × 43 picas. Starting from the top, the copy runs the full 27-pica measure to a depth of 12 picas. At this point, an illustration measuring 13 × 20 picas is to be inserted, flush with the right-hand margin. This size includes the necessary marginal space around the illustration. Beneath the illustration, the copy measures its normal 27-pica width and continues to the bottom margin of the page.

This gives the specifier three blocks of copy to consider. The first block runs the width of the page and down to the top of the illustration—27 × 12 picas. The block alongside the illustration measures the width of the page, minus the width of the illustration, and runs the depth of the illustration—14 × 20 picas. The remainder of the copy, which returns to the normal measure, will obviously have to be 27 × 11 picas. Thus, the page is composed of three blocks of copy: 27 × 12 picas, 14 × 20 picas, and 27 × 11 picas. Following is the way the copy is fitted:

1. Count the characters in the typewritten copy.
2. Select the typeface and size.
3. Refer to the appropriate copy-fitting chart and determine the number of characters that will fit into the 27 × 12 pica rectangle. Note this place on the typewritten copy. Then figure how many lines of the particular type will fit into the area.

4. Determine the number of characters that will fit into the 14 × 20 pica rectangle. Add this figure to the figure obtained in step 3, and note the place on the typewritten copy. Again, figure how many lines will fit into this area.

5. Determine whether the remainder of the copy will fit into the remaining 27 × 11 pica area. If it fits, the type may be specified as follows: Set in _____ point (size), _____ face. Set: _____ lines 27 picas (step 3); set _____ lines 14 picas, flush left (step 4); set _____ lines 27 picas (step 5).

If the job consists of a single page and the copy does not fit, try a smaller, larger, more condensed, or more expanded face.

Irregularly Shaped Copy.   If the margins of the copy are required to take on a specific shape, either of their own or to conform to the outline of some adjoining design, the typography must be specified line for line. An accurate characters-per-pica figure must be obtained for the face selected. The number of characters to be set in each line must be carefully counted and specified. This is done by inserting slash (/) marks in the typewritten copy, indicating the exact number of characters that are to fall in each line. Each line will be set containing the indicated number of characters.

The lines must then be aligned by the typographer to conform to the desired shape. The best way to specify such alignment is to make a careful tissue layout of the desired shape, indicating with ruled lines the exact length, alignment, and leading of each line.

The Requisites of Good Typography

Readability.   Layout design notwithstanding, the criterion of good typography is readability. Distortion for artistic effect, to the detriment of readability, is poor artistry. If it is *intended* to be read, body text should be easy to read.

Lower-case letters are easier to read than capital letters. This holds true even in headlines. However, this does not mean that the elimination of all capitalization increases readability further. The eye is accustomed to perceiving proper capitalization at the beginning of sentences and of individual words, and the elimination of this practice, even though artistically in vogue, makes reading more difficult.

Serif faces are easier to read than sans-serif faces. Although sans-serif faces may be used effectively for display copy, their use in lengthy body text should be approached with caution.

Body type that is too small is difficult to read; type that is too large is cumbersome and wasteful of space and paper. Text is normally set in 10- or 12-point type.

There is a limit to the distance an eye can travel along a line of type before it becomes tired and requires the stimulus of having to jump to the beginning of the next line. This is the reason why typography on wide pages is set in columns. Although there is no fixed rule, a good line width will contain from 40 to 50

INTERTYPE

AGATE	6 PT.	7 PT.	8 PT.	9 PT.	10 PT.	11 PT.	12 PT.

PICAS · INCHES

INTERTYPE COMPANY

A DIVISION OF HARRIS-INTERTYPE CORPORATION
360 FURMAN STREET, BROOKLYN, N.Y. 11201

ATLANTA · BOSTON · CHICAGO · CLEVELAND
DALLAS · LOS ANGELES · NEW YORK · SAN FRANCISCO
BERLIN · LONDON · TORONTO

INTERTYPE MATRICES RUN SMOOTHLY ON OTHER
LINE COMPOSING MACHINES

Courtesy of the Intertype Co.

A LINE GAUGE AND A PICA RULE (ACTUAL SIZE)

characters of the particular size face. Books in the 6" × 9" size range will often employ lines of about 60 characters, since the format is too small to accommodate two columns.

Letterspacing and Word Spacing. The use of letterspacing between lower-case letters is poor practice. Some letterspacing on lower-case display type of 36 points and larger is occasionally permissible, but it is wise to remember that lower-case type is *designed to fit close* and becomes hard to read when spaced out.

Lines set in capital letters, however, can often be improved by moderate letterspacing, especially when difficult letter combinations such as TY, TA, WA, VA, etc., occur. Straight vertical letters require more letterspacing than curved letters.

It is not necessary to attempt to specify the exact letterspacing that will be required. The typographer will do this when requested; most digital typesetters are designed to facilitate proper spacing.

Line and Paragraph Leading. Type that has been set solid is difficult to read, as it forms a tight mass that is hard for the eye to penetrate. Type with a large center body, and short ascenders and descenders, requires more line leading than type with long ascenders and descenders. As previously mentioned, normal body type (10 to 12 points) is seldom leaded more than two points; however, if more leading is desired, a fairly safe rule is to let the line leading equal the approximate word spacing. Whatever line leading is utilized, it must be kept consistent between all the lines.

Paragraph leading varies according to the nature of the copy, but it should be deeper than the line leading. Since there is no set rule of depth, the space between the paragraphs is an excellent place to locate a few extra points of depth in order to make copy fit. Paragraphs should not be leaded to the extent that they appear unrelated, and, once established, the leading should be consistent between each paragraph.

Formats

There are four major formats used for body-type composition:

Flush Left. All of the lines of type are aligned on the left side and are allowed to rag (fall naturally) on the right side.

Flush Right. All of the lines of type are aligned on the right side and the left side is allowed to rag.

Flush Left and Right (Justified). The lines of type are aligned on both sides.

Centered. The lines are centered over each other (as one sometimes sees in menus).

Most type is set in justified columns, but there is a current trend toward type that is set flush left, ragged right. Obtaining a right rag-edge that is aesthetically

PAGE
FORMATS

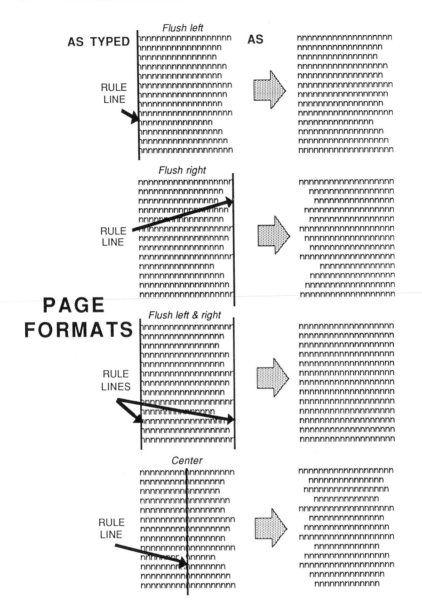

pleasing can be as problematical as justification and often requires a considerable degree of manipulation.

Type that is set flush right is considered difficult to read, as the eye has to search for the beginning of each line. This format has its use when the type is aligned with a square halftone positioned on the type's right.

Lines to be set in special shapes must be specified line-for-line.

Indention.   There are three types of indention: regular, flush, and hanging. *Regular indention* means that the first line of the paragraph is indented. The average line is indented one em—a longer line may be indented two ems; there is no set rule.

Flush indention means that there is no indention in the first, or in any other line of the paragraph. Flush indention makes smooth, even margins, but is more difficult to read than regular indention. When flush indention is used, there must be additional paragraph leading in order to serve as a break for the reader.

In the *hanging indention,* the first line is set to the full measure, and all the subsequent lines of the paragraph are indented. This type of indention does not require leading between paragraphs.

Initial Capitals.   Initial capitals are larger capital letters—often decorative—that are sometimes used at the beginning of an article or a chapter in order to lend interest and break up the monotony of the text.

A standing initial is one that aligns with the bottom of the first line and protrudes into the empty space above the line. In order to accomplish this, it is merely necessary to specify the face and size of the initial and the indention of the first line to correspond to the width of the initial. There should be no hole between the initial and the beginning of the line; therefore, such letters as T, W, V, F, and P must be kerned by the typographer in order to make a tight fit.

The set-in initial is one that is set into the first few lines of the composition, which have been correspondingly indented. The base of the initial should align with one of the lines of the text, and the line directly beneath it should come to the margin. The top of the letter should preferably line up with the tops of the letters in the first line. If this is not possible, the top of the letter should project above the top line; it should never be allowed to fall below it. The first word or phrase of the top line is often set in capital letters to provide an optical transition from the large initial to the body face, and to make sure that the initial is read as part of the first line.

Initial capitals should harmonize with the body type. Careful measurement is necessary for the specification of such initials. This measurement should be made with an actual specimen of the desired initial at hand, since, for example, a 30-point initial is not necessarily as high as three lines of 10-point type. The face and size of the initial, as well as the desired indention, must be specified.

It is possible to order the typography with merely the desired intention and to insert the initial by hand with either transfer or adhesive type. This is hardly worthwhile, unless a good many such initials are involved.

TYPE SPECIFICATION

There are no fixed rules for the way type should be ordered (specified) from the typographer. It is even possible, and often most practical, to order a few lines of type over the phone. If the type is encoded on a disk, it may be transmitted to the typographer with a modem, but the proper specifications must be either included or verbally transmitted. The important thing is that understanding communication should be maintained between the specifier and the typographer.

Instructions are generally marked with colored pencil, in order to make them stand out from the typewritten copy.

The best rule is to leave nothing to chance. Specify everything so that there will be no questions from the typographer. It is better to overspecify than to leave half the job open to guesswork. The typographer should be provided with the following information concerning *each typeface* to be set:

1. The type size.
2. The type family and face.
3. Specifications for capital letters, lower-case letters, or both.
4. The pica measure to which the lines are to be set.
5. Line-leading instructions.

Example:

10 pt. Times Roman ital., caps and l.c.

24 picas wide, 2 pt. lead

Pica width may be indicated by drawing a horizontal arrow above the typed copy, from margin to margin. The necessary information is inserted between the arrowheads. Type that is to be leaded by being cast on a larger body is indicated as a fraction: 10/11, 10/12, etc.

The procedure for marking copy is as follows:

1. All copy should be typewritten and proofread. If excessive handwritten corrections have been made, the copy should be retyped.
2. Number each page in the copy; mark "end'" on the last page of the copy.
3. Clearly indicate every different size, typeface, and measure. Use a colored pencil.
4. Indicate line leading in points.
   (a) If a measure and leading are indicated, the depth will be automatic and need not be noted. However, it should have been determined by the specifier for fitting purposes.
   (b) If the typeface is specified on a larger body, line leading automatically occurs and need not be further noted.
5. Indicate paragraph leading in points.
6. Indicate indentions, as they may not have been typed in the manner desired.
   (a) Regular indentions are indicated by square boxes representing ems.

> This is a regular indention. The beginning line will have been indented in order to make it easy for the eye to pick up the first line of the paragraph.

> The beginning line of the next paragraph will be spaced normally.
>
> ☐ ☐ The regular indention will be indicated in this manner.

(b) The copy probably will have been typed with regular indentions. Flush indentions are indicated by drawing an arrow from the first letter to the left edge of the copy.

> This is a flush indention. This results in a more massive, formal format, but it is more difficult to locate the beginning of the line.
>
> Thus, the spacing between the paragraphs will be increased.
>
> |←— The flush indention will be indicated in this manner.

(c) Hanging indentions are indented by drawing an arrow from the first letter beyond the left edge of the copy and noting the desired overhang in ems.

> Since it protrudes into the margin, the hanging
>   beginning of the paragraph is the easiest to locate of
>   the three formats.
>
> Paragraph spacing is normal in the instance of the
>   hanging indention.
>
> ☐ ☐ ←— The hanging indention will be indicated
>   in this manner.

7. An indication of copy alignment should be made. A vertical pencil line through the left marginal letters indicates that the copy should be flush left. A vertical line through the right end of the longest line indicates flush right. Use of both lines indicates flush left *and* right, meaning that the copy is to be justified. A vertical line through the center of the copy indicates that each line is to be centered over the next line—an equal number of characters to the right and to the left of the center character. In addition to the ruled lines, "flush left," "flush right," "flush left and right," or "center" should be marked next to the copy. The maximum allowable pica width of the composition should be noted.

8. Italicized words or sentences should be underscored once.

9. Capitalized letters, words, or sentences should be underscored three times; two underscores means small capitals.

10. Type to be set in the same size, boldface, may be underscored with a wavy line.

11. Note the point size of all rules (ruled lines) that are to be set by the typographer.
12. Mark "don't set" (or d.s.) on anything that appears on the copy sheet that is not to be set by the typographer, and circle it.
13. Indicate whether the type is to be made up or set in galleys.
14. If extra proofs are needed, indicate how many. Indicate whether or not repro proofs are required.
15. Include your *job number* with each order. This enables easy identification for both art and billing purposes.

PRODUCTION TECHNIQUES

A true feeling for typography requires a certain degree of taste as well as a sense of design. Typography is one of the most neglected aspects of the graphic arts. If one is incapable of seeing the difference between types or appreciating the subtleties of composition, there is little point in attempting to list the distinctions. Any of the methods are capable of producing readable type. The test of the specifier's and the typographer's skill is the ability to produce work that has quality.

Typography is billed on a time basis. This includes the time that is spent setting the copy, in make-up, in puzzling over the specifier's instructions, and struggling through poorly organized copy. Thus, the more the specifier can do in order to decrease the time that must be expended by the typographer, the less the job will cost.

The use of a great variety of typefaces in a single layout results in needless expense, since there is a minimum charge for each face. It is also considered in poor taste. A good rule is to limit the type to no more than three different faces per layout. Size, of course, may vary as required. Even though they are readily available, it is still considered poor taste for a desktop publisher to overindulge in the selection of type styles and sizes.

Typographers work on a union scale, which imposes strict charges for over-time. As a result, it is essential to give the typographer sufficient time to do the job so that no overtime work will be necessary. Many typographic shops employ a night shift. Since this is not an extension of the day shift but a separate eight-hour shift, there is no extra charge for overnight work. Work sent out at 5:00 P.M. will generally be ready at 9:00 A.M. the following day—without overtime charges.

The maxim for efficient production is: "Get the type out first." The type should have been set, proofread, checked for fit, and corrected by the time the mechanical artist is scheduled to begin pasting up the job.

Galley Proofs vs. Make-Up.   Galley proofs are proofs that are pulled from the type as it comes from the machine or from the output of an imagesetter, without regard for make-up. Complicated make-up by the typographer entails additional expense. The deciding factor between galley and make-up is time. It is cheaper to order galley proofs and to paste them up by hand, provided there is time to do so. When the job comes in at 5:00 P.M., and is due at 10:00 A.M. the next day, it is better to let the night typographer do the make-up so that in the morning the type can be rapidly pasted on the mechanical in a single piece. As a result of the advent of image-assembly systems, make-up (and the often-resultant elimination of paste-up) is a simple affair.

Photostatting Type.   Since type is line copy, it is practical to moderately enlarge or reduce type photostatically. Overenlarged type becomes ragged and necessitates hand retouching, and overreduced type tends to fill in and become unreadable. However, a glossy photostat, within a reasonable size range, can be as sharp and clean as the typography itself. All type that is to appear in reverse must be negatively photostatted—even if it has been set to size—for positioning on the mechanical. It may also be enlarged or reduced at the same time it is negatively photostatted. Thus, the photostat serves as an effective tool of the copyfitter.

It is well to keep in mind that when type is photostatted, over- or underdevelopment may adversely affect the weight of the characters. All photostats should be carefully inspected to make sure that this has not occurred. Photostats of type, especially body copy, should be carefully checked for dirt spots and sharpness of focus.

No area of *body text* should be photostatted to fit—unless it is to stand by itself—since photostatting reduces or enlarges the point size and makes it incompatible with the rest of the text. If the entire text must be enlarged or reduced, it should be done *photographically;* this provides a more accurate size control and there is less tendency toward paper shrinkage.

Some typographers supply photostat service. It is good to use such a typographer, since proofs can be photostatted immediately after they have been pulled. The entire job, type plus photostats, can be received at the same time—there is no further time spent in waiting for photostats.

Many typographers also have film type machines, which are used to set decorative headline faces. When ordering film type, it is more expensive to order the type in an individual size than to accept it in the size produced by the machine (about 35-mm strips). Often it proves economical to accept the work in strip size, gang it up, and photostat it to the desired size. This, too, requires accurate advance planning.

Checking Typography.   Upon receiving proofs from the typographer, the artist should perform the following functions:

1. Check the transparent proofs against the layout in order to determine if the copy will fit properly.
2. Have the typography proofread. More problems arise from typographical errors than for any other reason. It is safe to assume that there will be at least

one or two typographical errors in every sizeable type job. For this reason, the proof should be read promptly in order to allow the typographer time to make the necessary corrections. Every typographer proofreads the work; nevertheless, it should be rechecked by the specifier. If there is sufficient time, a duplicate proof should be submitted to the client for approval. Ideally, every job should be ordered with a sufficient time allowance for correction, or else the mechanical artist must be prepared to make paste-up corrections. *Corrections* are the rectification of errors made by the typographer, which are done at his or her expense. *Author's alterations* are changes made by the client after the first proofs have been pulled and are made at additional cost to the client.

3. Hot type repro proofs are usually still wet when delivered and smear easily. They should be immediately sprayed with fixative. Photographic proofs pose no such problem.

4. Many clients are in the habit of revising copy after it has been set. Thus, a revised proof may differ considerably in content from the first proof. Typographers have various methods of identifying revised proofs. When revised proofs are received, all previous proofs should be discarded in order to avoid any confusion.

5. Make certain that all hot type is left standing or that phototypesetter input tapes or disks are retained until the job receives its final approval.

Imperfect or Broken Characters. It is the responsibility of the typographer to discard worn or dirty type matrices. Linotype matrices can become nicked or damaged, as dirt will occur on the matrices of a photographic typesetter, and the imperfection will appear many times in the composition. There is less chance of this occurring on a digital typesetter.

Proofs containing badly broken type should not be accepted. Certain minor imperfections will occur due to inking and proofing, as well as processing. A good typographer will retouch broken characters. The alert artist should be constantly on the lookout for imperfections and should be able to retouch them. This is especially true in the case of photostat negatives made from type—the thin lines and the serifs have a tendency to fill in. These should also be retouched by hand. Type that has been excessively photostatted will tend to lose its sharpness.

Remember, a typographic bill is a charge for typographic services rendered *to your order and to your specifications.*

CHAPTER 13
THE PREPARATION
OF ILLUSTRATIVE
MATERIAL

When the layout has been approved and work on the finished art commences, it is the illustration—drawing or photograph—that is begun first. The illustration may take a longer time to execute than any other element of the job. The artwork should be undertaken as far in advance of the job deadline as possible, so the client can evaluate it and any necessary changes or corrections can be made. It is important to produce illustrative matter that satisfies the client, as this is the element of the finished art on which the greatest profit can be realized.

It may be necessary to photograph the illustration for inclusion in the mechanical art. The illustration should be finished before the mechanical is begun, so that time can be allotted for photography, as well as to make sure of a proper fit.

LINE ART

Line art can be produced by a variety of methods and techniques.

The Line Drawing

The simplest form of illustration to reproduce is the one-color line drawing. Such an illustration results in a printing plate that does not require the use of the halftone dot. In order to provide copy of maximum intensity for the platemaking camera, a dense black drawing ink is used. Each line is drawn in full value; there is no dilution of the pigment. There are five types of line drawing:

The Outline Drawing. The outline drawing is rendered with pen or brush and ink, with lines of uniform or varying thickness and without any solid or tonal areas. The character of the line is dictated by the type of pen or brush that is used and by the surface texture and absorbent qualities of the paper on which it is drawn.

The Line and Solid Area Drawing. The use of line and solid areas produces a drawing of strong contrast. There are no middle values. This type of drawing is usually rendered with brush and ink, since an attempt to fill in large areas with a pen destroys the paper surface. The dark areas in such a drawing should be well organized, so that the eye can make the difficult transition from white to black without the assistance of middle values.

The Line and Tone Drawing. A line and tone drawing is one in which intermediate tonal areas are used to form transitions between white and black areas, thus heightening the illusion of form or texture. Tonal areas may be produced by patterned pen or brush strokes or through the use of special shading films or papers that have been designed to aid in the rendering of such tonality. Although each line in the tonal area is full-value black, the eye measures the totality of white and black in these areas and sees them as gray tones in the same way it perceives the halftone dot.

There are various techniques for artist-produced tone:

Pen strokes provide a great variety of tonal and textural effects. The pen strokes may be free and loose or precise and mechanical. Ranging from closely spaced parallel lines to cross-hatching, stippling, and scribbly effects, they constitute a part of the vocabulary of the individual artist.

Brush strokes are bolder than the pen stroke and artistically more sensitive. The brush may be utilized for a wide range of tonal effects. The nature of the pen and brush stroke is left completely to the imagination and discretion of the artist, thus affording the artist the complete freedom of the medium.

Dry brush technique provides an interesting effect when a brush, from which most of the ink has been wiped, is dragged across the surface of rough-textured paper. This technique deposits pigment on the irregularly shaped spots of the paper surface, creating a stippled, feathery effect that lends character to both line and tonal areas. The resulting texture is determined by the speed of the brush stroke and by the roughness and absorbency of the paper surface. The paper may range from rough illustration board to watercolor paper, Japanese rice paper, or blotting paper.

Stipple or spatter may be used for tonal or textured effects. This is done by stippling directly on the drawing with a stiff brush, by applying the ink with a sponge, or by applying it with a swab of cotton or cloth twisted around the end of a stick or a brush handle. Spatter areas may be produced by rubbing an ink-filled toothbrush with a small stick, by rubbing a toothbrush over a fine-mesh screen, or by spraying the ink directly from the bottle with a fixatif sprayer or an atomizer. Care must be taken to keep the texture coarse.

Stipple or coquille board is commonly known as Ross board—after a well-known manufacturer. It is Bristol board whose surface has been embossed with thousands of tiny raised patterns. These boards are available in a variety of pattern styles, ranging from dots to irregular shapes. A tonal effect is accomplished by rubbing the surface with litho (grease) pencil. This deposits pigment on the high spots of the embossed surface pattern. The harder the pencil pressure, the more the pigment is forced into the intervening depressions and the darker the tonality becomes. Used for cartoons and newspaper illustrations, where speed is a critical factor, stipple boards produce a texture that is somewhat cliché, since the nature of the texture is determined by the pattern embossed on the board rather than by the discretion of the artist.

Scratchboard.   Scratchboard represents a unique art technique that can be used to duplicate the effect of wood engraving. The board is Bristol, coated with a thick white clay surface. The artist covers it with black poster paint or drawing ink and, with a scriber, scratches white lines into the black areas. The scribed line cuts through the black surface coating into the white clay layer, producing a crisp and precise line. Correction may be accomplished by reinking and rescribing, provided the original lines have not been scratched too deeply. If the surface is coated with drawing ink, care should be taken that the ink does not crystallize; this will cause the ink to flake off, resulting in unclean, ragged lines. A wide variety of scribing tools is available, including some that produce multiple lines.

Scratchboard is a crisp, precise medium, which, in skillful hands, can duplicate the technique of the black-line engraver. Beginners in scratchboard tend to blacken the entire surface and work in a white-line technique. The novelty of scratching the lines becomes too tempting, and soon the whole work becomes covered with tonal values, with little regard for solid blacks or whites. If a white-line technique is desired, it is simpler to execute the drawing on ordinary board in either pen or brush and ink and then make a reverse plate or order a photostat negative. The accomplished scratchboard artist generally works in a positive black-line technique, even when the background is to be black. This approach requires a bit more advance planning, but its mastery is well worth the effort.

Scratchboard is an ideal surface upon which to execute precise hand lettering—either positive or negative. The fact that the black pigment may be scraped away enables the letterer to clean edges to a razor sharpness.

The Line and Mechanical Tone Drawing.   Mechanical tone is textural tone that is produced either with prepared shading sheets, which are cut out and fastened to the illustration, or by drawing on an impregnated paper whose tonal pattern may be made visible by the application of a developing fluid. A line and solid-area drawing is made first. This drawing is always rendered in black ink, so that the mechanical tone will not appear in the solid areas. After the line drawing has been rendered, the mechanical tone is applied. The areas that will contain the tone should be carefully planned in advance, so that they will assist the eye in making the transition from white to black areas. There is little to be gained by covering the entire drawing with a tonal pattern.

Mechanical tones are uniform in their overall texture; each pattern produces a single tone that does not vary. The tones are available in a wide variety of patterns. It is not considered good practice to include too many tone patterns in a single drawing, and care should be taken that those used are compatible. As in any other type of tonal rendering, mechanical tone is used in an attempt to introduce clarity and illusory dimension to the drawing, not to decorate it to the point of confusion.

Since mechanical tone produces a regimented, rather than a random, pattern, its use imparts a precise appearance to the work; therefore, the line drawing should be executed with similar precision. It is an ideal medium for the rendering of hard goods, technical illustrations, and similar work. Mechanical tone finds widespread use in the production of black-and-white charts; it serves as a means of differentiation where the use of color is prohibited. There are several methods of applying mechanical tone:

Shading film consists of uniform tonal patterns, which are printed on transparent, adhesive-backed sheets. It is available in over 2,000 textures—parallel lines, dots, cross-hatching, stipple, etc.—in both positive and negative form. Each variety of texture is produced in different weights of line or dot, so that different values may be obtained with similar patterns.

The film is removed from its protective backing sheet and placed over the line drawing. It is cut to the desired shape with a razor blade or a frisket knife; the adhesive back will hold the shape temporarily in position while the remainder of the sheet is being removed. The film may be of the pressure-sensitive (self-adhering) variety, or it may be coated with a wax adhesive that can be activated by burnishing the film with the edge of a triangle or the back of a comb. Once burnished, the film becomes difficult to remove. Several manufacturers of shading film now produce their patterns in the popular "rubdown" format. Printed on acetate sheets, the patterns are transferred to the art by rubbing with a stylus or a burnisher.

In addition to shading film, there are many products on the market designed to assist the artist in the preparation of both line and comprehensive art:

Adhesive or rubdown sheets of borders, corners, arrows, symbols, designs, etc. These sheets can be custom-produced if the order is large enough.

Sheets of drawing and cartoons—architectural, industrial, and pictorial.

Charting and drafting tapes (used for making straight lines or for charts) available in a wide variety of thicknesses and colors—matte or gloss, transparent or opaque.

Courtesy of Paratone, Inc.

EXAMPLES OF ZIP-A-TONE® SHADING FILM PATTERNS

Dot screens in various percentages.

Transparent solid-color sheets—matte or glossy.

Opaque colored paper sheets and coated paper sheets—matte or glossy. Systems may be purchased enabling the artist to give matching instructions for four-color process matching.

Red film for overlays and separations.

Graph film.

Felt-tip markers in almost every conceivable hue, including warm, cool, and neutral grays.

Lettering (see page 163)—rubdown and cut-out.

Clip art or "swipe art" is line art that is sold in preprinted form. There are no restrictions on its reuse by its purchaser. It is an inexpensive means of acquiring competent—though cliché—line art. A wide variety of subject matter is available.

Most of this material is also available in many computer graphic software programs. A wide variety of textural patterns, designs and symbols, and clip art are provided by various manufacturers. Custom designs or logotypes can be created and programmed for the individual user.

The line drawing is produced by means of a line plate—there is no recourse to the halftone screen. It is considerably less expensive than the halftone plate. In letterpress, zinc plates are used for short runs; copper is used for longer runs for finely detailed work. Standard lithographic plates are employed for the line process. Unless the line drawing represents a minor element of the layout, line reproduction should not be attempted with the gravure process, since each line will necessarily bear a screen pattern.

If the plate is made from a film positive rather than a negative, the printed image will be in reverse values from the original art.

The criteria of good line drawing for reproduction are that the lines should be spaced far enough apart so that there is no danger of fill-in, and that they be thick enough not to disappear on the film negative or break away during the press run. Excessive areas of solid color tend to retain ink and eventually flood. Sizeable solid areas should be avoided.

Line art should always be prepared in black, regardless of the color in which it is to ultimately print. Care should be taken that the ink does not become diluted; neither should it be allowed to bleed because the paper is too porous. Fuzzy line edges, dirt, and fingerprints should be avoided. All preliminary pencil lines should be carefully erased. An artgum eraser is best for this purpose, since a kneaded rubber eraser tends to dull the luster of the ink. All artgum residue should be carefully brushed away.

Line art is preferably executed one and a half or two times the finished size, for the convenience of the artist. Reduction tends to minimize imperfections, but it is reasonable to expect that there will be no imperfections in professionally executed artwork. The final size that the art is to appear should always be kept in mind. This is especially important where tonal effects are present—those either drawn by the artist or produced with shading film. Too much reduction will cause these areas to fill in. Most shading film manufacturers provide charts that show their patterns in various reductions, enabling the artist to foresee what will happen to the artwork when it is reduced. Viewing the drawing through a reducing lens will help the artist anticipate troublesome platemaking problems. Enlargement poses no problem of fill-in, but lines that are too greatly enlarged may appear ragged and cumbersome.

All original art should be covered with a tissue overlay and a paper flap for production.

CONTINUOUS-TONE ART

Definitions

Continuous-Tone Art. Continuous-tone is the gradual flow of one tone into another, artistically known as blending. Continuous-tone art is positive art containing blending (black and white or color) that will require reproduction by means of the screened halftone dot. Pencil and pastel drawings, wash and opaque drawings, oil or acrylic paintings, and photographs all fall into this category. Such art is often incorrectly called "halftone art."

Square Halftone. A halftone whose entire area has a tonal value and whose edges have been finished off in either a square or a rectangular shape. A ruled border may or may not be utilized.

Silhouette Halftone. A halftone whose background has been removed, leaving the image in silhouette form. The silhouetting may be performed with white paint on the original copy, by opaquing the film negative, or by etching away the dot formations on the engraved plate or on the film positive. An outline is seldom utilized—the shape of the image is considered to be self-containing. Care should be taken that the values at the edges of the image are strong enough to provide a differentiation from the background on which it is to be printed. The silhouetting process is most effectively accomplished by the artist on the original art, since at this stage it is easy to determine whether any of the edges need strengthening. It is easier to observe minor details of the silhouette shape on the original art or photograph—details that might be obliterated when silhouetting on film or plate.

Vignette Halftone. A halftone whose outer edges fade off gradually into the background. This effect is accomplished by airbrushing the edges of the original art to blend into the background or by chemical (acid) reduction of the sizes of the outermost dots on the film positive or the engraved plate in order to achieve tonal gradation.

Dropout Halftone. Also known as a highlight halftone, this is a halftone in which certain areas are highlighted—the halftone dot is eliminated in order to permit the paper to show through as a contrasting or "highlight" effect. This is accomplished by dot-etching the film positive or reetching the engraved plate. The *magenta contact screen*, which contains dyed magenta rather than black lines, can be manipulated with filters in order to produce dropout areas on the film negative. Dropout halftones are considerably more expensive than regular halftones.

The dropout is much more effectively utilized for the reproduction of the artist's drawing than for the photograph. Dropouts in photographs, unless carefully handled, have a tendency to look contrived and artificial. Several manufacturers produce processes by which illustrations may be prepared for an automatic dropout and silhouette. The highlight areas are rendered with a medium that will fluoresce under ultraviolet light, eliminating dot formation on the film negative.

The Black-and-White Continuous-Tone Drawing

Any drawing utilizing a medium in which the value of the pigment becomes reduced—either by less pressure, dilution, or the addition of white pigment—is a continuous-tone drawing. Such a drawing must be printed by the halftone process.

To reproduce well, the pigment must be strong enough to record its tonal value on the film negative with a minimum of value loss. As a result, opaque pigment reproduces more faithfully than transparent pigment that has been smudged over the paper.

The Pencil Drawing. Pencil drawings are seldom used commercially, because the pencil is incapable of producing a black that compares with the strength and opacity of ink. With pencil, the value scale is condensed; the darkest pencil areas seldom represent more than an 80 percent value, and the highlight areas tend to become smudged, thus increasing their value. This gives the pencil rendering a flat, lifeless appearance, which will appear even more so when screened. If the job requires a pencil rendering, its value range should be spread as wide as possible in a deliberate attempt to obtain maximum contrast. The blackest areas may be reinforced with drawing ink and the highlights painted white. There is no point in making a pencil drawing for line reproduction—the value of the pencil line is not strong enough to ensure good reproduction.

It is possible to produce charcoal, crayon, or litho pencil drawings in either line or tone. The choice is dependent on the paper used—this governs the texture of the tonal areas. If the tonal texture is coarse, black, and has not been smudged, line reproduction is possible. Otherwise, a halftone plate must be ordered. In a line reproduction, some of the darker areas will fill in and some of the finer specks in the tonal areas will be lost. Charcoal and litho crayon drawings give better results than pencil drawings, because the blacks tend to be stronger.

The Black-and-White Wash Drawing. A wash drawing is a watercolor rendering that has been executed in a single hue. It is painted with transparent color in which the values are reduced by the addition of water. When so diluted, the color becomes more transparent, thereby allowing the paper to show through and reduce the color's value. It is possible to make a wash drawing using diluted drawing ink, but watercolor pigment is more finely ground and generally produces better results. The more diluted the color, the weaker it becomes and the less its ability to properly expose the film negative. Gray wash areas can be expected to lose 10 percent in value when screened. As a result, a wash drawing should be deliberately executed in a full value range so that it will not weaken too much when reproduced. If the lower-middle values are too subtle, the camera operator must overexpose to retain them and the upper-middle values. Properly executed wash drawings have a tonal subtlety that is ideal for the rendering of fashion drawings and soft-goods illustrations.

Wash drawings should be rendered on watercolor paper. Many artists make the mistake of attempting to render them on illustration board. Such board is mounted Bristol, and cannot absorb the excessive water required for the rendering of a light wash area. As a result, the paper surface is destroyed; the wash becomes difficult to manipulate and takes on a scrubbed or muddy appearance.

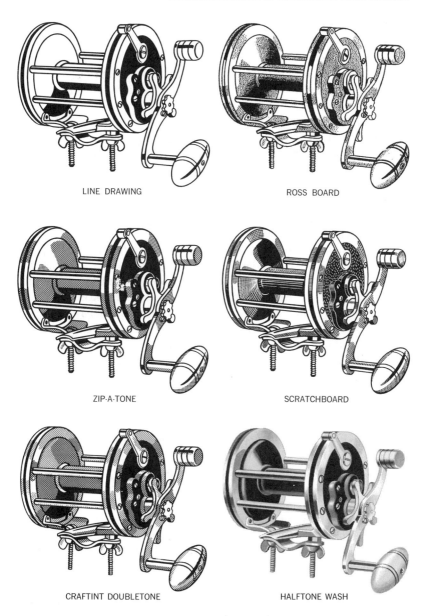

LINE DRAWING

ROSS BOARD

ZIP-A-TONE

SCRATCHBOARD

CRAFTINT DOUBLETONE

HALFTONE WASH

VARIOUS BLACK-AND-WHITE RENDERING TECHNIQUES

Wash drawings must be reproduced in halftone. The subtler the tonal values, the finer the screen that should be used. Newspaper advertisers utilize a good many wash drawings, due to the speed with which they can be executed. Since newspapers require a coarse screen, strong values are desirable. One-color wash drawings should be executed in black, regardless of the color in which they will ultimately print.

The Black-and-White Opaque Drawing. The most suitable medium for the rendering of continuous-tone art—from a reproduction standpoint—is opaque or "poster" color, also known as "designer's color." Poster color is often referred to as "tempera," which is inaccurate. Tempera is an opaque pigment that employs a colloidal medium, such as egg white, as a vehicle. Poster color uses water as a vehicle. Its values are reduced by the addition of white pigment. This assures a strong deposit of pigment, even in the lighter areas, producing the necessary strength for good reproduction.

Tubes of standardized opaque grays are manufactured for the retoucher and may be conveniently used by the illustrator. In the absence of these, black and white poster paint will suffice. Opaque color is more difficult to handle than transparent color. Care must be taken that solid areas remain flat and do not streak. This is accomplished by mixing the pigment to a proper consistency—approximately that of heavy cream. Edges, especially those of a high value contrast, are more difficult to soften or blend than with watercolor. It is often necessary to introduce an intermediate value in order to produce a smooth blending of color; such blending requires a high degree of skill and patience. Opaque paint is normally used for airbrush rendering. Use of the airbrush permits an extremely subtle blending of tonal values.

Opaque drawings are reproduced in halftone. Since stronger values are usually produced with opaque pigments, opaque renderings reproduce well with a coarse screen. Airbrush rendering should not be reproduced in coarse screen unless it has been executed with considerable contrast.

Dropouts

When continuous-tone original art is photographed through the halftone screen, *every* area of the negative receives a dot pattern, even in the lightest portions. In the normal halftone, the dot pattern present in the highlight areas can be minimized, but the pattern seldom disappears completely. Thus there are no pure white highlights.

Even a white background will produce a minimal dot pattern when screened. When halftone art is to appear as a silhouette, it must either be drawn on a white background, masked with a paper mask, or outlined with white paint. This will still produce a faint dot pattern, which must either be opaqued on the negative or be etched out by the platemaker. The platemaker may produce pure white highlights by opaquing, etching, or filtering with the magenta contact screen. This requires additional work on the part of the platemaker and results in considerably more expense than the normal halftone plate.

Multicolor and Full-Color Drawing

Media for color drawings include pastel, watercolor, opaque poster (designer's) color, acrylic, and oil. As in black-and-white drawing, the more opaque the pigment, the better it will reproduce.

It is possible to produce multicolor art in line. Line color may be pre-separated by the artist or camera separated by the platemaker. Preseparation entails few difficulties other than accurate registration of the color overlays. The number of colors that can be used is limited only by the patience of the artist and the budget of the advertiser.

Preseparation of continuous-tone art represents a considerably more difficult problem. Although there are methods by which this may be accomplished to some degree, continuous-tone color art is generally camera separated. It is always printed in halftone. Fake color process will give a full-color effect, but without any continuous tone; the various color areas will be flat, except for some modeling, which may be attempted with the black plate.

Full-color illustration destined for process printing may be prepared in any number and combination of colors desired. The purpose of the printed result will be the deciding factor between the use of three- or four-color process.

Most poor illustration results from inept execution and failure to serve the purposes of the advertiser, rather than from any nonreproducible qualities.

The work of an artistic genius is worthless if it does not meet the job deadline.

A common cause for the rejection of an illustration is the fact that it has been executed in an incorrect size. When reduced, it will not fit into its allocated area.

Good art should have a maximum definition between values. It is easy to be fooled by "contrasty" art. This may appear to be most dramatic; but the middle values, which should be clearly defined, succumb to the opposite ends of the value scale. Detail, which should be present in the middle values, is lacking.

Flat art is the opposite of contrasty art. It is characterized by a loss of detail, which should be expressed with darker areas. This is an undesirable situation and should be corrected by the introduction of greater contrast.

Paper has a strong influence on tonal reproduction. The grayer the surface, the weaker the highlight area. Hard, glossy paper produces the best highlight areas. The highlights become duller as the paper texture becomes coarser. Coarse paper will also cause black areas to become grayer.

THE COMBINATION DRAWING

There is one predicament the illustrator may inadvertently stumble into—one that cannot be solved by camera work. This is in the execution of the combination drawing—the drawing that is to print partially as line and partially as halftone. An example is the line illustration that has been supplemented with modeling or a tonal background.

The artist seldom encounters serious difficulty in the combination of type and halftone. Type is alien to halftone art and can hardly be positioned anywhere but on an overlay. It is, however, almost second nature to draw with pen or brush over a wash background or to model a line drawing with gray washes.

If such a drawing is to reproduce as line superimposed over halftone, the art must be separated. The wash must be painted on the illustration board with the line drawing registered over it on a transparent overlay. The wash rendering and the overlay will be photographed separately; one as halftone, the other as line. The resulting halftone positive and line positive will be used to produce a combination plate.

If the line and tone are not executed as separate art, but are drawn on the same board, the entire illustration will reproduce in halftone; the lines as well as the background will bear a dot pattern. In many cases, the screening of both line and wash is acceptable. However, some line work is so delicate that a dot pattern would destroy its character; retention of the line work as line is an absolute necessity.

If the artist unknowingly prepares such a drawing as one-piece art, there is no rescue by the camera operator. It is impossible to separate a black-and-white combination drawing. A black-and-color combination drawing may be camera-separated with an appropriate filter, but there is no method of filtering black from black.

Registration of line and halftone by the artist is easier to accomplish if the tone is rendered on an overlay on top of the line drawing. Unfortunately, there are few overlay materials that accommodate tone well—especially wash. Because of this, the tonal rendering is usually done on some suitable drawing surface and the line work is drawn on an acetate or vellum overlay. It is left to the ingenuity of the artist to devise a method of accurate registration.

In combination drawings, the line overlay is usually rendered with drawing ink. The tone may be rendered in transparent wash, opaque gray, pencil, crayon, or charcoal. The tone must be kept light enough so that the overprinting line will not be obliterated.

It may often be desirable to drop out the tone background behind the line art. If accurate registration is a problem for the artist, the dropout can be accomplished on the halftone film negative. Using the line positive as a guide, the opaquer can determine exactly where to obliterate the dots on the halftone negative. If such work is required, it should be carefully specified in the instructions to the platemaker.

PHOTOGRAPHY

Photographs, unless intended for conversion to some special linear effect, are printed with a halftone plate. Photographs intended for reproduction should be taken by a professional photographer. The "snapshot," except under unusual circumstances, is considered inadequate for the purpose. Sharply focused, well-lighted photographs reproduce best. The halftone process rarely improves the quality of a photograph. It compresses the value range, and a certain amount of detail is lost. If the original photograph does not contain sufficient detail, it will certainly not be brought out by the halftone process. As a result, areas lacking in detail must be clarified by the retoucher.

Lighting

Lighting is an important factor governing the suitability of a photograph for reproduction. The detail of an object, especially the definition of its texture, is seen in its middle-value areas. The eye resists making an abrupt transition from light to dark or vice versa. Middle values provide the eye with a comfortable means of moving from one extreme of light to the other.

Flat Lighting. Flat lighting is the direct frontal illumination of the subject. The large tonal masses become either too dark or too light. As a result, much detail is lost.

Side Lighting. Side lighting gives more illusion of depth, but the tones normally occur in large masses. The shadow edges merge with the background, and the light side of the subject tends to lose its detail.

Balanced Lighting. In balanced lighting, the subject is illuminated from the front quarter and the shadow areas are "filled in"—illuminated with a less brilliant light. This produces a photograph containing the full tonal scale. Light areas and adjacent shadow areas are properly separated by middle values, and there is sufficient detail present to identify the nature of the subject.

The criterion for determining the most suitable photograph for reproduction is good definition of its middle values. Since texture is observed in the middle values, it is most critical that the values be well defined; if so, the texture will be well defined. Darks and highlights can be intensified, but it is most difficult to clarify ill-defined texture, either photomechanically or by retouching.

When a photograph is to be silhouetted or retouched, the subject should be distinct from the background. This eliminates guesswork about the precise location of the edges. Important parts of an object are often eliminated by the silhouetter because they have become lost against the background.

If left to their own devices, photographers tend to print work on photographic paper that will look good. Sepia-toned, matte finish, or textured paper is not necessarily the best from the standpoint of reproduction. Glossy, white 8" × 10" prints reproduce best and are the easiest to handle.

When producing a halftone from a photograph, it is better to reduce than to enlarge; reduction makes any retouching less apparent.

Photographic prints should be kept in the same scale whenever possible. This enables the platemaker to gang up halftone art and reduce it all in one shot, rather than having to reduce each photograph separately with a different camera focus.

In order to prevent damage, photographs should be immediately mounted by the recipient. They should be rubber-cemented or dry-mounted (a process where dry-mounting tissue, cut to the size of the photo, is placed between the photo and the backing and pressed down with an electric iron or a dry-mounting press) on a durable mounting board. Once mounted, photographs should be immediately covered with a protective tissue flap.

All information written or stamped on the back of a photograph should be copied on the back of the mounting board before the photo is mounted.

Photographs received in a torn or cracked condition should be photocopied (if the negative is not available) so that the defect can be retouched.

Retouching

Retouching is not, as is sometimes implied, a method of misrepresenting or misleading, but rather the enhancement of a photograph in order to obtain maximum quality and efficiency from the various reproduction processes.

Retouching is accomplished with the airbrush, dyes, bleaches, or other chemicals. It is done directly on the positive photographic print. The prime function of retouching is to minimize the work of the photoengraver and the dot etcher in the production of halftone plates. Retouching includes the removal of photographic imperfections, the removal of undesirable or extraneous elements, the sharpening of contrast, and the accentuation of highlights. Retouchers may clarify detail, lettering, etc., and may restore lost edges. They also may add extra area to the photograph in order to alter its overall proportions. The majority of these functions may also be accomplished with a sophisticated computerized graphic system.

Photoprints

Also known as copy prints, photoprints are photographic copies of existing art or photographic prints. Photoprinters do not take original photographs. They may be called upon to duplicate a photographic print for which there is no existing negative or to make contact prints, in any quantity, from a negative. They may also produce screened Velox prints.

Rescreening

As previously mentioned, halftone proofs can be used as art for lithography. This is not so in letterpress. An occasion may arise when the only available art is a screened proof. It is possible for the photoprinter to copy this proof by keeping the camera slightly out of focus or moving the copy a fraction of an inch. This will cause the dots to merge and form some semblance of continuous-tone, which can be used as letterpress copy. There is a considerable loss of quality in this process, but it provides a possible solution for an emergency situation.

The Stock-Photo Service

Most photographs used for advertising purposes, especially color photographs, are taken expressly for their required purpose. A photograph taken by a competent professional is as expensive as a good illustration. There is an inexpensive source of photography upon which the producer of advertising art relies heavily. This is the stock-photo service.

The stock-photo service maintains a file of photographs of almost every conceivable subject. These range from photographs of historical landmarks to posed scenes of housewives in the supermarket. Large photo services publish catalogs of their available material. Reproduction rights to these photos are granted to the advertiser for a fee.

COLOR PHOTOGRAPHY

Early Color Photography

Early color photography employed projected transparencies which were produced by the color-additive process. This process, as previously mentioned, depended upon the addition of the primary hues of light—red, green, and blue—to produce the desired color image. The transparencies were laboriously produced by exposing three sheets of black-and-white film through red, green, and blue filters, converting the results to positives, and projecting them—in register—with appropriately hued lights.

Commercial applications of this principle were known as *screen-plate processes*, representing an attempt to produce a one-piece color transparency. Microscopic red, green, and blue particles—acting as filters—were deposited over a panchromatic film emulsion, resulting in a patchwork of negative separations on a single surface. Converting the negative panchromatic film to positive resulted in a mask, one which would block anything but the color that produced the original exposure. Projected with white light, the resulting mosaic of primary hues would add to reproduce the color of the original subject.

There were several variations of this process: *Lumiere Autochrome*, introduced in 1907, used heavy glass plates, covered by a mosaic of microscopic particles of dyed potato starch. In an attempt to transmit more light, *Agfacolor*, a faster German process, employed dyed particles of gum arabic as the filter screen. Faster yet, *Finlay Color* utilized a checkerboard screen of transparent squares, printed in the three primaries. Since the pattern itself was light-sensitive, no emulsion layer was required. The first process to use a film base rather than glass plates was *Dufaycolor*, a process which employed a screen, printed in an overlapping linear pattern and coated with a panchromatic emulsion.

The disadvantage of these processes was that when either printed or projected, the screen pattern was noticeable, often objectionable.

Modern Color Film

The subtractive method has produced the most successful color processes from the standpoint of simplicity of use and quality of result. The subtractive process makes use of the three secondaries, cyan, magenta, and yellow, and their ability to subtract the unwanted colors of light in order to produce the colors of the original subject.

Color negative film (print film) produces a transparent film negative whose hues are complementary to the subject. Available in a variety of film speeds, these negatives are used to produce reflection copy (positive prints), which are framed, mounted in albums, and so on. If taken with a camera which has a sharp lens and appropriate shutter speed, the resulting print may be used as copy for reproduction.

Color reversal film (slide film) produces transparent positives. In developing, the negative layers of the emulsion are reversed from negative to positive and dye is substituted for the silver in the appropriate layers.

Color reversal film is based on the coupler principle: the emulsion (silver bromide) is reacted upon by a developer, which reduces it to silver. The resulting oxidized developer will then react with certain compounds to form dyes. Thus, any light-sensitive layer of emulsion that has been exposed to a primary hue can be coupler-developed into its complement, forming the secondary hue necessary to produce a subtractive image.

The film negative consists of three emulsion layers superimposed on a transparent gelatin support (film). The top layer is blue-sensitive. Beneath it is a yellow filter layer used to prevent the blue light from reaching the lower layers, which are green-sensitive and red-sensitive, respectively.

In order to produce a transparent positive image, each layer must be developed and dyed with its complementary hue. Processing consists of chemically assigning the dyes to their proper layers. In processing, the blue-sensitive layer is dyed its complement, yellow; the green-sensitive layer is dyed magenta; the red-sensitive layer is dyed cyan.

These resulting secondary hues are subtractively combined either by projection or by viewing over a light source to produce a full-color positive image. Positive color transparencies are known as "*chromes*."

Color Prints

Color prints are positive color images that have been processed on white cellulose paper so they can be viewed without recourse to the projector or the light-table. A result of the subtractive process, they are made from color transparencies.

Most types of color print have a tendency to lose some of the color quality and fidelity of the original. As a result, separation negatives for process printing are preferably made *directly from the original transparency*. The prime reason for

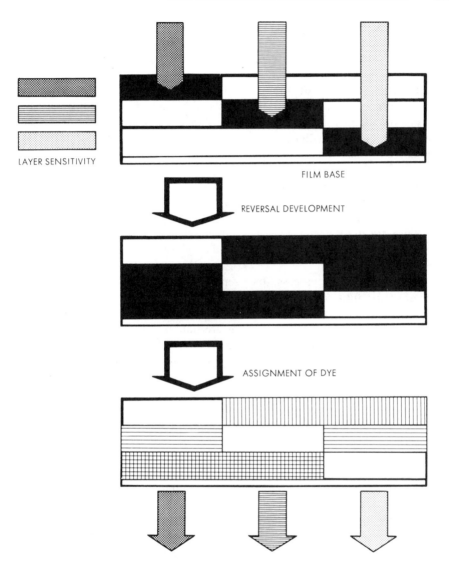

LAYER SENSITIVITY

FILM BASE

REVERSAL DEVELOPMENT

ASSIGNMENT OF DYE

COLOR REVERSAL FILM

THE ADDITIVE HUES REFLECTED FROM THE SUBJECT EACH EXPOSE A FILM LAYER SENSITIVE TO
THAT PARTICULAR HUE. THE LAYERS ARE REVERSAL-DEVELOPED AND COMPLEMENTARY-HUED DYES
(YELLOW, MAGENTA, AND CYAN) ARE CHEMICALLY ASSIGNED TO EACH LAYER. VIEWED
THROUGH A WHITE LIGHT SOURCE, EACH PAIR OF SECONDARY HUES COMBINES TO PRODUCE
THE PRIMARY HUES OF THE ORIGINAL.

utilizing a color print for reproduction purposes occurs when some form of color retouching is required or when some sort of hand-drawn retouching is necessary. Color prints are also used when it is necessary to produce a montage or a paste-up assembly.

There are two types of color prints used for reproduction—the indirect and the direct print. *Indirect prints* consist of chemically dyed separations that have been superimposed in exact register on a white base. They are expensive and represent the highest quality of print available for reproduction purposes. The most commonly used is the dye transfer.

The Dye Transfer. Dye transfers find use as reproduction copy. The original print is expensive, but once it has been produced, additional copies may be ordered at far less cost.

Since the dye transfer consists of three layers of dye rather than carbon tissue, it is more durable than the Carbro[1] and may be readily cut apart for paste-up assembly.

In the dye-transfer process, three separation negatives are exposed to three sheets of matrix film, forming a gelatin-hardened relief image. The matrices are then dyed magenta, cyan, and yellow. Registered with punched holes that position on pins, the dyed images of the matrices are transferred to white photographic paper. The matrices may be redyed and retransferred for the production of additional prints. The cost of a single dye transfer includes the production of the separation negatives and the matrix films. Once these have been paid for, additional copies may be had for merely the cost of the transferring operation.

Dye transfers are being used less and less for montage work, due to their cost. Montages are now produced with photocomp, a process that assembles color film positives on a single piece of film.

Photocomp. Photocomp(osition) can eliminate the need for an intervening color print when color retouching, picture retouching, or montaging is required. Undesired pictorial elements can be removed and backgrounds stripped into place. Line art may be drawn separately and placed into the composition in proper position and perspective.

Separate transparencies may be montaged together by masking with either photographic or hand-cut masks, resulting on a one-piece transparent positive, ready for color separation (see also page 139).

This operation can also be performed with a graphic computer system. Once scanned and stored as digital information, any number of images—photographic, art, or a combination of both—may be electronically merged into almost any conceivable combination.

[1]The Carbro is a positive color print consisting of three layers of dyed carbon tissue which are mounted in register on an opaque white cellulose base. The carbon tissue is photosensitized gelatin. The name Carbro is a combination of "carbon" and "bromide."

Direct Prints.   The direct print requires no separation; as a result, it is not nearly as expensive as an indirect print. Direct prints generally result in a color loss from the original transparency. There is further loss in the printing process; consequently they are not preferred as copy for color separation. But they can readily be color-retouched in an attempt to compensate for this tendency, making them an often acceptable medium in view of their relatively low cost.

Any number of copies of this type of print may be readily produced. This makes the direct print a suitable medium for short runs of color copy in which the expense of producing printing plates is not warranted. Full-color illustration, rendered in any color medium, is used as reflection copy for three- or four-color process printing.

SPECIAL PHOTOGRAPHIC TECHNIQUES

It is possible to convert continuous-tone art into single-colored or multicolored art, even into line art, through the use of a wide variety of photographic techniques. The application of these techniques is dependent upon the skill of the camera operator, rather than upon the preparation of the art, but the art director should be familiar with these techniques and their potential.

Black-and-White Conversion Techniques

These methods will produce the crisp visual impact of the black-line drawing, stipple drawing, or mezzotint, eliminating the laborious techniques of the original processes. Photo-line illustrations are finding widespread use because of their photographic fidelity to their subject, their sharp, dramatic image, and the resulting economies in both labor and halftone elimination. Black-and-white line art may be produced from continuous-tone original art in the following ways:

Line Conversion.   This technique converts a continuous-tone original into an image in which the middle tones have been eliminated; all tones appear as either solid blacks or whites. Contrasting developer and paper are used, both of which help to eliminate the middle values. It is possible to make a line conversion of continuous-tone art by placing acetate over the copy and tracing it with black drawing ink, making no attempt to duplicate the middle tones but resolving it into either black or white. The resulting line tracing serves as a film positive.

In either case, the subject matter should be appropriate; it must be capable of retaining its identity when reduced to this form. Excessive highlights will produce large white areas without detail; excessive dark grays and blacks will combine to form large, undecipherable areas.

The Single-Line Screen.   Single-line screens are contact screens that are placed over the film in the camera. The original copy—a continuous-tone positive—is then photographed through the screen. The result is a screened negative. A positive print may be made by either contact-printing or with a conventional enlarger, utilizing a continuous-tone negative. The screen is placed either between the negative and the paper in the contact-printer, or over the paper on the enlarger easel, and the image is projected through it.

The single-line screen consists of precisely paralleled lines running in one direction only. The line pattern may be horizontal, vertical, wavy, or arranged in concentric circles. Since there are no crossed lines, a linear rather than a dot pattern is produced. The resulting image is achieved by the variation of line thickness that occurs as value changes occur in the original. The result is similar in appearance to a black-line engraving or a tightly rendered pen-and-ink drawing.

Straight- and wavy-line screens are ideal for depicting machinery, glassware, jewelry, and other hard goods. The concentric-circle screen produces a bull's-eye effect that can be used to draw attention to a desired area, but its center should be skillfully located.

The Mezzotint Screen.   This screen contains a random grain pattern and is used in the same manner as any contact screen. A skilled camera operator can manipulate the screen with a great variety of results, ranging from a high-contrast (resembling a line shot) to a subtle flat gray suitable for a background. The standard screen is the equivalent of 75 lines per inch, and finer patterns of up to 150 and 225 lines per inch are available.

The Coarse-Dot Screen.   This is a coarsely ruled screen that exaggerates the halftone pattern to a point where the dots become obvious. This technique has attention-getting qualities that are particularly suitable for newspaper advertising or promotional pieces. Since the coarsest screen available is 50 lines per inch, dot enlargement is accomplished by making a screened negative at less than the desired size, making a contact positive, and enlarging this screened positive to the desired size. Results as coarse as 15 lines per inch may be obtained; obviously, considerable detail will be lost with such a dot size.

Special Effects.   The continuous-tone negative may be printed through any irregular texture that is capable of transmitting light through the interstices. This breaks the image into tiny, irregular shapes, as defined by the pattern. A wide variety of textural effects may be obtained by printing through loosely woven textures, such as cheesecloth, silk stocking, or wire-mesh screening. Sheets of shading film may be used. *Engraving and steel-etch* contact screens are available commercially. These screens may be utilized to form either a positive or a negative image effectively.

There are several new types of line conversion. They are less pictorial, perhaps, than their predecessors; but their objective is to attract attention, rather than to illustrate with a unique technique. *Photoline* is a conversion that captures enough detail to define the picture, yet eliminates extraneous detail. *Tone Line*

Courtesy of Chemco Photoproducts, Inc.

SPECIAL EFFECTS SCREENS

TOP: STRAIGHT LINE SCREEN.   CENTER: CONCENTRIC CIRCLE SCREEN.
BOTTOM LEFT: MEZZOTINT SCREEN.   BOTTOM RIGHT: STEEL ETCH SCREEN.

outlines every detail of the original, down to the grain of the original negative. *Continuous Line* has the appearance of a contour line, drawn, in outline form, around a particular tone value; the outline is retained, and the value is eliminated. *Photo Silhouette* is a stark and dramatic effect; it reduces the original to only the deepest and most significant tones.

Laserline™. Laserline, a new line-conversion/Velox process developed by Schaedler-Pinwheel of New York, makes laser-scan, special-effect line conversions from continuous-tone art without a camera. There are no negatives, no masks, no receiver papers. Prints are exposed directly with an amplified laser, scanning with extremely high resolution.

Photos and art can be rescaled, reproportioned, sharpened or softened, produced as a negative or a positive, or even flopped.

The system produces all of the special-effect line patterns, as well as eloxes up to 100 lines per inch. Each pattern can be adjusted to manipulate shadow dot or line sizes and to shift the middle values from light to dark without affecting the extremes.

Output is the original laser-exposed print, ready for paste-up on the mechanical art. Duplicate prints are produced by making a fine-line film negative of the original laser print and making contact prints from it.

Posterizing

Posterizing is a photomechanical process in which a black-and-white photograph, containing a full range of tones, can be reproduced with only a few flat tones. *Two-tone posterization* consists of the elimination of any middle tones. In this form, it is similar to the line conversion. *Three-tone posterization* utilizes black, white, and a single gray tone—obviously, a color other than black may be used. *Four-tone posterization* adds an additional middle tone. More than four tones are seldom used because the result is too similar to an ordinary halftone.

In order to produce a three-tone effect, the film is exposed to the copy only long enough to record the highlight areas. Following this, a 40-percent screen is placed over the film, and a second exposure is made in order to introduce a dot into the middle tones of the copy. The third tone—the blacks—consists of the tones that have not received enough exposure to form an image. The resulting negative can be used directly to produce a printing plate or a photographic print on high-contrast paper, which may be retouched or submitted for client approval. Posterized film positives may also be produced from continuous-tone negatives with a conventional enlarger, which projects them on either paper or film. This technique allows the picture to be observed during development, which can be varied to compensate for different exposures required by different types of subject matter.

Posterization need not be limited to the two-, three-, or four-tone range of a single color. In a two-tone posterization, a flat second color may be used, or the

LASERGRAIN POSITIVE TO POSITIVE

LASERLINE CONVERSIONS

LASERLINE LINE RENDERING

213

LASERLINE NEEDLEPOINT

LASERLINE CONVERSIONS

LASERLINE VERTICAL STRAIGHTLINE
POSTERIZATION

image may be printed on colored stock. If the second color is *printed*, it obviously allows for the possibility of a white dropout. A second color may be added to a three-tone or a four-tone posterization, either as one of the tones or as a solid tint added for dramatic effect. The ultimate would be four-color posterization in which each color printer is posterized, reducing each (magenta, yellow, cyan, and black) separation to one value, plus a solid. The overprinting solid areas represent the shadows, and the middle tones overprint to form color variations. The resulting loss of detail tends to dramatize what remains.

Black-and-White Printing Techniques

Special color toners—red, blue, green yellow, charcoal—may be added to ordinary black ink, enhancing the printed image with an added subtlety, literally a two-tone effect with a single color, black. These may be used to add warmth or coolness to a picture, to produce a seasonal effect, or to enhance some characteristic of the image.

Substituting *flat black* for gloss process black will provide good halftone reproduction *plus* a flat background, thus making the halftone stand out more effectively.

Variations of black—flat black, flat black plus matte varnish, gloss black, gloss black plus gloss varnish—can be used to create a variety of subtle enrichment for the printed piece.

A two-tone effect can be achieved with black ink if a second impression is utilized to overprint varnish, either clear or tinted. For example, gloss black with overprint varnish creates an extremely glossy image. Flat with an overprint of spot varnish (varnish in a selected area only) produces a glossy image surrounded by a matte background. Gloss black with tinted varnish imparts an additional tonal effect.

Multicolor Techniques

The Duotone Halftone.   The duotone halftone is probably the most popular of the two-color techniques. A duotone maintains contrast and tonal separation in both the highlight and the shadow areas, an effect that is not always possible in a one-color halftone. In order to produce a duotone, two halftone plates are made from a single black-and-white original photograph. A separate screened negative is made for each color. Each negative is identical, except that when the negative is made for the second color the lines of the screen are turned at a 30-degree angle from those of the first negative, so that the dots of the second color will appear *between* those of the first color, rather than becoming obliterated by falling directly *underneath* them. The resulting plates are printed, in register, on top of each other. The image produces a two-color effect. Thus, the duotone requires two halftone plates; if each plate were proofed separately, the image would be visible in the impression made of each color.

Most often, the first color in a conventional duotone is black. The mood of the picture may be substantially enhanced if the selection of the second color is appropriate. Different effects and emphasis can be created by varying the density and contrast of the two colors. Both colors may be printed in an equal value, or the value of either color may be strengthened. Equal value reinforces the detail found in the original photograph and creates a color that differs from either of the inks used. Strengthening the black results in even stronger detail; strengthening the color serves to enhance the mood.

The conventional duotone halftone has been subjected to many imaginative new applications. Some of these possibilities are:

The Halftone and Screen Tint (The "Fake" Duotone).   A similar but somewhat less dramatic effect may be obtained by printing a colored screen tint behind a black halftone. The screen tint is a uniform tone, carrying none of the image detail. One negative bears the halftone image; the other the screen-tint pattern. The screen angle of the tint is turned in order to avoid a moiré effect. The result appears as a tinted photograph, lacking the clarity and contrast of the duotone, although the tint may be mechanically dropped out in order to enhance desired areas. This process, known colloquially as the "fake" duotone, is considerably less expensive than the duotone halftone.

The Special Screen Duotone.   It is not necessary for either or both plates to bear a halftone image in order to produce dramatic two-color photographic art. *Printing a line conversion over a screen (dot) tint* or a *line conversion over a flat mezzotint pattern* has proved most effective. Obviously white highlights may be dropped out of either version. This addition of a color background has proved an ideal method for squaring-off line conversions in which the background has been lost. Any of the above-mentioned special line screens may be utilized in the production of two-tone art. For example:

Both colors are printed in *single-line screens*, superimposed over each other at right angles.

Both colors printed in *mezzotint screen*. It is not necessary to rotate one of these screens in order to avoid moiré; a slight displacement will suffice.

Both colors printed in *concentric-circle screen*. The center point of each is placed at a different location, and the resulting pattern radiates from the two points. The copy must be extremely appropriate.

Both colors *posterized*. Each color is resolved into two tones—a solid and a middle tone. The two colors are superimposed; one color is rotated to avoid moiré.

The Triotone.   The triotone is produced by superimposing three half-tone images. The triotone uses a black-and-white original and converts it into process-color halftones. Any three of the four process colors may be involved. The combination and strength of these colors call for skillful color selectivity and manipulation of the camera exposure in order to produce the desired effect. A black and two grays are also very effective.

The Duochrome. The duochrome differs from the duotone in that a full-color original is required for its preparation. The two printers utilized are *filter separated* from the original transparency or print. The duochrome gives the visual impact of possessing more color than a traditional duotone, even though it only possesses black and one color. Since the original of a duochrome is in full color, the camera operator has a full range of choice as to which color is to be filter-extracted. A color matching the subject may be selected, or a contrasting—even illogical—color may be chosen for an unusual or bizarre effect.

Even greater dimension can be added to the duochrome through the use of special screens. Combinations of single-line mezzotint screens, as well as posterization, can be combined to reflect almost any mood.

The Twin-Color Process. The twin-color process requires a full-color original, although in this case artwork as well as the photograph can be utilized. Twin color divides the spectrum into two colors, instead of three, yet retains a feeling of full color. The original art is filter-separated into orange-red and blue-green. When overprinted as solids, the two colors create black; when overprinted in equal tints, the result is a neutral gray. If the colors of the original are appropriate—a predominance of warm red-browns—remarkable results can be obtained. Both dot screening and special-effect screening can be utilized for this technique.

Fluorescent Ink. Finer grinds and improved color strength now permit fluorescent inks to be used in offset lithography. Halftones as fine as 133 lines may be printed. Some of the possibilities of this technique include:

A *line conversion* or a *special effects screen* overprinting a solid fluorescent color, with or without a white dropout.

A *posterization* over a fluorescent solid.

A *halftone screen* over a fluorescent solid, with or without a white dropout.

A *duotone halftone*—a black halftone over a fluorescent halftone. The individual halftones are made higher in contrast in order to provide maximum "show through" of the fluorescent color.

Metallic Ink. Metallic ink is not ideally suited for halftone reproduction, but it is possible to print a regular halftone or a special effects screen over a solid metallic ink background. Another possibility includes the combination of a black dot halftone with a mezzotint of the metallic ink. If kept coarse, the mezzotint pattern will not "fill," as it would in an attempt to print a halftone with a metallic ink.

Metallic ink requires a paper that will allow the maximum amount of ink to remain on the surface.

Full-Color Printing.   Four-color process printing is no longer limited to the traditional dot halftone screen. Four-color printing, utilizing mezzotint screens, is soft, yet dramatic. Normal separation negatives are screened to positives, using a fine mezzotint contact screen. Again, the screens do not need to be angled to the customary 30 degrees of four-color process; a slight displacement is sufficient. If a steel-etch screen pattern is combined with the regular halftone black printer, it will impart an antique look to the subject matter. Four-color posterization, as previously mentioned, is very striking. Full-color dot halftones can be printed with fluorescent ink, substituting fluorescent magenta and yellow for the conventional process inks. The result is more luminous and vibrant than a normal four-color impression. A fifth color—a solid metallic color in line—can be added to a four-color impression whose subject matter requires the look of actual metal that cannot be obtained with four-color process alone.

Additionally, gloss varnish, either as an entire overprint or a spot overprint, may be utilized to enhance four-color process printing.

Computer-Generated Effects.   The computer graphics system lends itself perfectly to the preparation of art for such printing techniques, because once scanned and digitally stored, original color art may be altered into most of the aforementioned combinations *before separations are made*, thus enabling an evaluation of any effect before a commitment is made to it.

CHAPTER 14
THE PREPARATION
OF MECHANICAL
ART

The initial step in the execution of a mechanical is "laying it out"—delineating its size with the proper types of lines. These are ruled with T-square and triangle in order to precisely define the areas in which the illustrations and the copy will be pasted. To lay out a job properly, the artist must know how pages are arranged on the press sheets, how they are bound, and how they are trimmed or cut to the desired size.

IMPOSITION, BINDING, AND DIE-CUTTING

Imposition

After pages are printed, they must be cut, folded, and bound. The bound copy may take a great variety of forms. In order to print both sides, cut, fold, and bind with the highest degree of efficiency—both in the saving of time and the elimination of waste—the printer must arrange the page forms on the press so that these operations may best be accomplished. This arrangement of the page forms is known as *imposition*.

Imposition is the responsibility of the printers; they will impose their pages properly, regardless of the order of their mechanical preparation. However, artists can expedite matters considerably if they are familiar with the practices of imposition and have learned to work in close cooperation with the printer.

The simplest type of printed form is the four-page folder. This is printed on both sides of a single sheet, which is then folded vertically in the middle. Pages 2 and 3 will print side by side, with page 2 on the left. On the back of the sheet, pages 1 and 4 will be printed, with page 4 impressed so that it will print on the reverse side of, or "back up," page 3. The mechanical flats are prepared in the following manner:

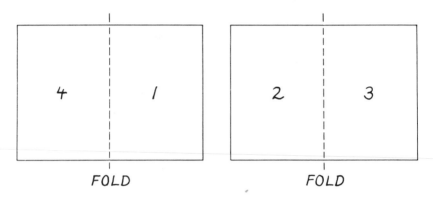

The four-page folder requires no binding. An eight-page folder, however, requires two sheets that must be bound—usually with staples—along the fold. The mechanical flats for an eight-page folder are prepared in this manner:

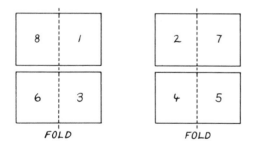

These flats are known as *engraver's flats*. This type of preparation is preferred by platemakers because they can shoot a negative of each two-page flat; they do not need to reposition the pages.

It can readily be seen that booklet pages occur in multiples of four. Thus, booklets must contain 4, 8, 12, 16, 20, etc. pages. It is not necessary to print on every page, but there can be no such thing as a booklet containing, for example, 5, 11, or 18 pages.

When preparing engraver's flats for more than eight pages, it is best to make up a paper dummy containing the desired number of pages. Each page is then numbered. When the dummy is taken apart, it will show the exact combinations in which the pages occur on the press sheet.

It is not always practical, from the standpoint of the artist, to prepare the flats in this manner. The layout may feature a complex design that runs across the entire spread. If this is the case, it is more convenient to prepare the art in facing pages. This may also prove easier for the client to visualize and evaluate than would engraver's flats.

An eight-page folder is laid out in *spreads* in this way:

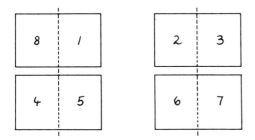

Since neither the front nor the back cover (pages 1 and 8) can be treated as part of a spread, they are laid out as they will appear on the plate. The platemaker shoots negatives of the spread and cuts them apart so that they can be imposed according to the requirements of the job.

The choice of the preferred mechanical format should be made after consultation with both printer and client. If artists prepare their flats in accordance with the printer's specifications, they are not directly concerned with the manner in which the printer imposes the pages; however, it is still pertinent for them to understand how it is done.

There are three basic types of imposition: (1) sheetwise, (2) work-and-turn, and (3) work-and-tumble. The type of imposition employed depends on the length of the run and the nature of the job. The purpose of imposition is the adaptation of the press setup and the paper size to the proportions of the job, so that a minimum of paper is wasted—to produce the job at the lowest possible cost on available equipment.

Sheetwise Imposition.   Sheetwise imposition utilizes two sets of plates—one set for each side of the job. Half of the pages are imposed on one set, the remainder on the other. The paper is printed on one side, allowed to dry, and then run a second time in order to print the back of the sheet. It takes 2,000 impressions to print 1,000 copies. The plates are imposed in the same manner as shown in the preceding diagram illustrating the preparation of the engraver's flat.

Work-and-Turn Imposition.   The object of work-and-turn printing is to allow the printer to print both sides of a given number of copies—1,000 for instance—with only 1,000 impressions. This is accomplished with paper cut to twice the desired size. All the pages are imposed on a single plate. In order to print a four-page folder, they are imposed this way:[1]

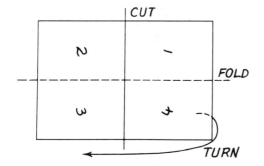

A total of 500 sheets is run through the press. The entire pile is then turned over, laterally, and rerun through the press. In the second impression, pages 1 and 4 will print on the back of 2 and 3; pages 2 and 3 will print on the back of 1 and 4. When the 500 sheets are cut vertically across, the other dimension of the paper is folded horizontally, 1,000 four-page folders will result.

Work-and-Tumble Imposition.   Work-and-tumble printing would also be utilized to print 1,000 copies with 1,000 impressions. It differs from work-and-turn in that it is applicable for jobs that are horizontal in format. Work-and-tumble is imposed this way:

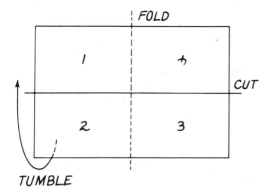

The pile of paper is turned over from bottom to top, instead of laterally. This again causes the proper pages to print on the backs of each other. The paper is cut horizontally across its dimension and is folded vertically.

[1]The diagram indicates the page positions as they will appear on the proof sheet. Many sources indicate the positions as they appear on the plate. It should be remembered that letterpress plates are imposed backwards-reading, and litho plates are imposed frontwards-reading.

It is possible to impose an 80-page book on a single sheet. This represents a considerable exercise in printing production, which no mechanical artist will ever be called upon to do. The mechanical artist prepares the flats as facing spreads or engraver's flats. Occasionally the artist will be called upon to prepare the flats in imposition for a smaller booklet. Broadsides and other mailing pieces may fold in some complex manner, but basically they are single sheets, printed on two sides. As such, they offer no problem of proper page imposition.

The *six-page folder* represents a unique problem for the mechanical artist. A six-page folder is not bound; the extreme right page is folded between the other two, as is a letter when it is inserted in an envelope. The *mechanical art* for a six-page folder is laid out this way:

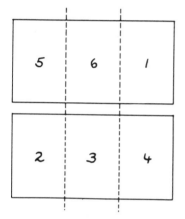

Page 4 is folded inward, covering page 3 and lining up with the right edge of page 2. If page 4 is not laid out *slightly narrower* than pages 2 and 3, the folder will bulge when it is folded. Obviously page 5 must also be made slightly narrower. If this is not done, the printer will automatically trim the inward-folding side of the sheet at least ⅛ inch to compensate for this tendency. If the artist is not aware of this necessity, vital material may be trimmed off.

Binding

After the sheets are printed they are shipped, still flat, to the bindery. The binder cuts, folds, binds, and trims the sheets into the desired format. The sheets are cut so that they may be folded, by machine, into signatures. The signatures are bound together; the trimming is done *after* the binding. In trimming, the cutting knives are aligned on the crop marks. This is the reason for bleed; there is ⅛ inch leeway to compensate for faulty binding or alignment of the knives.

The mechanical artist may be concerned with the way the work is to be bound. It may be necessary to allow adequate margins on the binding edge or to allow sufficient gutter clearance for the type of binding that will be used. There

TYPES OF FOLDERS

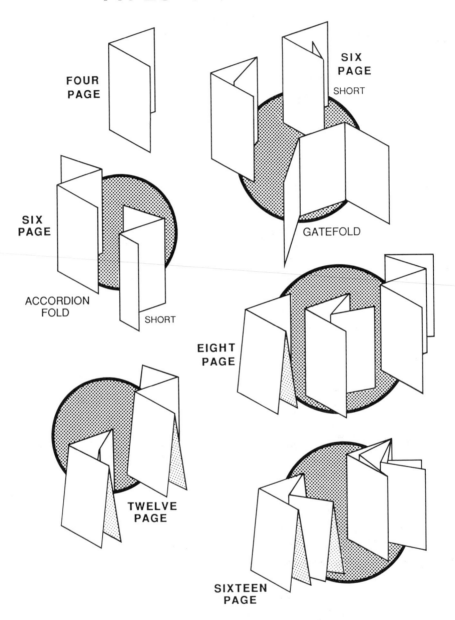

FOUR
PAGE

SIX
PAGE

SHORT

SIX
PAGE

ACCORDION
FOLD

SHORT

GATEFOLD

EIGHT
PAGE

TWELVE
PAGE

SIXTEEN
PAGE

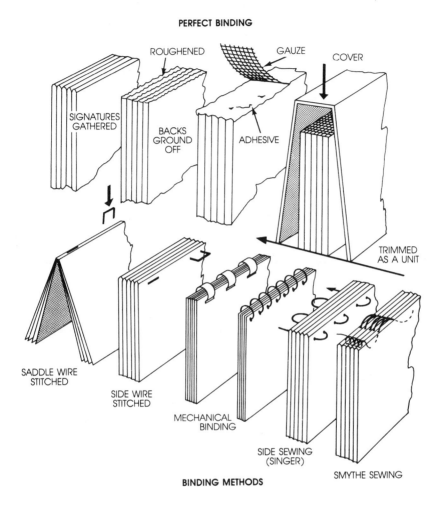

are no set rules; the printer will know the binding requirements, and the printer's instructions should be followed explicitly. There are several types of binding in common use.

Covers.   The self-cover booklet is one of relatively few pages whose cover is of the same paper as the inner pages; the cover offers no added protection for the contents. The *covered book* or *booklet* has covers made of a material that is more durable than the inner pages. The covering may range in quality from a slightly heavier paper to the finest leather.

Saddle-Wire Stitching.   Saddle stitching consists of wires or staples inserted through the fold, or saddle, of the pages. It allows the booklet to be fully opened but is impractical for the binding of a thick volume. Normal gutter allowances on the mechanical art will generally prove sufficient.

Side-Wire Stitching. Side-wire stitching consists of wires or staples punched from the front page through to the back page. These wires are inserted close to the fold and are clinched at the back. Since the pages of a side-wire stitched book cannot be opened flat, extra gutter allowance should be provided.

Perfect Binding. Perfect binding is an adhesive binding technique used for books that do not warrant expensive binding. Either signatures or folded pages are gathered together, and the fold edge is roughened. A hot, liquid adhesive is applied to the edge, and a gauzelike material (crash) is imbedded in the adhesive for extra strength. A separate cover (usually of thicker paper) is added while the adhesive is still wet.

Mechanical Binding. Mechanical binding requires the punching of holes in the paper so that metal or plastic wire or stips may be threaded through them. A typical variety of mechanical binding is the well-known "spiral" binding. Mechanical binding allows the pages to lie perfectly flat, but adequate gutter clearance must be left for the holes. As there is a great variety of mechanical binding devices, the required hole clearance should be carefully checked.

Looseleaf Binding. Pages that are bound together with removable rings or posts are called looseleaf. Ring binding may be opened flat; post binding may not. Since holes must be punched for either operation, proper clearance dimensions should be obtained.

The Sewed Book. Better books are assembled in signatures that are then sewed together with strong thread. The thickness of the signatures forms a wide spine to which the cover is glued. This method provides considerable strength and flexibility; the pages can be opened flat. The mechanical artist is seldom concerned with the preparation of a book that will be bound like this (Smythsewn).

Die-Cutting

Any irregular shape or design that cannot be cut with a straight cutting knife must be cut with a specially made die. Since there is no standard format for the die-cut piece, each die is custom-made to conform to the requirements of the job.

The die consists of a steel cutting edge, conforming to the outline shape of the job. The die is mounted on a plywood dieboard, cutting edge up, like a cookie cutter. Die-cutting presses are similar to printing presses; the platen printing press is often employed for die-cutting small work.

The die for a simple display or promotional piece is made to conform to the blue die-cut line on the mechanical art. The die-cutting of complex displays and folding boxes requires greater precision than can be accomplished by the average mechanical artist. In the case of such work, the folding shape—together with its required die—is usually designed and approved before the surface decoration is designed—at least before the mechanical art is begun. If this is the case, the mechanical artist will be provided with a *strike sheet*. This is a heavy cardboard sheet that has been struck by the die but not cut through. This strike sheet serves as a precise guide to the artist for the positioning of the mechanical art.

The printed sheet destined for die-cutting will also be imposed in a way that eliminates waste. In order to do this, several unrelated jobs may be run together. Since most die-cut jobs are not uniform in shape, it is not unusual for the mechanical artist to be required to alter a size slightly so that it can be more readily accommodated on the sheet.

INDICATION OF SIZE

Definitions

Size. Sizes are stated as width by depth; 9" × 12" is 9 inches wide by 12 inches deep. More production difficulties are encountered as a result of improper sizing of the mechanical art than for any other reason. It is imperative that before the mechanical is begun, the exact size should be determined.

Trim Size. The actual extremities of a piece of printed matter. In the case of an advertisement not occupying a full page, it is the total area—including margins—that the advertisement will occupy. In the case of a full-page advertisement (which will be trimmed after the publication is bound) or of a printed sheet, folder, brochure, etc., it is the final size to which the paper will be trimmed (cut). Trim size is indicated on the mechanical with *crop marks*, often with both blue outlines *and* crop marks.

Crop Marks. Crop marks are ruled *black* lines, placed at the four corners of the mechanical to indicate the actual finished size. These are retained on the printing plate and serve as guides for positioning it in a press form, or for aligning the cutting knives when the printed piece is to be trimmed. Crop marks should be ruled as *thinly and accurately* as possible. They should be placed no less than 3/16 in. from the corners (so as not to interfere with bleed lines), and should be no more than 1/2 in. long. Excessively long crop marks increase the size of the plate, adding unnecessarily to its cost. It takes eight separate crop marks—four vertical and four horizontal—to properly size a mechanical.

Bleed. An excess portion of the plate that extends *beyond* the trimmed edges of the sheet or page. It is utilized when a printed area is to appear to extend off the edge(s) of the page and is designed to eliminate white spaces between the printing and the trimmed edge caused by improper alignment of the trimming knife. It is not necessary to bleed on all four sides of the piece. When one side of a printed piece is to be bound or folded, bleed on the fold side is impossible.

Bleed Size. Normal bleed size is 1/8 in. This means an additional 1/8 in. on each side that is to bleed; thus, the bleed size of a 7" × 10" piece that bleeds four sides is: 7 ⅞" × 10 ⅞", or 7 ¼" × 10 ¼". If a 7" × 10" ad bleeds top, right, and bottom—leaving the left side for binding—the bleed size is: 7 ⅛" × 10 ⅞", or 7 ⅛" × 10 ¼". Bleed extremity is indicated by a *red* line ruled *outside* the trim line.

Plate Size. The overall size of the printing plate, including bleed—if any.

Black Lines. Any line on the mechanical that is supposed to print. Black lines are an integral part of the mechanical and require no further attention from the platemaker.

Light Blue Lines. Guide lines for trim sizes and shapes, as well as the indication of irregular trim (die-cut), folds, perforations, etc. These lines are for the convenience of the artist and for the alignment of the folding or the cutting machinery. They will not appear on the negative, as light blue does not photograph on normal film.

Red Lines. Lines that are used to indicate the size, shape, and position of all halftone, tint (Ben Day), and color areas. These lines should be strong, clean, and accurate. Red lines indicate to the platemaker that work, such as stripping or opaquing, is to be done. Red lines will appear on the negative, but will be removed after they have served their purpose and will not appear as lines on the plate.

Fold Marks. Dashed black lines that are used to indicate the extremities of a fold. Placed *outside* the trim line, they are kept at approximately the same distance as crop marks and are the same length. These, also, will be retained on the plate, as a guide to the folder. The actual fold line is indicated within the mechanical as a thin, dashed blue line. Such an indication is not always necessary but sometimes serves as a guide for positioning copy so that it will not fall across a fold.

Perforation Lines. Short-dashed blue lines that are placed inside the mechanical and are used to show the exact location and alignment of perforations. The length of the individual dash need not be precise, as the perforation die is a manufactured item and is not made photomechanically from the lines on the mechanical.

Die-Cut. Any irregular shape or design that requires cutting with a specially made die; a shape that cannot be cut with a straight blade.

Die-Cut Line. A solid blue line on the mechanical art indicating the shape in which the job is to be die-cut. The cutting die is handmade to conform to this line.

Gutter. The inside margin between the printed matter and the fold or the binding.

Double Spread. Two facing pages in a publication.

Live Matter. The printed message of a piece, which should be kept sufficiently within the trim to preclude any possibility of being cut off. Live matter should not extend into the gutter.

Agate. A unit of measurement: ¹⁄₁₄ in. or 5 ½ points. The agate is used in the measurement of the depth of newspaper advertisements. Mechanical artists should have an agate ruler as part of their equipment. This unit of measurement is often supplanted by the pica.

The Determination of Correct Size

The mechanical artist should always check the proper authority to make certain of the correct size. This should be indicated on the layout; if it is not, it is the responsibility of the mechanical artist to find out the correct size. Measurement of the layout is not sufficient—the layout may be off a fraction of an inch, or the paper may have shrunk or stretched.

Information is available for determining the proper size for every magazine and newspaper published in the United States or Canada (see pages 232–33).

Magazine Size Requirements

Specifications for sizes of advertisements in individual magazines are listed in guides published by the *Standard Rate and Data Service*. Sizes are given for double spreads, full pages, and fractions of pages, depending upon the mechanical requirements of the publication. Both bleed (or plate) and trim sizes are given, as well as gutter allowances. Some publications list the maximum allowable area of nonbleeding live matter.

A double spread, which cannot be printed on the same sheet unless it is the center spread, is prepared as a single, double-width mechanical. The plate is cut when it is received by the publication. Double gutter allowances—one on each side of the center line—should be made, but no bleed should be inserted *between the pages*. Lateral bleed should be at the extreme left and right only.

Unless front, inside front, inside back, back, or center-spread insertions are purchased (at additional cost), it is impossible to predetermine the exact location of one's advertisement. As a result, mechanical requirements (trim and bleed) are specified to compensate for any possible location. In a thick staple-bound publication, the pages nearer the front and back must be wider in order to accommodate the wrap around the back edge or spine. To compensate for this extra width, extra bleed (left and right) is specified. Gutter allowances should be carefully observed, lest the live matter become jammed too close to the binding for readability.

Since it is impossible to predetermine whether a single-page advertisement will appear on the left or on the right, bleed should be furnished on *both sides*. The gutter bleed will be trimmed off the plate by the publication. Gutter allowances should be observed on *both* sides of the advertisement.

Rescale Mechanicals

Often an advertisement will be scheduled to appear as a full page in one publication and as a half page in another. All the material included in the larger advertisement must also appear in the second. If there is no proportional relation-

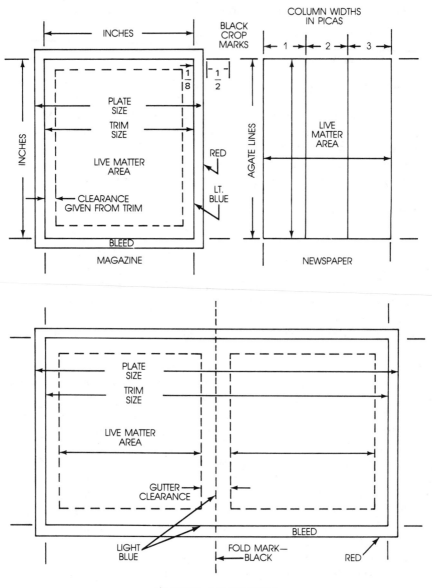

MAGAZINE—DOUBLE SPREAD

MECHANICAL FORMATS

BLEED

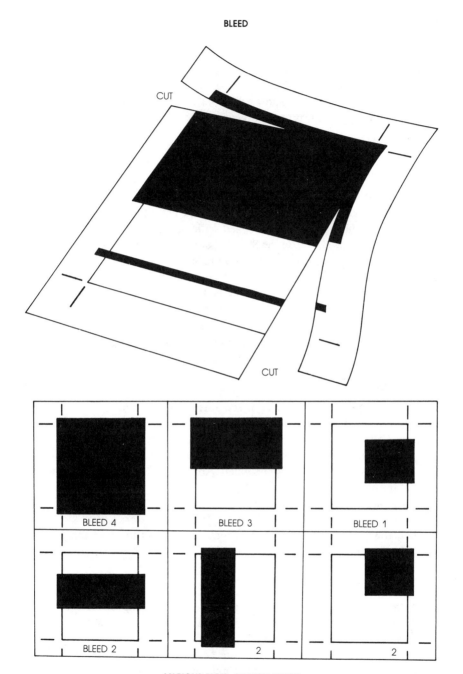

VARIOUS BLEED COMBINATIONS

ship between them that will permit camera reduction, a separate layout and an individual mechanical must be prepared for each.

It is often practical to use a single mechanical for the production of plates for several various-sized publications. Suppose, for example, an advertisement is to appear, full-page, in four different publications. The plate sizes required are: 4" × 5", 8" × 10", 8 ½" × 10 ½", and 7 ¾" × 9 ¾". All four plates may be produced from a single mechanical, if proper allowances are made:

1. A basic mechanical, 8" × 10", is prepared.

2. The 8" × 10" plate may be made from a same-size negative.

3. The 4" × 5" plate may be made by camera-reducing the negative 50 percent, since this is a proportional reduction.

4. In order to accommodate the 8 ⅓" × 10 ½" plate, the margins or bleed of the original mechanical are extended ¼ in. on each side. The live matter remains the same size as in the 8" × 10" advertisement; it merely "floats" in the larger size. A separate set of crop marks, preferably in a different color for easy identification, is added to the original mechanical to indicate the extra enlargement. A same-size plate is made, which is then cut to the size indicated by the second set of crop marks.

5. Provided the live matter pasted on the original mechanical is kept within a 7 ¾" × 9 ¾" area, a third same-size plate may be made and cut down to the reduced size. A third set of crop marks should be added to indicate this size. The live matter may be tight, but this is often tolerated if it eliminates the need for an extra mechanical.

If the presence of three sets of separate crop marks becomes confusing, the same effect may be accomplished by cutting a paper mask to each desired plate size and hinging it in position over the mechanical.

Care should be taken that there is no confusion between plate size and trim size—both should be clearly indicated. Appropriate bleeds should be calculated for each size variation.

Obviously, if the publication prints in offset, it is film, rather than plates, that is sent to the publication. If this is the case, care should be taken that any enlargements or reductions are in the same scale as the mechanical art.

Newspaper Size Requirements

Newspaper size requirements are specified in the *Print Media Production Data* volume published by the *Standard Rate and Data Service (SRDS)*.

Newspaper advertisement widths are measured in *columns*, and depths are measured in *agates*. An *agate line* is one column wide and one agate deep. Publishers' rates are quoted at so much *per agate line*. In former days, most newspaper columns were 2 inches wide, 8 columns to the page; but with modern formats and tabloid sizes, column widths vary considerably. The column width for every newspaper in the United States and Canada, both daily and weekly, is specified in SRDS. Sizes are also specified for full and half pages.

Column widths for newspaper were formerly specified in inches; they are now specified in picas. It is also important to know the *number of columns* in a specific newspaper.

If the column width for a newspaper is specified to be 1 $1\frac{1}{26}$ in. wide, two columns are 3 ⅜ in. wide, etc.

Newspaper advertisements are referred to by their total linage—the width (in number of columns) multiplied by the depth (in agates). An advertisement that is 1 column wide by 100 agates deep is a *100-line ad* (1 × 100); one that is 2 columns wide by 100 agates deep is a *200-line ad* (2 × 100), etc.

However, an advertisement that is 1 column by 200 lines (1 × 200) is also a 200-line ad. So is one that is 4 columns by 50 lines. Although the charges for these variously shaped 200-line ads would be the same, it is good to know the proportions the client favors.

SCALING AND POSITIONING OF ILLUSTRATIVE MATTER

Scaling Illustrative Matter

Illustrations or photographs are seldom submitted in the same size that they will appear on the mechanical. Such art, which cannot be pasted in position on the mechanical, is known as *separate art*. It is necessary for the camera operator to enlarge or reduce this separate art to the required size and strip it—in negative form—into the master flat. The area into which each piece of separate art is to be stripped must be carefully indicated on the mechanical; each piece of art must be keyed so that there is no mistaking its proper location.

Before its position is indicated, the art should be scaled to the mechanical size in order to determine its proportional adherence to the requirements of the layout. Width and depth enlarge or reduce in direct ratio to each other:

Example:

$$\frac{\text{Width}}{\text{Desired Width}} = \frac{\text{Depth}}{\text{Desired Depth}}$$

$$\frac{12}{6} = \frac{8}{4}$$

Obviously, to alter this ratio photographically would result in distortion. Therefore, it is the manner in which the picture is to be framed or "cropped" that is of concern to the mechanical artist. If an illustration is in silhouette or vignette

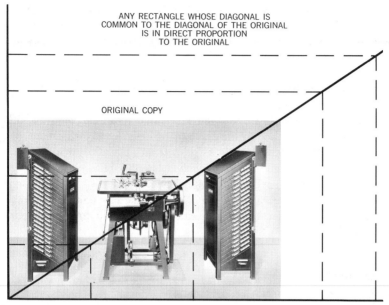

ANY RECTANGLE WHOSE DIAGONAL IS
COMMON TO THE DIAGONAL OF THE ORIGINAL
IS IN DIRECT PROPORTION
TO THE ORIGINAL

ORIGINAL COPY

SCALING WITH THE DIAGONAL

The Ludlow Typograph —
Photo courtesy of
The Ludlow Typograph Co.

form, it has no frame; it can be enlarged or reduced at will to fit within the desired area. A square halftone has definite edges that are often subject to alignment with other elements of the layout. If the proportions of the original are not conducive to such alignment, they must be altered so that they will be. The determination of the proportions that will result from a predetermined enlargement or reduction is known as *scaling.*

The proportionally reduced or enlarged dimensions of a scaled rectangle may be determined with a circular proportional scale. However, the scale provides only the dimensions of the new rectangle; it provides no visual means to decide *where and how the illustration will be cropped* if its proportions must be altered to fit the mechanical art.

Since proportional alteration is dictated by the nature of the illustration, a visual scaling method is more desirable—one that can be shifted at will over the original art in order to visually determine the best possible cropping.

Visual scaling is based upon the principle that any new rectangle whose diagonal coincides (in angle, not length) with the diagonal of the original— whether in enlarged or reduced form—*is in proportion to the original.* This type of scaling will enable the artist to visualize the area the art will occupy when enlarged or reduced.

Visual scaling, using transparent tracing tissue, is accomplished in the following manner:

1. Place a piece of tracing tissue over the original; with T-square and triangle, rule a pencil line along the bottom horizontal edge and the left-hand vertical edge. If the original is an irregular silhouette or vignette shape, draw a rectangle about its extremities.

2. Rule a diagonal through the original rectangle—from lower left to upper right corner.

3. Determine the dimension that is more critical to the layout of the mechanical—depth or width—and mark the desired measurement on the corresponding ruled line on the tissue. With a 90-degree line, project this point to the diagonal. With another 90-degree line, project the point on the diagonal to the adjacent edge—the other ruled line. The resulting rectangle will be in proportion to the original.

4. If the rectangle determined by this process is adequate for the purpose of the layout, it means that the original—enlarged or reduced to the critical dimension—will fit without alteration of its natural edges. Crop marks are then placed at the corners of the original, and the size to which the original is to be enlarged or reduced is clearly indicated between them with a blue-pencilled arrow.

If, when scaled to the critical dimension, the proportions are found unsuitable, the shape of the original must be altered—either by trimming or by adding extra area—to conform to the desired proportions of the layout. For example; suppose a photograph that must occupy the entire width of the layout, when scaled to the desired width, is found to be so deep that it will infringe upon the copy area. It is made to fit within the desired space in the following manner:

1. Take the scaled rectangle (on the tissue), position it over the mechanical, and reduce its depth by ruling a horizontal line at the point where the bottom edge of the photograph should ideally occur.

2. Rule a new diagonal from the upper right-hand corner to the point where the new horizontal intersects the left-hand edge.

3. Replace the tissue over the original so that this newly established lower left-hand corner coincides with the lower left-hand corner of the original.

4. By projecting the *right-hand vertical edge* of the original to the newly established diagonal, and then projecting this point of intersection horizontally to the left-hand edge, a new rectangle—*showing the portion of the original that is in proportion to the desired size*—will have been established.

5. If depth is the critical factor, and the width of the original must be cropped to maintain it, the desired width is ruled on the scaled rectangle. A new diagonal is drawn, and the new width is scaled back to the original.

6. The advantage of working on tissue paper is that, once the cropped dimensions have been determined, the tissue may be shifted over the original in order to ascertain which border(s) can be most practically trimmed off.

SCALING

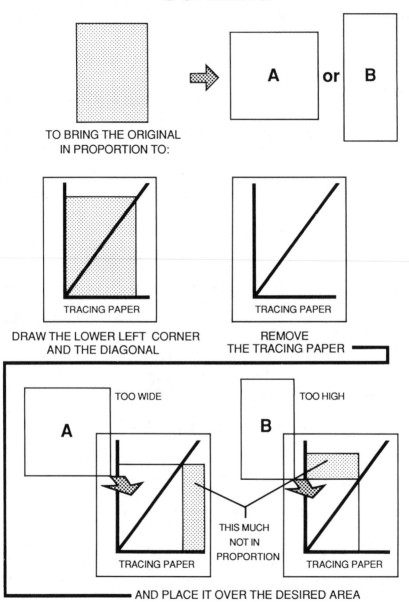

TO BRING THE ORIGINAL
IN PROPORTION TO:

A or B

TRACING PAPER

TRACING PAPER

DRAW THE LOWER LEFT CORNER
AND THE DIAGONAL

REMOVE
THE TRACING PAPER

TOO WIDE

A

TOO HIGH

B

THIS MUCH
NOT IN
PROPORTION

TRACING PAPER

TRACING PAPER

AND PLACE IT OVER THE DESIRED AREA

2 x

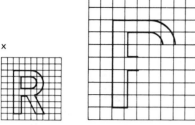

IN ORDER TO ENLARGE
A COMPLEX SHAPE WHEN
NO LUCIDA IS AVAILABLE,
DRAW A GRID OVER THE
ORIGINAL, ENLARGE THE GRID,
KEEPING THE SAME NUMBER
OF SQUARES, AND DRAW EXACTLY
WHAT APPEARS IN EACH SQUARE.

x

IT TAKES A LOT OF TIME TO DO THIS—
THEREFORE, DO THIS:

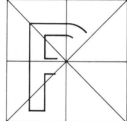

PROPORTIONALLY ENLARGE
THE OVERALL SHAPE, THEN DRAW
THE DIAGONALS AND INTERSECT
THEM WITH HORIZONTALS
AND VERTICALS.

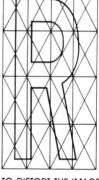

IF GREATER RESOLUTION IS REQUIRED—
CONTINUE TO DRAW DIAGONALS

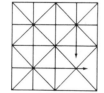
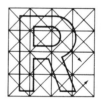

SCALING IRREGULAR SHAPES

TO DISTORT THE IMAGE,
DEVELOP A DESIRABLY
PROPORTIONED RECTANGLE
AND REPEAT THE DIAGONAL
PROCESS.

Obviously, edges should be cropped where the subject matter is of least importance.

7. Since it is seldom desirable to destroy a photograph or illustration by physically cutting away portions, crop marks are placed outside the edges. When sized between the crop marks and reduced or enlarged accordingly, the cropped area of the original should occupy the desired area on the mechanical. If the photograph or illustration must be cropped with no margin for error, it can be masked by cutting an opaque paper frame to the desired size and hinging it in position over the original.

8. Artistic judgment should be utilized when an artist is deciding which portions of a photograph or illustration can be sacrificed by cropping. The portions of a photograph that are to be cropped should be its least important areas. Care should be taken not to trim off vital detail, tops of heads, hands, etc.

9. It is often necessary to *add* to a photograph in order to obtain the desired proportions. This is accomplished by reprinting the photo—in its original size—on larger paper. This provides a much wider margin around the photograph; therefore an extra area may be added without encountering a paper edge. The retoucher is employed to add the additional area. The scaling should be planned so that the retoucher's job can be accomplished in the least complex area; it is simpler to airbrush a tone representing sky than to extend a detailed foreground. The job should be planned so that it is necessary only to add to one side; the cost would be double if the retoucher were required to add to *both* sides.

10. Illustrators should be fully aware of the size and proportions in which their work will appear and should keep their drawing within the required proportions.

11. If art is to bleed, *the bleed area should be taken into consideration when one is scaling*. If, due to the nature of the art, all of it must remain within the trim area, a satisfactory bleed area can often be accomplished by adding a compatible gray tone to the edge(s) in question.

12. Scaling and cropping is readily accomplished with a computerized image assembly system. Images are scanned into the system, where they may be scaled and cropped at will. The obvious advantage of the system is that variations may be tried without permanently altering the original image.

Positioning Illustrative Matter

Once the illustration or photograph has been properly scaled and cropped or marked, its position must be clearly indicated on the mechanical art. This indication aids the platemaker in stripping the separate art into its proper location on the flat. It may be done by any of the following methods:

Photostats in Position. Photostats of the illustrative matter, reduced or enlarged to the desired size, may be pasted directly on the mechanical art. This method provides foolproof identification of each piece of separate art and clearly indicates where any cropping will occur. It also enables the client to visualize the finished result. When photostats are pasted up like this, bleed should be included. If, for any reason, it is necessary to include a ruled edge for the convenience of the stripper, the photostat is brought almost to the ruled line and deliberately cut with a ragged edge. This leaves the ruled line standing clear. The ragged edge indicates that the stripped-in illustration will terminate at the ruled line. In order to prevent any possibility of the photostats being mistaken for art in position, *"Not for Repro"* should be clearly marked on each photostat.

Red Keyline with Blue-Line Identification.   A red keyline is drawn on the mechanical, indicating the extremities of the area into which the illustration is to be stripped. If the area is irregular or is a silhouette shape, its proper outline should be determined by enlarging or reducing it to the mechanical size with a camera lucida. The resulting shape is then traced onto the mechanical and indicated with a red line. The stripper uses this red line as a guide, removing it from the negative after the illustration has been stripped into position.

The details of each stripped-in illustration are often indicated with a blue-line drawing of its essential elements, which will readily identify it. To do this, the image is brought to the desired size with the camera lucida. The essential elements are roughly traced and transferred, in blue line, onto the mechanical art. This method gives positive identification of every strip-in. The blue identifying lines do not appear on the film negative.

Red Keyline with Letter Identification.   A red keyline is drawn on the mechanical art. If there is no pictorial means on the mechanical for identifying which halftone strips into which location, each should be appropriately "keyed." A letter or number, written in blue pencil on the border of the separate art and within the keyline on the mechanical, identifies the proper piece to be stripped into each area. This method affords the greatest possibility for stripping errors and provides no visual predetermination of the finished result. It is, however, the most economical method; there is no expenditure for photostats, and no time is spent in making blue-line facsimiles of the illustrations.

Platemakers prefer to receive art that will automatically produce "windows" (clear areas surrounded by black) on their film negatives, into which the properly sized halftone negative can be stripped. Platemakers do not like to *cut* holes in their film to accommodate halftones, because the cut edges cast undesirable shadows.

Thus, when platemakers receive art with halftone positioning indicated by photostat or red keyline, they will cut red film to the delineated shape and adhere it to the mechanical art before photographing it. This will produce the desired windows on the film negative. It will also result in an additional stripping cost.

The extra stripping cost may be eliminated if the windows are prepared for on the mechanical. This may be done in the following manner:

1. Place red film *over* the in-position photostat. The stat may still be viewed through the film, but the camera will record *only* the film, not the photostatted image underneath, leaving the desired window in the negative. This will also avoid the possibility of the position stat's being shot as finished art.
2. Adhere red film in the area that would normally be defined with the red keyline. Key the halftone with an appropriate notation *underneath* the film.

3. Cut a piece of black paper to the shape of the halftone and position it on the mechanical. This is more time-consuming than cutting film, and it affords no opportunity to properly identify the halftone.

Sizing Illustrative Matter

Each illustration or photograph should be marked with the size of the negative that must be made in order to strip it into the flat. This saves considerable calculation for the camera operator. One size indication, either width or depth, is sufficient. The words "Reduce to" or "Enlarge to" should accompany the size indication. If the illustration is to bleed, the bleed should be taken into consideration when sizing. Many illustrations have been photographed to an indicated size, only to be found to lack sufficient bleed area.

Specifying the Screen Size

The screen size should be marked on each piece of separate halftone art that is submitted to the platemaker. The screen size must be kept consistent throughout a job; screen sizes do not vary from illustration to illustration or from page to page.

The artist should consult the printer in order to determine which screen size is most suitable for the paper on which the job will be printed. The general rule is: The rougher the texture of the paper, the coarser the screen must be. Offset lithography can print a finer screen on a rough-textured paper than letterpress can.

Indications of both size of art and size of screen should be made in blue pencil on the margin of each piece of separate art. If the job is to reproduce in line, it should be so specified.

THE SCREEN PRINT OR VELOX

A screen print is a photographic contact print made from a screened halftone negative. Since screen prints were often printed on "Velox"—a Kodak photographic printing paper—the name Velox has become a generic term for the screen print.

The screen print is used to provide art that can be pasted in position on the mechanical—art that, since the image has already been screened, can be photographed by the platemaker as line art.

The negative for the screen print is made from a continuous-tone photograph or wash drawing in the same way as the halftone negative. The resulting screened negative is contact-printed onto photographic paper, rather than onto a sensitized printing plate. The result is a *photographic print* in which the image has been reduced to the appropriate dot patterns.

The screen print, which is ordered to the actual size it is to appear on the printed result, is pasted in position on the mechanical. When the mechanical, with all Velox art in position, is submitted to the platemaker, *a line shot is made*. There is no need for the platemaker to use a halftone screen; *the dot pattern has already been established.* The platemaker makes a line negative of the copy. Since the screen prints are positioned on the mechanical, no stripping is required. The line negative makes a perfect copy of the existing dot patterns, which may then be produced on the appropriate printing plate.

When the screen-print negative is first made, it compares in quality with the flat-etched halftone. The entire area, even the white background, bears a slight screen pattern. The highlights are not pure white, nor are the blacks solid. The Velox negative, normally produced, has not been dropped out. It may be dropped out by the following methods:

Hand Retouching. The screen print is returned to the mechanical artist, who, upon positioning it on the mechanical art, silhouettes it with white paint, restores the dropout highlight areas with white paint and fills in the solid areas with black paint. It takes considerable skill for this operation, especially in the restoration of edges and thin black areas. Any slipshod work on the part of the artist will be incompatible with the precise nature of the dot structure and readily noticeable.

The artist has no means to alter the dot patterns in the middle-value areas. Any attempt to do so will result in objectionable irregularities of the screen pattern.

Automatic Dropout. This is effected by the photographer. Two negatives are shot—a screened negative and a contrasting line negative in which the white areas appear as solid blacks. A contact print is made by superimposing the two negatives. The line negative serves as a mask for the silhouette and dropout areas, eliminating the screen pattern in these areas of the print. There is an additional charge for a dropout screen print.

When one is ordering screen prints, both the size of print and the size (lines per inch) of screen must be clearly specified, as well as the number of prints required.

The screen print must be ordered and the mechanical prepared to the actual size it will appear on the printed result. Any enlargement or reduction of the screen print will also affect the dot size. If a 110-line screen print is pasted on mechanical art that is to be reduced 50 percent, the resulting image will print 165 lines per inch—too fine for normal reproduction. If the art is enlarged 50 percent, the resulting image will have 55 lines per inch—too coarse for anything but a newspaper advertisement.

The advantage of a screen print is the resulting economy. Although the printed result resembles a flat-etched halftone, it has nevertheless been *reproduced as line art.* Line plates are considerably cheaper than halftone plates. Its disadvantage is that, since there is no means of dot alteration, the screen print lacks the quality that can be attained in a good halftone. The dropout highlights tend to appear coarse and artificial, and there is little subtlety in the tonal areas. As a result, screen prints are most often employed for newspaper reproduction, where halftone quality is not such a critical factor. Photographs destined for screen-print reproduction should be heavily retouched in order to provide sufficient contrast.

When a screen print is being mounted on the mechanical, it should never be *cut* to the desired silhouette shape. The photographic emulsion tends to chip off along a cut edge, forming a ragged dot pattern. The print should be silhouetted with at least a ½-in. margin of white paint, and the print cut out around the outer edges of the white. This will serve as protection for the actual edges of the image. A square print should be handled in a similar way. It is difficult to produce a good vignette effect with a screen print.

REVERSE COPY

All areas where type or art appears in reverse—white copy on a black background—are preferably prepared as such on the mechanical art. The first step in the production of the reverse-copy area of the layout is the ordering of a glossy negative photostat of the copy. If it is of type, it should be carefully inspected to make certain that none of the lines have filled in. If the type has delicate serifs or an illustration has particularly delicate lines, the photostatter should be instructed to expose the photostat a little less in order to produce a stronger reverse image. Extremely small type should not be printed in reverse.

A reverse area must assume some sort of shape; this shape should be drawn or ruled in black outline by the artist and filled in with black ink. The negative photostat is then cut out and pasted in proper position within the black shape. The cut edges of the photostat should be blackened so that they will not appear on the platemaker's negative. All rubber cement should be carefully cleaned off.

Often there is no time to order negative photostats. In this instance, the type or art is pasted on the mechanical in positive form, to be reversed by the camera operator. Where camera reversal is required, a tissue overlay—clearly indicating the desired result—should be included with the job. If an area is to be camera-reversed, it should not be filled in, but delineated by the artist with a thin red outline, or *keyline*. The camera operator makes a film positive; the red keyline appears on the positive as a black line. The opaquer paints *up to this line from the outside*. The resulting black-silhouetted positive art is stripped onto the negative flat. In reverse to the negative flat, it will appear as a reverse area when printed.

Some mechanical artists will paste a negative photostat within a red keyline, leaving the cut edges of the photostat deliberately ragged in order to indicate that the opaquer is to fill in the space between the edges of the photostat and the keyline. The opaquer will do this with red film on the mechanical, so that it will not be necessary to make a film positive.

Often a reverse panel or area will bleed. When this occurs, it is necessary to indicate the location of the trim line. If the panel involved is rectangular and merely bleeds off one or more of the square edges of the job, crop marks, located

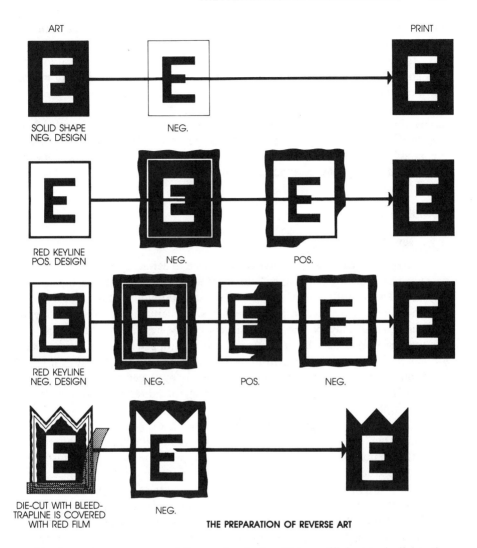

ART

PRINT

SOLID SHAPE
NEG. DESIGN

NEG.

RED KEYLINE
POS. DESIGN

NEG.

POS.

RED KEYLINE
NEG. DESIGN

NEG.

POS.

NEG.

DIE-CUT WITH BLEED-
TRAPLINE IS COVERED
WITH RED FILM

NEG.

THE PREPARATION OF REVERSE ART

outside the extreme corners of the mechanical, will be sufficient to indicate the trim line. If the trim is an irregular die-cut and the reverse area bleeds off its edge, the exact die-cut line must be indicated. This is done by means of a *trap-line*.

The trap-line is a *blue* line used to indicate a construction line—a die-cut edge, a fold line, or a perforation guideline falling *within a reverse area*. The blue line, whatever its purpose, is ruled or drawn in the usual way. The outline of the reverse shape is drawn in black in its proper location. When the reverse area is filled in, the solid black is painted *almost* up to both sides of the blue line.

The edges of the black panel adjacent to the blue line are deliberately made ragged. This ragged edge is a signal to the stripper that the area must be filled in before the plate is made. This may be done in advance, if the artist strips red film over the trapped blue construction line. The line will still be visible under the red film, but neither the trap nor the line will appear on the negative.

In this manner, the construction line is retained on the mechanical to serve as a guide for the proper alignment of the trimming knives, the folding mechanism, or the cutting die.

Unless there is a specific reason for doing otherwise, reverse art should be prepared with photostatically reversed copy and with all solid areas painted in by the artist. This requires the least work on the part of the platemaker. If it is prepared in any other manner, the artist should know how much extra work will be required of the platemaker and the effect it will have on platemaking costs.

SCREEN TINTS

Ben Day

"Ben Day" has become a generic term used to denote a screen tint of a color produced by reducing an area, or "block" of solid color, to a uniform pattern of tiny dots. The tonality is regulated by the size and proximity of the dots.

Screen tints are used to provide emphasis to certain portions of the layout. The background may be screened; the copy may be screened; solid copy in positive or reverse may be either surprinted or dropped out of a screen background. The screen tint differs from the halftone screen in that there is no tonal variation within an area. Screen tints are generally produced by the platemaker to the artist's specifications, but they can also be applied directly on the mechanical with Craftint or Zip-A-Tone.

The original Ben Day was a mechanical shading process developed by Benjamin Day in 1881. It is a line medium used for introducing tonal patterns into a line illustration, to reduce the tonal value of type or the lines of an illustration, or as a background tint panel or shape.

In the original Ben Day method, the shading pattern was applied directly to the letterpress plate using equipment leased from the parent firm. Ben Day antedates shading film and is available in a wide variety of patterns—dots, lines, cross-hatches, stipples, etc.—but the uniform dot pattern is the one most generally used. Unless otherwise specified, the term "Ben Day" implies a dot pattern.

Screen tints are described in percentiles of 100, in multiples of 10, with 0 percent representing white and 100 percent representing solid black.

In current usage, particularly in offset lithography, master negative pattern sheets are purchased by the platemaker. These are reproduced as thin film positives and are stripped into position on the flat.

There are four possible screen-tint combinations:

1. Tint background—black copy surprinted. Produced from positive art.
2. Tint background—white (reverse) copy dropped out. Produced from negative art.

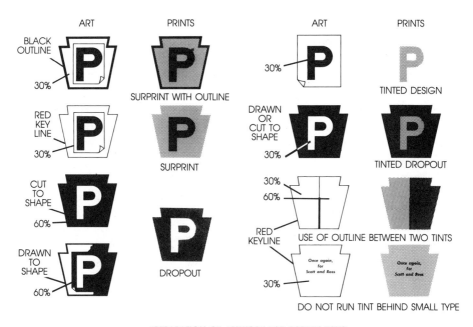

PREPARATION OF ARTWORK FOR SCREEN TINTS
SCREEN PERCENTAGES SHOULD BE INDICATED IN LIGHT BLUE

3. Tint copy—white background. Produced from positive art.

4. Tint copy—black background. Produced from negative art.

When the copy is to surprint on a background of black dots, a *red line* is used on the mechanical to delineate the screened area. The screen positive (black dots) is stripped onto a film positive of the art within the delineating lines. A negative is made for platemaking, and the lines are removed by opaquing.

When the copy is to drop out of a screened background, it is prepared as a reverse panel. This produces a transparent area, or "window," on the negative onto which positive dot film is stripped. The resultant proof will be a background with a white dot pattern, bearing dropped-out copy.

When the copy itself is to be screened, positive art is provided. This also produces transparent areas on the film negative onto which positive dot film is stripped. In the resultant proof, the copy will appear with a white dot pattern.

When screened copy is to appear on a black background, a reverse panel is provided. The positive dot film is stripped onto a film positive of the reverse panel. Thus, in the printed result, only the copy will bear the screen, and the background will remain solid.

Each area of the mechanical that is to receive a screen tint should be carefully marked with percentage of tint and color of ink. This should be done in blue pencil on the art itself.

If there is any possibility of confusion about *exactly* where the screen tint is to be stripped, the screened areas should be carefully indicated with blue pencil on a tissue overlay.

There are several precautions that should be taken in the utilization of screen tints:

1. If positive copy is used, background tints should be light enough to keep the copy legible. Screen-tint charts generally show the effects of copy surprinted on various screen percentages.

2. If reverse copy is used, the background tint should be dark enough to carry the copy.

3. Screen tints have a tendency to print 5 to 10 percent *darker* than specified. This tendency should be taken into consideration when the specification is made.

4. It is not advisable to run a tint behind type that is less than 8 points in size; the dots will tend to obliterate the letter structure of type that is extremely small.

5. Screen areas cannot be effectively butted together, since the variation in angle will produce a ragged edge. Adjacent screen patterns should be separated with a black holding line.

6. One screen superimposed on top of another produces a moiré pattern—a wavering pattern that is uneven in tone.

The Preparation of Artwork
with Shading Film

Shading film is a transparent, adhesive sheet bearing a printed pattern, which may be applied over artwork and removed from the undesired areas. Removal is accomplished by scraping off the dots with a stylus or by cutting them away with a razor blade.

Shading film may be fixed to the mechanical itself in order to produce a screen tint area. This results in the elimination of stripping charges. The film is placed on the art, cut to the desired shape, and attached by burnishing it with a triangle or the back of a comb. If air bubbles should result, they can be released by pricking them with a divider point. Shading film is most practically applied to line illustrations. This keeps the process directly under the control of the artist and enables the artwork to be presented for approval in the exact form it will appear in when printed.

The following procedures should be followed when attaching shading film to the mechanical art:

1. Check to make sure there are no imperfections in the printed film.

2. White dot patterns are impractical for application over reverse areas, or on top of line copy. Although they may appear opaque upon initial examination,

they are seldom opaque enough after they have been burnished. The result is a gray dot that is unsuitable for sharp reproduction.

3. Make certain that, if there is to be any reduction in the printed size of the art, the pattern will accommodate this reduction without filling in. Most manufacturers provide charts showing the various patterns in reduced size.

4. Make sure there are no pencil lines or dirt under the film. The wax backing of the film readily attracts dirt.

5. Do not attempt to attach film over cut edges. When burnished, these edges will distort the pattern and will be picked up by the camera. This possibility may be eliminated by fastening the film, in registered position, on a transparent overlay; however, a stripping charge will result.

6. Except in an attempt to produce a cross-hatched effect with single-line patterns, films cannot be effectively applied on top of each other; a moiré pattern will generally occur.

MECHANICAL ASSEMBLY

Mechanical assembly ("paste-up") is the preparation of the elements of the layout for the platemaker's camera; the "final assembly" of the art. The mechanical may be prepared as camera-ready art—with all elements pasted in position; or it may be submitted as a mechanical plus separate art—with the position of all strip-ins indicated on the mechanical with red keylines.

The elements of the layout are pasted on a sheet of illustration board known as the *flat*. This may or may not have overlays, depending on the nature of the job.

An increasingly popular surface for paste-up is 60 to 70 lb. offset stock. It is thinner than most business cards, but thicker than bond stock. This material does not readily support overlays.

Preprinted paper (idiot paper) consists of offset stock bearing printed light-blue guidelines, either to define a standard format size or to minimize the need for a T-square.

Three colors are used in the execution of the mechanical; each has a definite purpose:

Black. Anything that is to appear on the printed piece is prepared in black on the mechanical.

Red. Thin red lines are used to indicate the size, shape, and position of halftone and screen areas. Red lines are used to indicate the outlines of reverse panels that have not been filled in. These lines will be used by the platemaker to strip in separate art, or as a guide for opaquing. After their use, they will be removed by the platemaker; they will not appear on the printed result.

Light Blue. Instructions for sizing, tint percentages, screen size, stripping instructions, etc., are written on the mechanical (or on a tissue overlay) in light blue pencil. Light blue lines are used to indicate shapes and positioning for the convenience of the artist in assembling the mechanical. They will not appear on the platemaker's negative. Die-cut lines are indicated in blue, since the die is not made photomechanically. Light blue shading is often used to indicate Ben Day areas; this may be done directly on the flat or on a tissue overlay.

Referring to pages 227–29 for the appropriate definitions, the principal steps in the assembly of mechanical art as follows:

1. The mechanical should not be commenced until the layout has been approved by an authorized person.

2. Mechanical art should not be commenced without knowledge of the exact size.

3. The job is "laid out" on the flat, either in actual size or in a logical multiple of the actual size. Actual size is always preferable. The job should be laid out with generous margins on the flat in order to provide adequate room for registration marks, instructions, etc. The trim size is first ruled with T-square and triangle, using a well-sharpened hard pencil. The size should be exact: $\frac{1}{32}$ in. is a critical factor in mechanical art, especially where accurate registration is required.

4. Thin black crop marks are ruled at the corners of the job. Fold marks, if any, consisting of thin black dashed lines, are appropriately located. After these have been ruled, the pencilled trim lines may be erased or reruled as light blue lines to serve as a guide to the artist in properly pasting up the elements of the mechanical. Traditionally, all colored lines on the mechanical were ruled with ruling pen and colored ink. It is now possible to buy *"repro pens"*—black, blue, and red ball-point pens capable of ruling the clean lines required for mechanical art. These are not to be confused with ordinary colored ball-point pens, which are incapable of producing a clean enough line for this purpose.

5. The halftones are then scaled and positioned (see pages 233–40). A thin red keyline is drawn on the mechanical, indicating *exactly* where the halftone will be stripped in. Any blue-line identification of the halftone is drawn at this time. Bleed—the excess portion or safety area that extends beyond the trim size—is added. It, too, is defined with red keyline. Normal bleed is $\frac{1}{8}$ in., but it is always good to check. If the mechanical is being prepared in an enlarged size, the bleed must be proportionally increased.

A good practice is to complete all the pen work on the mechanical before applying any cement; a stray glob of rubber cement that has not been cleaned may play havoc with a subsequently ruled pen line. After the pen work has been completed, the photostats (if any) used to indicate the position of the halftones may be pasted on the mechanical. These may be cut to actual size (including bleed, if any) and pasted in position. They may also be mounted within the red keyline area, with their edges cut ragged, ¼ inch or so short of the line. This provides a precise ruled line to serve as a guide for the stripper, and still assures visual identification of the halftone. To cut the photostats to the exact size and then rule a red keyline immediately adjacent to the cut edge is redundant.

All photostats used to indicate halftone position should be marked "Not for Repro," or "Position Only," or defaced in some manner to indicate to the platemaker that they are not in-position continuous-tone art.

Since screen tints are stripped into the negative flat, their position should be indicated in the same manner as a halftone—with a red keyline. The desired percentage for each area should be indicated with light blue pencil— *on the artwork* (see pages 245–46).

6. The mechanical artist is responsible for the execution of any irregular shapes—balloons, cartouches, bursts, borders, underlines, dashed rules, etc.—that appear on the layout. These should be done cleanly and precisely. If the shape is complex, it may be drawn on the thin Bristol and pasted in position. This prevents spoiling the flat if a mistake is made. Dashed lines are usually drawn by ruling a solid line and breaking it evenly with white paint. If a complex border design is required, a short portion may be drawn separately and additional portions duplicated with photostats. The photostats are then pieced together.

7. All type proofs, lettering, line art or photostats of line art, logotypes, trade marks, photostats used to indicate position, and any other material photostatted to size, are pasted on the mechanical. All material should be "square"— in perfect alignment with the top and bottom edges of the flat.

    Paste-up is accomplished with *thin* rubber cement; a mixture of one part cement to four parts thinner works best; it permits easy removal if changes are necessary. It is true that a carelessly executed mechanical can still be reproduced, but many firms are judged by the appearance of their mechanical art. An untidy mechanical is an invitation to check thoroughly for further discrepancies. In order to improve the appearance of mechanical art, all material to be pasted up should be cut square with a straightedge, rather than cut haphazardly with scissors.

    In paste-up, rubber cement is applied to both surfaces, and they are allowed to dry before being joined. Material cemented while still wet has a tendency to shift and may eventually become stained, since trapped cement does not always dry properly. Cement the entire type proof and the entire mechanical. The type proof is placed, face up, on a cutting board.

    Good cutting surfaces for paste-up include:

    Chipboard. Chipboard is cheap cardboard. The backing of a pad or a spoiled piece of illustration board are also suitable.

    Pressboard. This is the same material as a notebook cover. It has a slick surface, and proofs do not adhere readily to it.

Plastic Sheets. Lucite, Plexiglas, etc., make good cutting surfaces but are readily marred by cutting. These sheets may be placed upon a light-table.
Glass. Glass is good when a back-light source is needed. It quickly dulls the cutting blade; therefore, a hone should be kept handy.
Linoleum or Vinyl Floor Covering. On such surfaces the blade will last longer, and the proof will not adhere. It is most economical to purchase remnants.

The blocks of type are cut out with a razor blade and a steel-edged T-square. The dried rubber cement will hold them in position on the board until they are ready to be transferred to the mechanical. This practice keeps small type from becoming lost and serves as a check to make certain that all the type has been transferred to the mechanical art. The transparent type proof is used to predetermine the proper fit of the type. For those who prefer it, a one-coat rubber cement is available. This cement need not be applied to both surfaces but only on the back of the type proof. It remains tacky, never drying completely. Its disadvantage is that unless the cutting board is kept meticulously clean, all sorts of debris will adhere to the tacky cement. Thus it is best to immediately protect the cement with a sheet of waxed paper. When the artist is cutting out the type, the waxed paper too often remains adhered to the back of the proof. The advantage of one-coat cement is that since no cement need be applied to the mechanical, there is no need for cleanup. One-coat is most useful in adhering small pieces in areas where it is imperative that no cement be smeared over the adjacent type.

The type or photostat is aligned on the mechanical by placing the T-square along the base of the bottom line and maneuvering the piece into position by holding an upper corner. Tweezers are indispensable for this purpose. A large block of copy may be slip-sheeted (a tissue placed underneath the upper portions to prevent adhesion) until it has been lined up. If for any reason the material must be removed after it has been attached, thinner should be used to loosen the cement. The area should be liberally flooded with thinner; a small oil can is ideal for this purpose. If a cemented piece is pulled up without the use of thinner, bumps of cement will form and make smooth replacement difficult.

Wax proofs are proofs to which an adhesive wax has been applied by a special machine. There is a variety of tabletop machines available for applying wax to the back of repro proofs, stats, copy prints, etc. The machines vary in the pattern in which they apply the wax; some coat evenly, some apply the wax in stripes, wavy lines, etc. There is more variation between brands of waxes than brands of rubber cement.

Once the waxed copy is positioned on the mechanical, it is covered with tracing paper and burnished with a roller or a blade burnisher. The edge of a triangle will serve as a substitute. The friction melts the wax and adheres it to the desired surface. Given a wax that matches the adhering quality of rubber cement, the advantage is obvious—there is no surplus cement to clean off the mechanical. Waxed proofs also work well on acetate. Wax proofs are generally more popular with printers than with art departments.

8. Hot-type proofs should be sprayed with Krylon, Spray-Fix, or some other fixatif before paste-up. Proofs remain wet for some time and are easily smudged if not sprayed. Cold-type proofs need not be sprayed.

It should not be taken for granted that all type has been set square. If it has not been properly composed, the lines may not be precisely parallel. This should be checked, and, if necessary, the offending lines cut apart to make certain of their accurate alignment.

The mechanical artist is responsible for the checking and repair of smudged or broken type characters. Excessive cases should be returned to the typographer. It may be assumed that the copy has been proofread; nevertheless, the artist should be on the alert for typographical errors. Do not assume that phototypesetting does not contain broken characters.

9. All excess rubber cement, pencil lines, dirt, eraser residue, etc., should be thoroughly removed. It is easy to spot unremoved rubber cement if the flat is held at an angle to the light. There is no excuse for mechanical art's not being properly cleaned up.

10. All separate art not indicated by photostats on the mechanical should be keyed for positive identification.

11. The printing size should be clearly marked on the mechanical. Both bleed and trim sizes should be indicated.

12. All screen tint areas should be indicated with light blue pencil on a tissue overlay. This serves not as the actual art—the keylines on the mechanical do this—but as a visual indication to the stripper of *exactly* where the screen tint is (and is not) to be stripped.

13. There should be a blank tissue sheet hinged over each mechanical flat and over each piece of separate art. These are provided for marking corrections so that there is no temptation for anyone to mark on the actual art.

14. Both mechanicals and separate art should be further protected with a paper flap. Brown wrapping paper is often used for this purpose.

15. Mechanicals and separate art should bear the name of the source and the number that has been assigned to the job.

OVERLAYS

The overlay is a transparent or translucent sheet that is positioned over the mechanical flat. It is used to position material that cannot be conveniently pasted on the flat or to position elements of the design that are to print in an additional color.

PREPARATION OF
SURPRINT ART

PREPARATION OF
DROPOUT ART

PREPARATION OF
MORTISED ART

SEPARATION OF
MULTICOLOR ART

SEPARATION OF
LINE AND WASH

USES OF OVERLAYS

The overlay must be registered. Registration entails providing markings that will enable the overlay to be replaced exactly in its original location or will enable a plate made from the overlay to be printed precisely over the underlying impression.

Registration marks are thin 90-degree cross-lines, drawn with a ruling pen. They are first drawn on the flat on at least three sides of the artwork. They should not be too far from the edges of the mechanical; neither should they be close enough to extend into the bleed area. They should be no longer than ¾ in. After the overlay has been securely taped in position—hinged across the top edge with a single strip of tape—the registration marks are drawn on the overlay exactly on top of those on the flat. The registration marks on each overlay should be slightly shorter than those on the flat or overlay beneath. This enables the artist to make certain that the marks are directly on top of each other. The thinner the marks and the more accurate their superimposition, the more exact the registration will be. Registration marks preprinted on transparent tape are available; however, a much thinner and more accurate line can be drawn with the ruling pen. Platemakers have various types of printed multiple marks that are used to provide accurate registration for multicolor work. The fact that they will be used by the platemaker does not excuse the artist from providing precise registration marks; it may be necessary to remove and replace the overlay before it reaches the platemaker.

The material used for the overlay depends on the kind of work that is to be done on it.

Transparent acetate affords the most accurate registration, but it is a difficult surface on which to rule lines. Frosted acetate has a better surface for ruling lines but is more difficult to see through, especially when several overlays are required. Heavy tracing vellum is ideal for pen work, but affords even less visibility. It is possible to buy treated clear acetate that will readily accept pen lines, but it is extremely expensive.

Overlays are used for the following purposes:

1. The positioning of art or type that is to be either surprinted or dropped out of a halftone background.

2. The preparation of line and halftone combination drawings.

3. The delineation of Ben Day areas when the nature of the paste-up makes it difficult to rule keylines or paint solid areas on the flat. These areas may be indicated on the overlay with either red keylines or solid areas of red film.

4. The location of alternate copy. For example, a brochure may be printed in which the name of the dealer changes in each area of distribution. The copy for each of these changes is registered in position on a separate overlay. In instances when, for certain reasons, prices or other information may vary, alternate copy is positioned on an overlay.

5. The preparation of preseparated color art, in which a separate overlay is made for each color that is to be printed.

THE USE OF RED FILM

Red film is finding increased use in the preparation of mechanical art. The red film will photograph on the negative as if it were black. But, because it is transparent red, it can be seen through, and it is thus easier to position over an element on the flat or to register in proper position on an overlay. Bourges film has an advantage in that the color may be scraped off the film base with a special stylus; it is easier to *scrape* textural strokes than to cut them. Rubylith and Amberlith are films used by the printing industry for masking, stripping, and other purposes. Rubylith is red and Amberlith is orange, but in function they are identical. Amberlith, though less "light-safe," is easier to see through.

Red film is self-adhering and is easily cut to the desired shape. A swivel knife is preferable, but any sharp pointed blade will suffice. Small pieces, once cut, can be lifted off the work with a small piece of cellophane tape.

Red film may be utilized by the artist for the following functions:

1. Red film eliminates the need for painting large areas. It is difficult to produce large, solid black areas on any of the previously mentioned overlay materials; they will chip from clear or frosted acetate, and will cause vellum to wrinkle. Film will neither curl nor warp.

   The area to be rendered solid, on either the flat or the overlay, may be outlined with ink and then filled in solid with film. The ink will not be differentiated from the red film by the camera (and on the negative); neither will any corrections or repairs made to the film with black ink. If the solid area is a square-cornered panel, the artist should be aware that it is easier to *cut* meticulously square corners than to *rule* them. Thus, the entire panel may be cut from red film if so desired.

2. Red film can be used to convert a photograph to line. Film placed over the photographic print can be cut to the shapes, which will print solid in the resulting line conversion.

3. Red film can be used to provide separated overlays for multicolor line art. It may also be used as a separation for adding screen tints to a line drawing.

4. Red film can be used to silhouette photographs.

5. Red film is used to prepare "windows" on the mechanical art. Art prepared with rectangular film areas representing square halftones will produce transparent rectangles—known as windows—in the negative. The actual halftone negatives are then stripped (taped into position) in these windows. The advantage of this technique is that there are no holes, therefore no cut edges in the negative, which would cast undesirable shadows on the plate.

   If photostats are used to indicate the position of the halftones on the mechanical, the red film may be placed over the stat and cut to the same size. The underlying stat can be viewed through the film, but the camera will not penetrate the film, thus leaving a transparent window on the film negative.

A number of additional techniques are available to the stripper, such as:

1. Faking a square halftone from silhouette art.

2. Reducing the background density of a photograph.

3. Staging (cutting back by chemical alteration) photographic backgrounds. The film serves as a mask, providing greater control while the background is being staged.

4. Separating color.

5. Preparing mortise shapes.

6. Creating a solid-color area (or a dropout) in the second color of a duotone.

COLOR PRESEPARATION

Color preseparation is the preparation of artwork with a separate, accurately registered overlay for each color that is to be printed. The platemaker makes a negative of the flat and of each overlay; there is no need for the printer to become involved with filter separation and opaquing.

Good color preseparation is completely dependent on the skill and accuracy of the artist; there is no prepared medium that will ensure foolproof results. Preseparation is undertaken in an attempt to eliminate the cost of camera separation and to allow the artist to maintain closer control of the job. It allows the artist to execute and thus be paid for work that might otherwise be done by the platemaker. Preseparation and camera separation require a similar expenditure of time for their execution. Camera separation is more expensive because of the photomechanical equipment involved; preseparation requires no special equipment. Most printers prefer to have art submitted in preseparated form. Printers realize their profit from the use of their presses, not from their camera-art department.

Poorly executed preseparation may cause registration problems that will prove difficult to repair. This could result in more expensive complications than if the job had been originally camera-separated. The preseparation of mechanical and illustrative art should be entrusted to an artist who has a reputation for craftsmanship.

The Preseparation of Mechanical Art

Color separation of mechanical art involves line separation of two or more colors, plus whatever additional effects may be obtained by the addition and/or superimposition of screen tint areas. There are two types of registration involved: *loose register* and *hairline register*. A job is in loose register when the component colors never print less than $1/16$ in. from each other. Hairline register occurs when two color areas meet, with neither overlap nor white space between. If the second color is considerably darker, it is possible to have a hairline of overlap for safety's sake.

The simplest variety of line separation involves a typographic layout that is to print in two colors. The caption and the logotype will print in red, while the body copy prints in black. Since no type area touches any other type area, there is no problem of hairline registration. It is a simple matter to paste all the black-plate type on the flat and all the red-plate type in registered position on an overlay. Negatives of both the flat and the overlay will be made, and a plate will be produced from each negative. Should the plates print slightly off-register, it will be scarcely noticeable.

The inclusion of a red panel or some other design shape will not complicate the job unless it must print in hairline register with some element of the black plate. When this occurs, the overlay must be carefully registered, and the edge of the area on the overlay must coincide *exactly* with the edge of the adjoining area on the flat underneath. A ruling-pen line that is too thick provides sufficient latitude to throw the job off-register.

Any solid or Ben Day area is indicated on an overlay in the same manner as it would be indicated on a one-color mechanical—with either a solid area or a red keyline. Most hairline registration of solid-color areas is accomplished with red film. It is possible to cut a more precise edge than can be ruled or drawn with a pen. If a panel or shape is cut slightly off-register, it can readily be picked up and shifted into position. Film can easily be trimmed or patched to produce a more accurate registration. Some red film, such as Bourges, is manufactured so that the color may be deliberately scraped off. This may be used to great advantage in complex line separation, but when using such film, one should take care that the pigment is not accidentally scratched.

Every overlay that is to print in a color should bear a color swatch—a sample of the color in which the plate is to print. The swatch should be at least 1" × 2", sizeable enough so that it may be easily matched by the printer. It is not necessary to provide a swatch for a Ben Day tint, so long as one is provided for the solid color. Color swatches may be hand-painted, cut from colored paper, or cut from the samples provided for this purpose in an ink sample book or the Pantone Matching System (PMS). It is the responsibility of the printer to match the color accurately. However, if a sample of *printed color* is submitted, care should be taken that it is a flat *solid* color. A process color or a varnished color may be difficult to match.

The Pantone® Matching System (PMS).   Considered a standard by the graphic arts industry, PMS is a system for accurately specifying color. The use of color swatches and/or reference numbers enables the artist, printer, and client to communicate clearly about color.

Pantone color reference books show samples of 500 hues on coated and uncoated stock, tints of each of these hues in 10 to 80 percent, and ink-mixing formulas and process-matching percentages for each hue. There is also a color selection for film and foil printing.

Color markers, opaque and translucent sheets are available that are compatible with the system.

The Preseparation of Illustrations

Line drawings are separated in the same manner as mechanical art. Each additional color is drawn on an overlay in either loose or hairline register. As in the preseparated mechanical, accuracy of registration is a critical factor. If each overlay is hinged—with tape—to a different side of the art, the sequence of the overlays can be changed so that any overlay may be worked upon on top of any other overlay.

Various additional color combinations can be obtained by the superimposition of screen tints. In the separated line drawing, solid areas are prepared as such; tint areas are prepared with red keylines and are stripped in by the platemaker. The use of shading film on a separated line drawing is impractical; the dot pattern is too coarse, and a moiré effect will invariably result.

Fake Process. The purpose of fake process is the creation of a full-color effect through the use of superimposed screen tints rather than with halftone process plates. Since the plate that utilizes screen tints is a line plate, it is considerably less expensive than a true process plate.

Fake process jobs are preseparated by the artist. The artist who prepares fake process art should have a set of color charts. These charts, published by various sources, contain small swatches printed in almost every conceivable hue and value. Each color is arranged on the chart so that its component percentages of the process hues can be readily determined. The artist selects a particular color area that is to appear on the printed result, noting the component percentages. For example, the color selected may contain 80 percent yellow, 40 percent cyan, and 20 percent magenta. The artist must then produce, either by drawing or by cutting film, an identical, accurately registered area on each overlay. Each area must then be marked, in blue pencil, with the percentage of the screen that is to be stripped into the area. The resulting surprint of the three screened areas will produce the color that was originally selected.

The screened areas of fake process produce flat tones: there is no modeling. In an attempt to produce some degree of tonal variation, the black plate is often drawn in tone and printed in halftone. Fake process art may be prepared in either of the following techniques:

1. A black line drawing is made. Three overlays are registered over the line drawing: one each for magenta, yellow, and cyan. The screen percentages of each desired color must be determined, and a solid or keyline area must be produced in register, on every applicable overlay. Each must be marked with the correct screen percentage found on the color chart.

2. A black tone drawing is made, rather than a line drawing. This will afford some degree of modeling when the flat color areas are printed over it. The black drawing should be kept light in value so that there will be a minimal discoloration of the surprinting hues.

Halftone Preseparation. Some artists produce preseparated art with a set of accurately premixed gray paints—one for each tone percentage.

The artist first makes a thin-keyline drawing in black. A line plate is made from the drawing and several proofs are pulled, *in blue ink*, on illustration board. Since all proofs are pulled from the same plate, they are identical and thus in perfect registration. The artist then designates a proof for each process color and paints in the appropriate areas with the proper percentage of gray. Provided the artist paints accurately within the blue lines and the percentage calculations are correct, the result will be superior to a fake process job. Since the separations must be reproduced in halftone, the artist has the opportunity to introduce blending into any desired area.

Preseparated art may be prepared with color sheets. Transparent color sheets are available in the process hues and in various percentages of the process hues. The sheets are printed as continuous tints, rather than as screen tints. As a result, any multicolor illustration preseparated with color sheets must be reproduced in halftone.

Since the sheets are printed in color, they provide a visual method of preparing preseparated art. The color may be scraped from any desired area with a plastic stylus or may be darkened with special water-soluble colors or modeling pencils. Separations are prepared in the following manner:

1. A key wash drawing is prepared in black.

2. Bourges sheets—either solid color or a percentage of the solid color—are registered over the key drawing. If a great variety of tint percentages is required, it may take more than three overlays to produce the job.

3. The desired color combination is effected by either removing, darkening, or leaving untouched the appropriate area of each overlay. Since the artist can see through any or all of the overlays, there is constant visual control over the work. The color that appears through the combined overlays is the color that will appear on the printed result.

CHAPTER 15
PRODUCTION FOR THE PRINTING PROCESSES

Much has been written about the best methods of producing art for the various printing processes. In actuality, properly prepared art should present few difficulties for any of the processes. Many artists feel that the printing will somehow minimize their mistakes. No printing process can perform miracles if the art is poorly executed or if poor plates are supplied. If slipshod work, clearly evident on the mechanical art, is no longer present in the printed result, it is because someone—usually the stripper or the opaquer—has rectified it. Such additional work is, of course, billed accordingly. It is reasonable to assume that there is no excuse for imperfections in professionally prepared art.

The following is a list of criteria for well-prepared art regardless of the printing process to be employed:

1. All copy should be proofread.
2. Sizes should be exact.
3. The art should be clean. Rubber cement, dirt, fingerprints, and pencil lines should be carefully removed. All art should be protected with a paper flap.
4. Line copy should be prepared in black, regardless of the color of ink that will be used to print the job. The black should be black, not gray. Line art should be clean and sharp. Lines should be heavy enough to stand up during the

press run and spaced far enough apart to avoid fill-in. Bleeding lines, resulting from the use of soft paper, should be avoided.

5. Continuous-tone copy should have well-defined tonal areas. These areas—which are where the texture is evident—should be cleanly rendered; scrubbed or muddy tone does not reproduce well. Photographs should not be over-retouched.

6. Broken type should be repaired. Smudged type should be replaced.

7. All elements of the mechanical art should be "squared up" with T-square and triangle. No printing process can realign copy that has been carelessly pasted in position.

8. All overlay material should be accurately registered. No printing process is capable of registering inaccurate preseparation. Material for the dropout, the mortise, or the surprint should be submitted in the manner that will require the least amount of photography on the part of the platemaker.

9. All separate art should be keyed for positive identification. Its position on the mechanical art should be delineated with either photostats or precisely ruled lines. The required enlargement or reduction of every piece of separate art should be clearly indicated.

10. No instructions should be left to guesswork. Instructions for every desired operation should be clearly written on the art in a pertinent location. Whenever possible, it is better to write instructions on the base art rather than on an overlay. Overlays are torn off during photography and may get lost. All instructions should be written in *blue pencil*.

11. Every screen-tint area should be carefully marked with the tint percentage and the color of ink desired. A swatch of the desired color(s) should be attached to the mechanical art. A tissue overlay, showing the color and location of all screened and solid-color areas, should be provided.

The best printed results are obtained when artists make an effort to learn the manner of preparation preferred by the individual printer for whom they are preparing the art. The following preferences of the printer should be ascertained in order to prepare the art in the most efficient manner:

1. Whether the printer (or the platemaker) prefers "in position" or separate art.

2. Whether photostats or keylines should be used to indicate the position of separate art.

3. Whether color and tint areas should be indicated by solid areas or with keylines.

4. How line/halftone combination art should be prepared.

5. Whether the art should be camera-separated or preseparated; whether the artist or the platemaker should be paid for the separations.

6. Whether the pages should be prepared in spreads (facing pages in numerical sequence) or as engraver's flats (the sequence in which they are imposed on the press sheet for cutting and folding).

7. When the press run is scheduled. Missed deadlines mean idle presses—an expensive occurrence for all concerned.

Additionally the artist should ascertain, either from the printer or the client, the following information concerning the job:

1. The exact finished size.
2. The number of colors in which the job will be printed.
3. The process that will be used to print the job.
4. The size and type of press the printer intends to use.
5. The type of paper on which the job is to be printed.
6. The quantity desired.
7. The screen size that will be used for the halftones.
8. The manner in which the printer intends to impose the plates.
9. The manner in which the job is to be cut. If it is to be die-cut, whether or not the die already exists, and if so, whether there are strike sheets available.
10. The manner in which the job is to be folded, bound, stitched, or mounted.

PRODUCTION FOR LETTERPRESS PRINTING

Advantages of the Process

Letterpress is an excellent medium for the reproduction of line, halftone, and color art. Printing plates are extremely durable and readily withstand long press runs. Proofs of letterpress plates can be readily supplied.

Existing letterpress plates can be cut apart and rearranged for further use. Printing may be accomplished from metal type without recourse to the reproduction proof. Letterpress plates may be converted for lithography; letterpress material can be often designed with this further purpose in mind.

Disadvantages of the Process

Except in the case of newspaper art, which utilizes a coarse screen, letterpress halftones must be printed on quality paper.

There is an additional charge for all halftone work. Continuous-tone art must be supplied for halftone printing. An exception is the screened Velox print, which is etched as a line plate rather than as a halftone. Screen prints are used extensively in newspaper advertising but are seldom employed for quality fine-screen printing.

The letterpress plate is expensive. Any error requiring the production of a new plate is a costly one. Ease of correction is often mentioned as an advantage of the letterpress process: this is true only when actual type, which is easily replaced, is used for printing. Correction of a letterpress *plate* is a difficult and expensive operation.

The Preparation of Art for Letterpress

Mechanical Art.   Most letterpress-printed advertising material is produced from mechanical art. Since halftones are often engraved separately, it is not necessary to paste continuous-tone art in position on the mechanical. Line art is either drawn or photostatted to size and pasted in position.

Small advertisers with limited art facilities will often provide the newspaper with illustrative matter but request that the newspaper set the type. In this instance, no mechanical art is required; a layout is sufficient.

If metal type and separate engravings are used for letterpress printing, actual mechanical art need not be produced. A paste-up—using galley proofs and key-lines to indicate the position of the illustrations—may be supplied as a guide for page makeup.

The engraver should be consulted in order to ascertain whether art for the surprint, dropout, or mortise should be overlaid on the separate art or on the mechanical.

Photographs and Wash Drawings.   The fine-screen letterpress halftone can be produced with remarkable fidelity to the original art. Other than the normal requirements for good halftone reproduction, there are no special procedures for the preparation of photographs and wash drawings for letterpress printing.

There is, however, a considerable difference between the preparation of art for magazine (110-line screen) and for newspaper (55- to 65-line screen) reproduction. Newspaper reproduction requires better-defined contrast—preferably employing no more than four tonal values. Retouching for the 110-line screen is kept subtle; retouching for newspaper screen should be strong. However, excessive retouching will not save a poor-quality photograph.

Line Copy.   No special preparation is required for letterpress line work. Excessive reduction should be avoided, although fine-line detail is easily held in letterpress.

If metal type is used for printing, a proof of the composition should be carefully examined in order to make certain that there are no broken characters.

Newspapers are reluctant to print large areas of solid black—especially reverse backgrounds. The printing of such areas requires excessive ink that will oversaturate the newsprint and retard drying. Most newspapers will arbitrarily screen any solid black areas they consider too large.

PRODUCTION FOR LITHOGRAPHY

Advantages of the Process

Offset lithography is the most economical method of printing in quantity. This does not mean, however, that lithography is never expensive, that it is always less expensive than *any* form of letterpress printing, or that it is an inferior medium. In lithography there can be a wider range of quality than in any other printing process. There are lithographers whose speciality is cheap one-color handbills. There are lithographers who print four-color process on coated stock. There is poor letterpress and poor gravure, but it never looks quite as bad as poor lithography. Good lithography rivals the best efforts of the other processes.

Some of the factors that affect both the quality and the price of lithography are:

1. The artistic integrity of the lithographer.
2. The type of plate employed.
3. The type of press used to print the job.
4. The amount of effort expended in dot-etching or color correction.
5. The kind of paper used. Lithography can print halftones well on a cheaper grade of paper than letterpress can, but lithography does not require the use of a cheaper grade of paper.

The lithographic plate is inexpensive, but there is considerable difference between the cost of a presensitized paper plate and a deep-etch plate. Plates, duplicate plates, and multiple-image plates take less time to produce than do plates for the other processes.

It is possible to print previously screened material with lithography. This practice should be approached with caution, because there is a noticeable loss in halftone quality. If high-quality work is preferred, it is just as desirable to submit continuous-tone art for offset lithography as it is for any other process.

Lithography is especially adaptable for large-sized work, such as posters and displays. The plate lays down an ink film of even thickness on large work—work that would pose a serious makeready problem in letterpress printing.

Disadvantages of the Process

Offset litho plates are not easily corrected. This disadvantage is overcome by the inexpensiveness of the plate. Should a mistake be found on the plate, the correction is made on the negative; the old plate is discarded, and a new one is made. The expense of a new plate is small compared to that of a letterpress or gravure plate.

Mechanical art must be prepared if standard photomechanical procedures are utilized. However, the film output of an image assembly system can be utilized directly to produce litho plates.

There can be considerable paper waste until the inking and dampening mechanisms have been properly adjusted for the press run.

The Preparation of Art for Lithography

Mechanical Art.   Mechanical art for lithography and mechanical art for the letterpress *plate* are prepared in a similar manner. The lithographer would prefer to have all the continuous-tone art pasted in position. This is seldom practical; the original continuous-tone art is generally too large for the mechanical. Line art is pasted in position, as it is for letterpress.

Material for both the litho plate and the letterpress plate is assembled in film-negative form, with the exception of deep-etch plates, which require positives. Mechanical art that has been prepared for expeditious negative assembly is suitable for either process. As in letterpress, it is best to know the preferences of the platemaker.

When a halftone proof is used for litho art, it should be pasted on the mechanical to be reproduced same-size. Reduction will cause the dot pattern to fill in; enlargement will make the pattern too obvious.

Photographs and Wash Drawings. Some artists, especially retouchers, once felt that the softness of the offset blanket impression warranted overemphasis of the tonal areas of continuous-tone art. Modern lithographic techniques have rendered this practice unnecessary.

Line Copy. Line copy is prepared in exactly the same manner as for letterpress. Line copy for lithography should be particularly clean. If any undesirable material appears on the negative and goes unnoticed by the opaquer, there is no way of routing it off the litho plate.

Since lithographic plates cannot incorporate letterpress type, reproduction proofs must be utilized on the mechanical art. These should be carefully checked for broken characters, smudges, and other imperfections.

PRODUCTION FOR GRAVURE

Advantages of the Process

Gravure is an excellent medium for the reproduction of properly prepared continuous-tone art, both in monotone and in color.

The paper used (newsprint) is comparatively inexpensive. Gravure plates are costly, but this cost is balanced by the saving in paper cost that is realized over a long press run.

Gravure is a simple system; presses can be started rapidly. There is little paper waste—half that of lithography. Presses are very fast, and gravure cylinders are extremely durable.

Disadvantages of the Process

Since the entire gravure plate carries a screen, line work—especially type with thin lines and serifs—has a tendency to look hairy.

Elements of the design, once etched, cannot be altered or shifted. Due to the speed of the rotogravure press, hairline register is difficult to maintain.

The paper stock used for gravure cannot be relied upon to produce any artistic effects.

It is impractical to use materials (negatives, plates, halftone proofs, etc.) from other printing processes.

The Preparation of Art for Gravure

Mechanical Art.   More special precautions should be taken in the preparation of art for gravure than for either letterpress or lithography. In gravure there is no counterpart of the line and halftone combination plate—all of the gravure plate is halftone. Thus, anything submitted as line on the mechanical art must be prepared with the knowledge that it will bear a screen on the printed result. In effect, line work is silhouette halftone. The center of the line fills in, but the dot pattern is evident at the edges. *Any* line elements of the mechanical art that are too thin are in danger of becoming ragged in appearance.

Once a gravure cylinder has been etched, it is impossible to shift units or make major changes. As a result, all type, lettering, line art, logotypes, etc., should be submitted as a single mechanical.

If drawings or photographs are to be submitted as separate art, an accurate indication of position should be included on the mechanical.

Guide lines for tint areas should be indicated with red keylines and with instructions to delete the lines from the negatives. Neither Ben Day nor shading film is applicable to the gravure process. Second colors should be painted in red or black on acetate overlays or applied with transparent sheets of red film.

The paste-up should be neat and accurate. Carelessly cut and pasted edges will cause additional retouching costs.

Photographs and Wash Drawings.   Gravure is essentially a tone medium. It is used most advantageously as a medium for the reproduction of the color photograph.

Many publications that are printed in gravure also contain signatures (sections) that are printed in one- or two-color letterpress. This enables an advertiser to insert an advertisement in the publication, using duplicate plates of a letterpress advertisement that may have been used elsewhere. A one-color line advertisement is best run in this section.

If advertisers wish to advertise in full color in a gravure publication, they must purchase gravure plates for that purpose. The quality of the printed result may justify the additional cost of a set of gravure plates.

Photographs submitted for gravure should be printed on smooth paper. Extra-flat or extra-contrasting prints should be avoided; the middle tones should be rich and sparkling. If several photographs are to appear, they should not be of varying contrasts. Excessive enlargement or reduction should be avoided.

Wash drawings should be held to the same tonal range as photographs. The lightest printable tone should be a good value step away from the white of the paper. Gravure stock has a certain grayness; this should be allowed for in the drawing. Wash drawings that contain two types of black pigment—for example, a drawing rendered with both lampblack and drawing ink—should be avoided.

Line Copy. Fine line copy should be checked with extreme care in order to make certain it will accept the gravure screen.

Excessive reductions should be avoided. If they are necessary, they should be photographically reduced and retouched. Actual-size drawings are ideal for the process.

Delicate line work should be restricted to one color. It is difficult to maintain hairline register on the rotogravure press: the slightest off-register will cause thin lines to blur if they are overprinted in two colors. Off-register on reverse backgrounds will cause the edges of the background to bleed into the lines.

The use of typefaces with delicate thin lines and serifs should be approached cautiously. There should be no imperfections in the type proofs utilized for the mechanical. Body type should be no smaller than 8 point. Reverse type should be heavy enough to ensure that it will not fill in, especially if it is to be dropped out of four-color process plates, because it is difficult to maintain register in high-speed rotogravure.

Special attention should be given to type surprinting over a panel or a background. The background should be light and contrasting in color. Type should be printed in one color only. Type to be surprinted or dropped out should not be overlaid on the artwork, but should be placed *in position on the mechanical.*

PRODUCTION FOR FLEXOGRAPHY

Advantages of the Process

Plates are inexpensive.

Flexography will print on a considerable variety of substrates.

Makeready costs are lower than for other printing processes.

Copy changes can be made during a press run.

Rubber printing plates will outlast electrotypes.

A plate roller can print a continuous pattern, which can then be cut to a desired length.

Fast-drying inks enable checking immediately after printing.

Spot varnishes and heat-sealing materials can be easily printed by flexography.

Ink coverage is excellent. Process inks have not been standardized; it is better to submit a color chip for matching. Flexography uses tint inks rather than screen tints.

Plates are easily stored.

Disadvantages of the Process

Stretching in both plates and substrate material must be compensated for in the mechanical art.

Correction is time-consuming.

Depending on the substrate material, the potential for off-register printing should be compensated for in the artwork.

The Preparation of Art for Flexography

Design. Design elements should be kept away from areas prone to excessive rubbing in folding, forming, or filling, and from areas to be stamped, taped, or glued.

Large solids and fine details should be avoided if they are to be printed on a single press station.

Shapes within shapes should be avoided, as they might emphasize poor registration.

Images printed on plastic should be kept away from the portions that are to be heat-sealed.

Copy should be designed to print on a colored background rather than bare plastic. If the enclosed product supplies the background color, a design color should be chosen that will not obscure or be dulled by that background.

Opaque inks cover most substrate surface colors better than transparent ones. Transparent color has a tendency to become stained by the color underneath.

Textiles are not generally printed with flexography, unless it is with special inks and plates.

Mechanical Art. Shrinkage must be considered when the mechanical art is prepared. Shrinkage occurs in three areas of rubber platemaking:

1. The original relief pattern plate.
2. The plastic matrix.
3. The rubber printing plate.

Magnesium originals do not shrink, while zinc shrinks substantially from the heat required by matrix-making. Zinc shrinks more cross-grain than it does with-grain. Grain direction must be kept consistent in multicolor printing by checking the grain direction as indicated on the back side of the plate material.

Matrix shrinkage will vary according to brand, and it should be checked against the dimensions of the art, negative, and pattern plate.

Rubber plate materials shrink when vulcanized and stretch when the plate is curved around the press cylinder. A vulcanized rubber plate containing no shrink control laminate will shrink from 1 ½ to 2 percent across each dimension. If fabric, plastic, metal, or paper laminates are incorporated into, or bonded onto, rubber plates, shrinking will be minimal.

Shrinkage can be computed mathematically, but there are enough variables so that the printer should be considered the final authority for the correct sizing of the mechanical art.

Since the dimensions of the package itself are usually determined before the design treatment is created, the mechanical artist should take care to determine the exact specifications of the package:

1. Determine the sizes of the surfaces to be printed.
2. Determine the locations of folds, die-cuts, perforations, slots, seams, etc.
3. Determine the federal labeling and packaging requirements for the job.
4. Know the configuration of the package when it is filled.
5. Acquire a dummy package if at all possible.
6. Acquire a sample of the substrate material.

When four-color process is employed, a black trap-line can be used effectively to surround color areas in order to "clean up" any edges that may tend to print off-register.

In package printing, type changes for weight, ingredient, price, or recipe changes can be:

1. Mounted with the other plates of the same color on the press cylinder.
2. Stripped into the negative or mortised into the relief plate.
3. Located on an overlay on the mechanical art.

PRODUCTION FOR SILK SCREEN

Advantages of the Process

The silk-screen stencil is inexpensive to produce. A hand-operated process requiring no expensive printing equipment, silk screen is an ideal medium for an extremely short run. It is practical to use silk screen to print as few as 50 copies. Automatic equipment is available for quantity printing.

Silk screen will print on virtually any surface. Special inks and paints can be used, many of which would provide difficulties for any other printing process.

Disadvantages of the Process

There are certain artistic limitations to the process, because it is essentially a medium for printing line. Halftone silk-screen printing has made considerable progress, but there is no comparison with the capabilities of the other processes.

Although silk screen is a very versatile medium, the equipment has neither the speed nor the stamina for book, magazine, newspaper, or other comparable types of printing.

The Preparation of Art for Silk Screen

Mechanical Art. Mechanical art should be supplied to the silk-screen printer, but it is seldom as complex as that submitted for the other printing processes. Since halftones are to be avoided if possible, there is no problem of stripping; there is no counterpart of the combination plate. The use of screen tints is a questionable practice. It is more practical to print a second color, if any color variation is desired.

A one-piece mechanical, to size, with all elements pasted in position, will generally prove sufficient.

Continuous-Tone Art. As previously mentioned, the printing of halftones should be avoided, unless there is no other method of solving the problem. If silk-screen printers are located who can provide evidence of their ability to print halftones, their advice, and theirs alone, should be followed for the preparation of the artwork.

Line Art. Silk screen is an excellent line medium. The artist should ascertain whether the printer plans to use photographic or hand-cut stencils. If the use of a photographic stencil is planned, the line art is prepared in the normal way. It need not be drawn to size; it can be reduced when the film positive is made.

If the screener plans to use a hand-cut stencil, the art should be made actual size. It may save time if the artist realizes that *only outlines need be provided.* There is nothing to be gained by filling in lettering, designs, etc.; the screen-cutter needs only the outline to serve as a guide for cutting. It is even possible to submit art that has been outline-drawn in pencil.

When producing line art in color, the printer needs preseparated art only if photographic screens are to be used.

Screen-cutters are artists in their own right. They are able to make accurate hand-cut separations of any color art submitted to them. Good screen-cutters are capable of converting a photograph or a continuous-tone color rendering to the flat-color technique of the process, making the appropriate separations. Their judgment may be superior to that of the artist who is accustomed to working in tonal values.

PRINT MEDIA PRODUCTION

In the past, when most publications printed with letterpress, it was only necessary to send them the proper size plates. Today, with publications printing in a variety of processes—mostly offset—print media requirements are more complex.

Specific production information for all U.S. business publications, consumer magazines, farm publications, and newspapers is contained in *Print Media Production Data,* published by the Standard Rate and Data Service. Pertinent information included is broken down into the following categories:

A. Magazines
   1. Personnel
   2. Mechanical requirements—printing process, trim size, binding method, colors available, dimensions, ad page (width and depth)

3. Bleed—plate size, live matter dimensions
4. Printing specifications—originals and duplicates, screens, color requirements, extra charges for conversions, requirements for special issues
5. Geographic/demographic editions
6. Inserts
7. Issue and closing dates

B. Newspapers
1. Personnel
2. Printing processes
3. Mechanical requirements—number of columns, column width (in picas), page size (in inches), screen, acceptable materials
4. Color requirements
5. Closing times

Preferred materials and acceptable material refer to the form in which the advertisement should be submitted to the publication. The materials are listed in order of preference, and not all preferences are similar. Most magazines and newspapers are printed with offset lithography. A few consumer magazines and Sunday newspaper supplements print with gravure. Some newspapers and a very few magazines continue to print with letterpress. Advertising material is submitted to them in the following way:[1]

Magazines—Offset Lithography. Magazines printed in offset prefer the submission of film. The publication will specify whether the film is to be positive or negative, whether the image should be frontwards- or backwards-reading, and whether the emulsion side should be up or down. Acceptable also are camera-ready art, repro proofs, and letterpress conversions such as Scotchprints, Cronapress conversions, and Brightype.[2]

Gravure Publications. These require fully retouched continuous-tone positives.

Magazines—Letterpress. These require original copper relief plates or electrotypes.

Newspapers—Offset Lithography. Offset-printed newspapers accept camera-ready art, Veloxes, film negatives, Scotchprints, and Cronapress negatives.

Newspapers—Letterpress. Letterpress newspapers prefer camera-ready art, Veloxes, and repro proofs. Virtually no newspaper currently utilizes the stereotype process.

---

[1]Not listed in any preferential order.
[2]See page 50 for definitions.

PRODUCTION WITH PROCESSED IMAGES

The following pages chart the ways processed images—on film or on paper as produced by either the photostat or the diffusion-transfer process—can be used for various aspects of production.

Paper Positives

1. Use dye (Dr. Martin's) to color the background behind a black design.
2. Dye the background, and chemically remove the design—this results in a white dropout.
3. Indicate halftone art on a layout.
4. Make a paper negative (photostat).
5. Reduce or enlarge type or line art for reproduction on the mechanical.
6. Indicate the cropping and position of a halftone on the mechanical: "Not for repro" or "Position only."
7. Prepare overlay art for a surprint.
8. Make a continuous-tone glossy print for photoretouching.
9. Make continuous-tone prints for montage assembly.
10. Make a posterization, a line, or a Laserline conversion from a glossy, continuous-tone original.
11. Image-set proofs for pasting on the mechanical art.

Paper Negatives

1. Dye a dropout design on a black background.
2. Dye the dropout design, and chemically remove the background—this results in a colored design on a white background.
3. Make a paper positive (photostat).
4. Prepare reverse line art on the mechanical.
5. Prepare overlay art for a dropout.
6. Gang up negative images to create a multiple positive image.
7. Make corrections or alterations on line art and revert to a paper positive so that the corrections will not show.
8. Respace lettering or type.
9. Flop an image.

Film Negatives

1. Make litho or dry-offset plates.
2. Make relief plates for letterpress or flexography.
3. Strip a screen tint onto a design.

PAPER POSITIVES

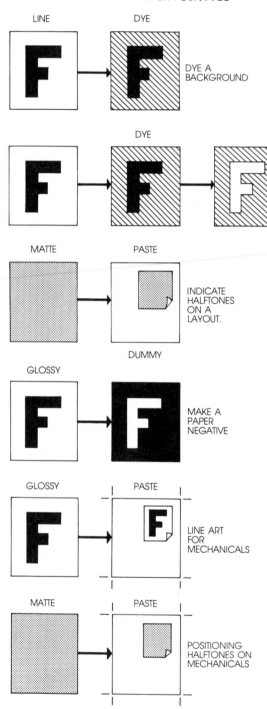

LINE   DYE

DYE A
BACKGROUND

DYE

DYE
BACKGROUND
BLEACH
DESIGN

MATTE   PASTE

INDICATE
HALFTONES
ON A
LAYOUT.

DUMMY

GLOSSY

MAKE A
PAPER
NEGATIVE

GLOSSY   PASTE

LINE ART
FOR
MECHANICALS

MATTE   PASTE

POSITIONING
HALFTONES ON
MECHANICALS

PAPER POSITIVES (cont.)

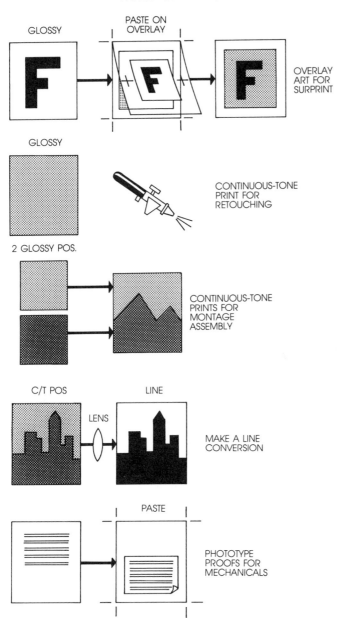

GLOSSY

PASTE ON OVERLAY

OVERLAY ART FOR SURPRINT

GLOSSY

CONTINUOUS-TONE PRINT FOR RETOUCHING

2 GLOSSY POS.

CONTINUOUS-TONE PRINTS FOR MONTAGE ASSEMBLY

C/T POS

LINE

LENS

MAKE A LINE CONVERSION

PASTE

PHOTOTYPE PROOFS FOR MECHANICALS

4. Make a screen print (Velox).
5. Make a line positive paper print.
6. Make a continuous-tone positive paper print.
7. Make a line positive transparent film.
8. Make a continuous-tone positive transparent film.
9. Make a halftone positive transparent film.
10. Generate photographic type image.
11. Make Color-Key® transparent proofs of multicolor or process color separations.
12. Make positive projection transparencies.

PAPER NEGATIVES

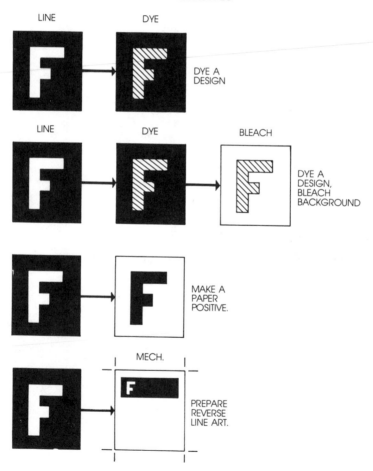

PAPER NEGATIVES (cont.)

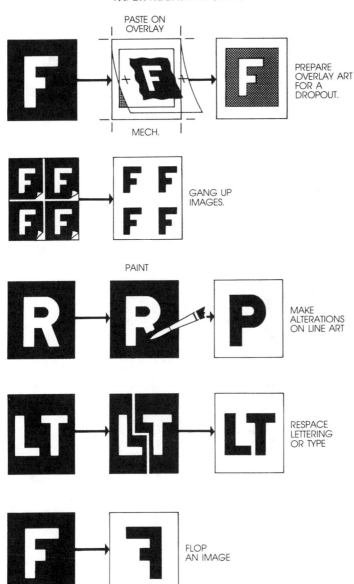

PASTE ON OVERLAY

MECH.

PREPARE OVERLAY ART FOR A DROPOUT.

GANG UP IMAGES.

PAINT

MAKE ALTERATIONS ON LINE ART

RESPACE LETTERING OR TYPE

FLOP AN IMAGE

FILM NEGATIVES

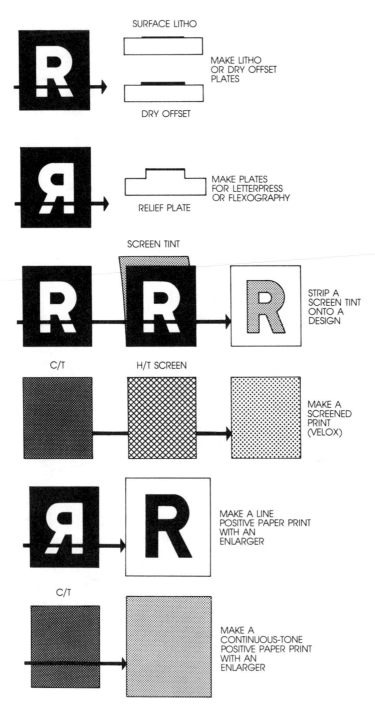

FILM NEGATIVES (cont.)

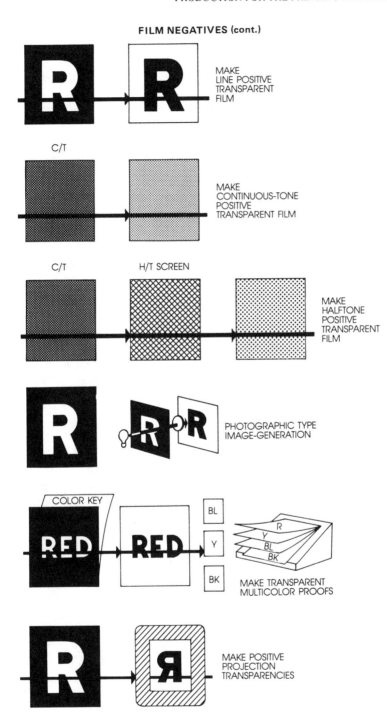

MAKE
LINE POSITIVE
TRANSPARENT
FILM

C/T

MAKE
CONTINUOUS-TONE
POSITIVE
TRANSPARENT FILM

C/T   H/T SCREEN

MAKE
HALFTONE
POSITIVE
TRANSPARENT
FILM

PHOTOGRAPHIC TYPE
IMAGE-GENERATION

COLOR KEY

BL

Y

BK

MAKE TRANSPARENT
MULTICOLOR PROOFS

MAKE POSITIVE
PROJECTION
TRANSPARENCIES

Film Positives

1. Make deep-etch litho plates.
2. Make reverse letterpress plates.
3. Make gravure plates.
4. Strip a screen tint into the background of a dropout design.
5. Surprint a design on a screen tint.
6. Make a negative paper print.
7. Make a photographic silk-screen stencil.
8. Check phototypesetter/image-setter type for fit.

FILM POSITIVES

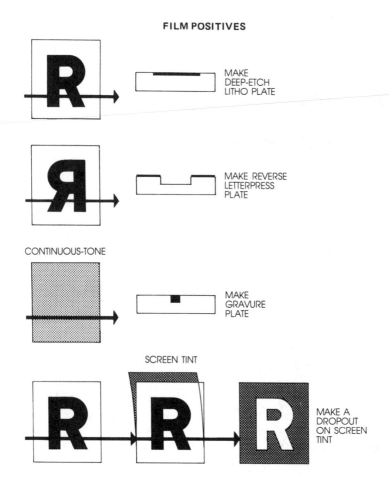

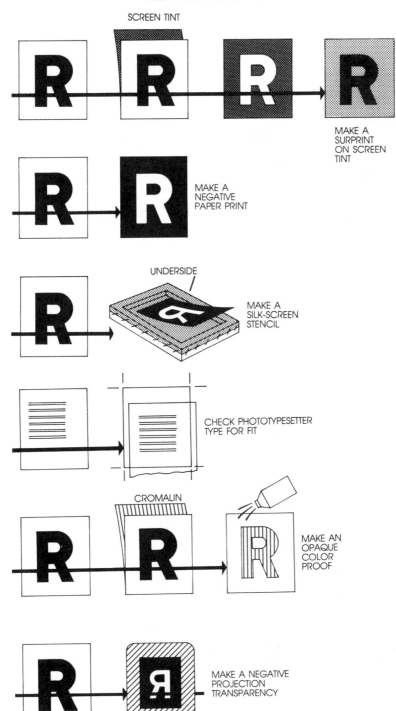

SCREEN TINT

MAKE A
SURPRINT
ON SCREEN
TINT

MAKE A
NEGATIVE
PAPER PRINT

UNDERSIDE

MAKE A
SILK-SCREEN
STENCIL

CHECK PHOTOTYPESETTER
TYPE FOR FIT

CROMALIN

MAKE AN
OPAQUE
COLOR
PROOF

MAKE A NEGATIVE
PROJECTION
TRANSPARENCY

COMBINATIONS

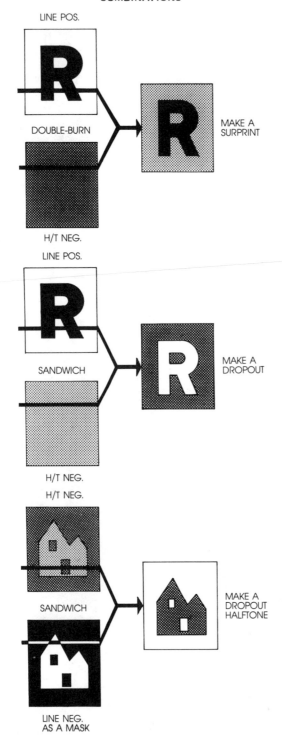

COMBINATIONS (cont.)

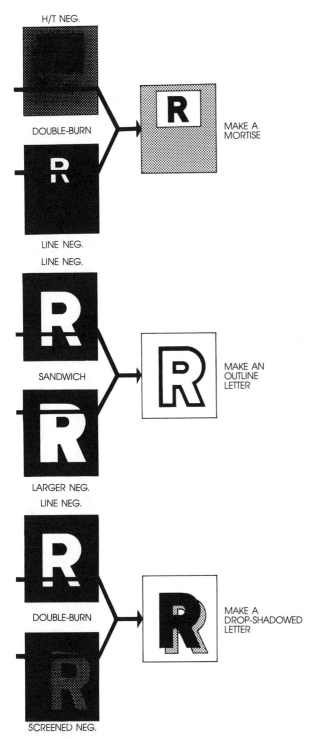

H/T NEG.

DOUBLE-BURN

LINE NEG.

MAKE A
MORTISE

LINE NEG.
LINE NEG.

SANDWICH

LARGER NEG.

MAKE AN
OUTLINE
LETTER

LINE NEG.

DOUBLE-BURN

SCREENED NEG.

MAKE A
DROP-SHADOWED
LETTER

9. Make a Chromalin® opaque color proof.

10. Make a negative projection transparency.

Combinations of Transparent Film

1. Line negative and halftone negative. Double-burn to make a surprint combination plate.

2. Line positive (from negative art) and halftone negative sandwiched to make a dropout combination plate.

3. Line negative and halftone negative sandwiched. Line negative serves as a mask, producing an automatic dropout for a plate or for a Velox.

4. Halftone negative and line negative. Double-burn to make a mortise.

5. Line positive of type or lettering and a slightly larger line negative of the same, sandwiched to form a positive outline letter. A contact film positive may be used to produce a reverse outline letter.

6. Line negative of type or lettering and a same-size screen negative. Double-burning with the screened negative shifted slightly down and to the right will produce a black letter with a screened drop-shadow.

CHAPTER 16
PAPER

The first practical, easily handled writing material was developed by the Egyptians sometime between 2500 and 2000 B.C. It was produced from the split stalks of the papyrus plant, which were cross-laid and pounded together with a stone, and the name of this material provided the derivation of the English word paper.

The immediate predecessor of modern paper was developed by the Chinese in the first century. Pulp fibers, reduced from the inner bark of the mulberry tree, were formed into sheets by floating them in water and allowing them to settle and dry. It has since been demonstrated that almost any fibrous plant can be made into paper of one quality or another.

The Chinese process was a closely guarded secret for nearly 600 years. The Arab conquest of Samarkand in A.D. 704 introduced papermaking in the Western world; it soon spread to the remainder of Europe. The first American paper mill was built near Philadelphia in 1690.

During the seventeenth century, all paper was made by hand, generally from the reduced fibers of hemp, linen, and cotton rags. The rags were reduced to pulp by the action of a water-driven stamping mill. The pulp was then floated in a vat of water and seined onto the surface of a wire screen. Shaking of the screen by hand felted (matted) the pulp as the water drained off through the mesh of the screen. Sheets of matted fibers were removed and sandwiched between pieces of felt, where excess water was removed by pressure. The individual sheets of paper were then hung over rods to dry. Naturally, this process was expensive and limited in production.

In 1798 a Frenchman, Nicholas Louis Robert, conceived the principle of making paper with a moving endless wire screen. Robert took his patents to England, where they were sold to Henry and Sealy Fourdrinier. The Fourdriniers developed the first practical papermaking machine in 1804. Present-day papermaking machinery still bears their name.

Rags were the source of fibers for the Fourdrinier process until 1840, when Gottfried Keller, a German, invented a method of reducing wood to pulp by mechanically grinding it with a revolving stone. In 1867, Benjamin Tilghman, of Philadelphia, furthered the technology of pulp reduction by the introduction of an acid process for separating the fibers. It took many years to overcome the imperfections of this process, but by the end of the nineteenth century, chemical wood pulp was becoming commercially usable. This is the process by which the bulk of modern paper is manufactured.

THE PAPERMAKING PROCESS

The Raw Materials

Paper is a matted web of cellulose fibers. Almost any organic matter with a suitable fibrous structure can be manufactured into paper. The nature of fibers from different sources makes it difficult to categorize minor differences, but the following classification should be adequate:

Rag Pulp. Rag pulp is made from new, unlaundered, and undyed cotton rags. This pulp yields almost pure cellulose, which produces a strong, durable paper.

Vegetable Fibers. Esparto (Spanish and Algerian grasses), straw, and bamboo (which may be considered a gigantic straw) are chemically reduced to pulp. The chemical treatment of bamboo, a more complex fiber, is necessarily the most severe. Cardboard is made from straw and wood fibers.

Jute. Jute (plant fibers), in the form of old bagging, is chemically reduced for use in the manufacture of strong, cheap papers when whiteness is not a requisite.

Reclaimed Pulp. Used paper is reclaimed by submitting it to an alkali solution to dissolve the ink. It is then chemically reduced to pulp form.

Mechanical Wood Pulp. Mechanical pulp is ground, rather than chemically treated. Logs are ground into tiny particles resembling fine sawdust. These are mixed with water and floated onto the screen of the papermaking machine. Spruce, balsam, and hemlock are the principal sources. Mechanical pulp is used for newspaper stock.

Chemical Wood Pulp. Chemical pulp is wood chemically treated for the purpose of removing gums, resins, and other undesirable substances. The result is pure cellulose fiber. The type of chemical reduction process utilized is determined by the nature of the wood fiber. Long-fibered pulps are needed to provide paper with strength and durability. Varying mixtures of long and short fibers produce different degrees of bulk, opacity, and smoothness. Short fibers produce the best formation, matting closely with a minimum of pores, but paper made exclusively from short fibers will not hold together for prolonged use. The following are the principal processes for the chemical reduction of wood fiber:

The Sulfate Process. The reducing agent (or "cooking liquor") in this process is a modified form of caustic soda, which provides a pulp suitable for bags or wrapping paper (kraft paper). Pitch-bearing woods, such as pine, are generally used; they provide the longest and the strongest of the pulp fibers.

The Sulfite Process. In this process, calcium bisulfite is the reducing agent. Long-fibered coniferous (evergreen) woods are used. The resultant pulp responds well to bleaching. Sulfite pulp is used for writing papers.

The Soda Process. In this process, fibers are reduced with caustic soda (sodium hydroxide). Short-fibered deciduous woods (seasonal, such as poplar) are utilized. Pulp manufactured by this process is used extensively for book papers.

Alpha Pulp. This pulp is an extremely white, purified fiber that is utilized as a substitute for rag stock. Alpha pulp is considerably superior to ordinary pulps.

The logs are ground into small uniform chips and are screened free of dust. The chips are placed in acid-resistant, brick-lined tanks called *digesters*. The cooking liquor is pumped in under controlled temperature (steam). The process separates the pure cellulose fibers from their incrusting impurities; the cellulose is subjected to repeated cleanings until all such impurities have been eliminated. When thoroughly cleaned, fibers are bleached white with chloride of lime.

Semi-Mechanical Pulp. Mechanical and chemical pulp are combined to produce an intermediate pulp with a high strength and a high yield.

Thermo-Mechanical Pulp. Since mechanical grinding of the logs causes damage to the wood fibers, the thermo-mechanical method utilizes hot pressurized steam to reduce the pulp. This method substantially increases the pulp's strength.

Papermaking Machinery

In order to form fibers into paper, small clusters must be broken into individual fibers, and the walls and ends of the fibers must be frayed and conditioned with various nonfibrous ingredients.

The fibers are beaten in water in order to fray them so that they will mesh together (or "felt") more strongly in the paper. The *beater* is an oval-shaped vat in which the pulp is circulated and beaten with blunt bars. These bars are mounted on a revolving drum and rotate against a bedplate of similar but adjustable bars. The bars in the bedplate may be set for the type of treatment required for the character of the paper that is to be made from it.

Various nonfibrous materials are added to the pulp while it is being processed in the beater. Some of these materials are:

Sizing.   This reduces moisture penetration and acts as a binding agent that prevents fuzzing from the pull of sticky ink or erasure. It gives the paper a greater hardness. Rosin, starch, wax, animal glue, and silicate of soda are frequently used. Different amounts of sizing are used for different purposes.

Blotting paper is unsized.

Mimeo, newsprint, and gravure stock are slack-sized for fast ink penetration.

Uncoated book stock is medium-sized—enough to prevent moisture-absorption wrinkling, but not enough to retard ink-drying.

Writing, litho, and offset stock are hard-sized in order to bind the fibers and prevent absorption.

Fillers.   These are fine particles of clay, calcium carbonate, talc, calcium sulfate, and titanium or zinc pigments that are used to fill up the spaces between the fibers—increasing density, opacity, and smoothness. Titanium imparts additional whiteness; clay readily accepts polishing.

Dyes.   Pigments and aniline dyes, necessary for the manufacture of colored paper, are introduced at this point in the processing of the pulp.

Alum.   A weak acidifying agent used to hold the sizing and fix the dye on the fibers.

The pulp, with its additives, proceeds from the beater into the *Jordan engine* or "Jordan." The Jordan consists of a horizontal conical shell, with a plug that revolves within it at high speed. Protruding bars exert an action similar to that of the beating process, which reduces the fibers to a more uniform length.

Recently beaters have been replaced with faster, more efficient machinery and are now used only for mixing purposes; however, the basic function of the new equipment remains the same.

The fibers are now ready to pass through storage vats and into the papermaking machine.

The *"wet end"* of the papermaking machine, the end into which the treated pulp or "stock"—now about 1 percent pulp and 99 percent water—is pumped, is known as the *Fourdrinier section*. The stock is forced through microscopic

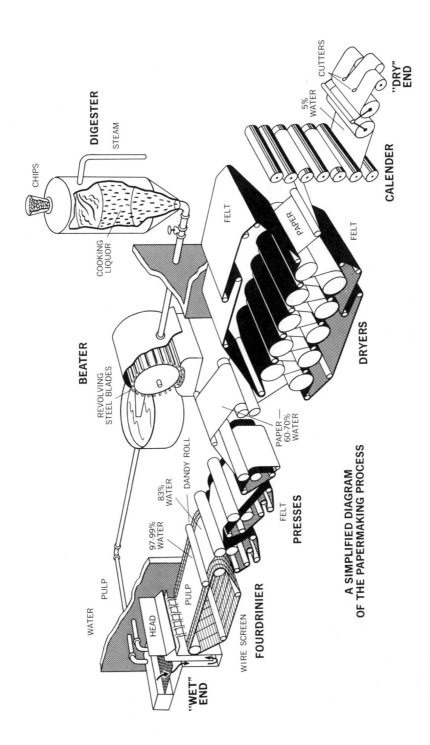

A SIMPLIFIED DIAGRAM
OF THE PAPERMAKING PROCESS

straining slots onto the finely woven wire mesh of the moving, endless Fourdrinier screen. This screen vibrates constantly and interweaves and mats the fibers. The fibers tend to flow lengthwise in the direction of screen travel, but the shaking somewhat disrupts this tendency and disperses the fibers in all directions. Perfect formation of the fibers without any directional tendency (grain) is possible only in handmade papers. Thus, the grain of the paper is in the direction of screen travel.

The *dandy roll,* located atop the wire screen, is of great importance. Covered with a wire mesh similar to the screen, it imparts the first surface pressure to the *top* of the paper. The dandy roll is also used for watermarking and laid marking.

The Watermark.   The watermark is a distinctive design, or an imprint of the manufacturer's name, which becomes an integral part of the paper, visible when held up to the light. The watermark design, formed from wire, is attached to the dandy roll which impresses it *into* the still wet paper. The watermarking of currency, postage stamps, or other negotiable papers is undertaken to discourage counterfeiting. "Watermarks" on less expensive papers are often printed from raised letters on a rubber sleeve fitting around one of the press rollers of the papermaking machine. These are characterized by a sharper, more artificial appearance than a genuine watermark. A genuine watermark is usually a sign of a superior product.

Laid Paper.   Laid paper bears an imprinted design of unequal mesh, consisting of parallel wire marks, intersected at 90-degree angles by heavier "chain" marks. The chain holds the wires together laterally and its marks are spaced at wider intervals than the wire marks are. The chain marks, readily distinguishable, follow the grain of the paper marks, and the overall pattern appears as a continuous watermark.

Wove Paper.   Paper not characterized by laid marks is called *wove paper.* In wove stock, the nature of the paper surface is determined by the equal mesh of the woven-wire Fourdrinier screen and by the woven felts that carry the paper through the first stages of smoothing and drying. The dandy roll helps give the topside of the paper an appearance as much like the underside (wire side) as possible.

Laid paper shows more textural variation between "front" and "back" surfaces than wove paper.

The paper, which is now being formed on a continuous roll, or *web,* is now strong enough to pass, unsupported by the wire mesh of the screen, into the *press section* of the machine. The web is picked up by a continuous strip of wool felt, which carries it through multiple pressing and smoothing rollers called *presses.*

The top surface of the paper is known as the *"felt side"*; the underside, bearing the pattern of the screen, is known as the *"wire side."* The felt side of the paper accepts printing better than the wire side. The condition and the cleanliness of the wool felt is an important factor in paper quality.

The paper moves between pairs of rollers—one brass or solid granite, the other rubber—where it is squeezed to a greater density. The first two pairs are arranged so that both sides of the paper are worked on, reducing the possibility of dissimilar sides in the "finished" paper. If a third press is utilized, the felt is often removed, and it becomes a smoothing press. This flattens the surface without polishing it. The surface "watermark" is imprinted at some point in the press section.

From the presses the paper travels unsupported to the drying section. Drying is a carefully controlled process. As it passes into the dryer section, the paper still retains about 62 percent of its original moisture. It travels over steam-filled drums, securely held by a continuous roll of cotton or asbestos felt. The web is gradually dried to a moisture content of 4 ½ to 6 percent.

Once dry, the paper is ready for finishing. It is subjected to a variety of additional operations, which will be discussed in conjunction with textural characteristics.

VARIETIES OF PAPER

Definitions

Stock. Paper.

Ream. A ream is 500 sheets of paper.

Basis Size. The standard size of any particular grade of paper. Of course, paper may be manufactured in any size. The basis size is the size in which it is normally and most conveniently produced.

Basis Weight. The designation (in pounds) given to an individual sheet of paper, based upon the weight of one ream of its basis size. For example, the basis size of book stock is 25" × 38". The designation "25 × 38—basis 70" means that 500 sheets of this paper weigh 70 lbs. An individual sheet of this paper is known as 70-lb. stock; it may also be known as "substance 70."

Grammage. In the metric system, the basis weight of paper is stated in grams and is known as grammage. Grammage is measured in *grams per square meter,* or g/m^2. The basis weight of the paper is multiplied by a metric constant of 1406.5 and divided by the number of square inches in the basic sheet.

Caliper Thickness. The thickness of a heavy stock as measured with a micrometer. To measure this, fold the sheet into four thicknesses, measure with a micrometer, and divide by four.

CLASSIFICATIONS OF PAPER

There are three major classifications of paper: book, writing (or business), and cover paper. Of the wide variety of finishes contained within these categories, some are accomplished on the papermaking machine, others in separate operations. The machine finishes range from rough antiques to a smooth English finish. The separate processes produce supercalendered (further smoothed with rollers), coated, or fancy embossed surfaces.

Typical basis sizes of the major classifications are:

Book Stock. The basis size of book stock is 25" × 38". Basis weights range from 45 to 120 lbs.

Writing Stock. The basis size of writing (business) stock is 17" × 22". Basis weights of bond papers range from 9 to 24 lbs.; ledger papers range from 24 to 40 lbs.; and manifold (onionskin) is made in a 9-lb. weight.

Cover Stock. Cover stock has a basis size of 20" × 26" and generally comes in 50- and 80-lb. weights. Heavier cover stock is measured in caliper thickness (thousandths of an inch—.010 in., .012 in., .014 in., etc.).

Book Stock

Book stock possesses qualities desirable for book and fine magazine work. It may be roughly classified in the following categories:

Antique Finish. Antique finish is similar to the paper of early printing days. Paper in the antique category is machine finished—produced in the papermaking machine and not requiring additional finishing. Rough in comparison to other book papers, due to the minimum of smoothing pressure, it is usually sized to a moderate degree. Its absorbency depends on the amount of sizing mixed with the pulp. Antique is used for books, programs, and some forms of advertising. There are several subcategories of antique stock:

Eggshell Antique. A rough paper with a surface resembling an eggshell's. It is produced on wet presses, using special felts.

Text. A high-grade antique, smoother than eggshell, used for quality books, booklets, and brochures. It is often watermarked and deckle-edged (feathered and untrimmed). Wove and laid stock is most often found in antique and text papers.

Vellum Finish. Classic vellum is paper of finer quality than parchment, made from calf skins. Vellum finish is the smoothest grade of the antique category, finished to resemble genuine vellum. It is available in the following grades:

Paper Vellum. An imitation of classic vellum, made from high-quality rags; it is used for fine book editions and documents.

Japan Paper. This is made from the bark of the paper mulberry in imitation of classic vellum.

Offset Stock.   Related to the antique group, offset is a smooth, uncoated book stock, generally with a text or vellum finish. It is ideal for fine-screen offset lithography and will accept line work without difficulty. Offset stock is sized on both sides to prevent curling from the moisture inherent in the lithographic process.

English Finish (E.F.).   Having a nonglare, slightly roughened surface, English finish is a further development of machine finishing. It is so universally preferred for advertising and sales-promotion printing that many paper houses stock no other finish in the book-stock category. English finish has a high clay content; its fibers are short, allowing the papermaking machine to impart extra smoothness. E.F. produces good results with 120-line halftones and is especially manufactured for lithography and gravure.

English finish is *calendered*. A stack of five to nine heavy iron calender rollers is incorporated into the dry end of the papermaking machine for the purpose of ironing and smoothing the fibers. The paper may be threaded through all or some of these rollers, depending on the degree of smoothness desired. The rollers are driven by friction, and the resulting slippage adds to the gloss of the finish. The paper passes through the machine calender rollers only once.

Supercalendered Stock.   Supercalendered stock has a smooth finish, with less bulk and opacity than English finish, and is known colloquially as "super." Used for magazines and booklets, it will accept halftones of 120- to 133-line screens.

Super stock is finished by a stack of calender rolls *independent* of those in the papermaking machine. In the supercalender, steel rollers alternate with cotton or paper-surfaced rollers. The paper is dampened by steam, then polished by the friction of the steel rollers and the softer-surfaced ones. Super stock is sent through the calenders twice—once for each side—and may be sent through four times for an exceptionally high finish.

Coated Stock.   Coated stock has a smooth, shiny finish ideally suited for the printing of 133- to 150-line halftones. The finest coated stock will accept halftone screens of up to 200 lines.

Coated stock is finished by a supplementary operation that also takes place outside the papermaking machine. The coating emulsion adheres to, rather than being incorporated in, the structure of the paper. The coating—a white, milky substance—is a mixture of white China clay (kaolin), calcium sulfate, and aluminum oxide together with whitening agents, such as barium sulfate, titanium oxide, or zinc sulfide. The adhesive agent is casein glue, a skim-milk derivative.

The web of paper passes through a vat containing the coating substances, after which it is dried by hot air and rewound. The coating does not dry glossy; high- and medium-gloss finishes are produced by supercalendering. Coated stock ranges from enamel (super glossy) to dull (smooth, but without gloss).

A coated paper retains more ink on its surface, resulting in more brilliant, denser color. Thus, matte-coated paper is an alternative to dull-coated or uncoated papers. It reproduces halftones well, because the coating keeps the ink on the surface for maximum density and brilliance. Coated matte is ideal for printed pieces that require a nonglare surface but also holds good ink gloss for sharp halftones and brilliant color.

Machine-coated stock is coated while the stock is still on the papermaking machine. *Conversion-coated* stock—generally better and more expensive—is coated off the machine. *Blade-coated* stock is an on-machine coating. Excessive coating is applied and smoothed with a flexible blade, producing a matte finish. *Cast-coated* stock affords the highest gloss—similar to a glossy photographic print. Expensive, it is produced by pressing the paper against a polished chromium drum.

Litho stock, coated on only one side, is common; recently two-sided litho stock has come into use.

Writing Stock

Writing stock is exactly what the name implies—paper used mainly for written (or typewritten) communications and for the keeping of written records. Writing stock is hard-sized to prevent absorption, since it is apt to be written on with a pen. Writing stock is divided into the following categories:

Flat Stock.   Flat stocks are calendered writing papers, ranging from cheap memo paper to fine stationery.

Bond Stock.   Bond stock has a rough, nonglare surface that accepts both printing and writing ink. It is used for stationery, office forms, catalogs and booklets. The finest bonds are made from rag stock and have a snap or "rattle" when briskly shaken. High-grade bonds, with their nonabsorbent qualities, accept letterpress printing with difficulty, but good results may be obtained with both steel engraving and offset lithography.

Top-grade bonds are generally watermarked and are available in a wide variety of colors. Bond finishes include regular, laid and wove, glazed, dull, cold pressed, cockle, and ripple.

Corrasable® Typewriter Paper.   Paper with a surface that will readily accept erasures.

Business Paper.   Business paper is a single type of paper formulated for use with four types of copying equipment: electrostatic (Xerographic), mimeograph, spirit duplicator, and offset lithography. It is usually 20-lb. stock which is manufactured to generate less lint than bond.

Ledger Stock.   Ledger stock is used for account books, office forms, and quality letterhead printing. It is made from longer-fibered pulp than bond in order to withstand folding. Glare-free, smooth-finished for writing and ruling, and sized for maximum erasure resistance, it has a high rag content, which makes it both strong and durable. Ledger is not suitable for fine-screen halftones, unless they are printed by offset lithography.

Manifold Stock (Onionskin).   Thin but strong, manifold is used for second sheets (carbon copies), sales books, and records where less bulk is a requisite. It is also used for lightweight airmail sheets.

Carbonless Paper.   Paper that will produce duplicate copies without the traditional interleaving of carbon paper.

Cover Stock

Cover stocks are heavier, stronger, easier-folding stocks, available in a wider variety of colors than any type of printing paper. Able to withstand rough handling, they are used for announcements, booklets, catalogs, mailing pieces, and pamphlet covers. Unsuitable for letterpress work in halftone, cover stocks readily accept line letterpress and offset (both line and halftone).

Cover stock is available in a great number of finishes, ranging from antique to imitation leather and cloth. More common finishes include:

Antique. Unfinished, with a rough surface.

Coated. Surface-coated with a smooth, glossy finish.

Crash. A finish similar to coarse linen.

Embossed. An overall, textured design pressed into the paper.

Laid or Wove. Impressed with the pattern of the wire and/or the dandy roll.

Metallic. Paper with a metallic surface.

Pebble. Pressed between steel rollers that impart a surface pattern.

Plate. A fine, smooth, hard finish obtained by rolling between plates of zinc or copper.

Ripple. Pressed between sheets of sulfite pulp or embossed rollers that produce an irregular texture suggesting ripples. The finish is glossy, but rough.

Additional Varieties of Stock

News Stock.   Commonly referred to as "newsprint," news stock is 70 to 80 percent mechanical pulp and therefore lacks permanence and strength. News stock is slack-sized and therefore highly absorbent—a quality that helps the ink dry.

The resins and gums that remain in the ground wood cause news stock to be chemically affected by light and air. As a result, newspapers intended to be preserved (in libraries, etc.) are printed on rag-content paper.

Roto Paper.   Roto paper is newsprint specifically made for the gravure process. Soft and absorbent, it is capable of handling the fluidity of gravure ink. The cheapest variety is unsized. Normally slack-sized, it will accept both line and the 150-line gravure screen.

Computer Paper. Continuous letter size (8 ½" × 11") sheets with perforated, detachable side-strips which enable the paper to feed through a dot-matrix printer. Paper for a laser printer does not require these perforations.

Bristol Board. Bristol board is a heavy, stiff printing paper used for announcements, postcards, index cards, display cards, menus, etc. It has an excellent surface for the printing of quality booklets and brochures. Bristol is manufactured in several varieties:

Plain Bristol. A surface similar to English finish, but stiffer and heavier in weight.

Index Bristol. A plain, stiff paper, used for index cards or file dividers.

Coated Bristol. A stiff paper, coated for quality halftone printing.

Cardboard. Cardboard is a heavy, durable board used for box manufacture. Faced with a thin sheet of calendered or coated stock, it is used for boxes, posters, and counter cards. Made from a cheap pulp filler, sometimes reinforced with straw fibers, its thickness is developed by pasting plys (layers) together with a multicylindered machine. Faced cardboard will accept letterpress, lithography, or silk screen—depending upon the quality of the facing sheet. Unsurfaced cardboard is ideally printed by flexography.

Parchment (Genuine). Genuine parchment is extremely expensive and is made from the skin of sheep or goats. It is used for important documents, diplomas ("sheepskins"), certificates, etc.

Parchment (Paper). Paper parchment is an imitation of genuine parchment made from a waterproofed, extremely high grade of bond paper.

India (or Bible) Paper. India paper is a quality paper, similar to English finish but very light in weight. It is used in fine books, bibles, dictionaries, and encyclopedias—in instances where compactness is a desirable factor.

Safety Paper. Safety paper is paper designed to show up any attempt at erasure or alteration. Used for checks, money orders, or other items of negotiable value, it is chemically treated or printed with a surface design which is readily affected by water, bleach, chemicals, or erasure.

Kraft (Wrapping) Paper. Kraft paper is a strong, unbleached brown paper made from long sulfate fibers. It will not accept halftones, but may be printed in line—particularly with rubber flexographic plates.

Art Papers

There are several types of paper that find general use in the production of advertising art. The illustrator may employ a wide variety of papers in an attempt to produce unique textural effects, but the following papers are normally used by the art department:

Tracing Paper. Tracing paper is a thin transparent paper used for making preliminary drawings, laying out lettering, scaling drawings and photographs, etc. The transparency of the paper allows the artist to retrace readily and thus refine the work. Tracing paper is not suitable for ink drawing; the ink will make it wrinkle. A drawing made on tracing paper is transferred to drawing paper or board by blackening the back with a soft pencil or a graphite stick. The surplus graphite is rubbed down with a rag or a paper towel. Retracing the lines with a hard pencil transfers an image of the drawing onto the desired surface.

Tracing Vellum. Tracing vellum is heavier in weight and somewhat less transparent than tracing paper. It is available in several weights. Ink will not wrinkle vellum unless it is applied in large areas; its transparency permits tracing from an original layout or sketch in order to render finished line art. It is used for line drawings, lettering, and separation overlays.

Bristol Board. Bristol boards are high-rag-content boards used for illustration and lettering. Bristol comes in 1-, 2-, and 3-ply thicknesses, laminated for extra strength and permanence. *Plate-finish Bristol* is extremely smooth and is used for precise line work. *Kid-finish Bristol* has a medium finish, which is suitable for continuous-tone drawings and loose brush-and-ink lettering or illustration.

Bond Paper. Bond paper has a medium finish that is neither kid nor plate; it is ideal for layout purposes. Three grades of bond are used by the artist: layout, medium, and heavy bond. Layout bond is transparent enough to allow the artist to trace and revise previous work. It readily accepts pastel, charcoal, or colored pencil and is used for rough layouts. Heavy bond is used for line illustration, lettering, finished layouts, and masks for photographs or illustrations.

Marker Paper. Contemporary layouts are most often rendered with felt-tip marking pens. These have a tendency to "bleed." Bleeding through to a clean sheet underneath is not always disastrous, but bleeding laterally will cause the lines to spread and thus ruin the layout. Although many pads purport to accept marker ink without bleeding, this is not always true. A marker pad should be first tested with the particular marker one intends to use.

Illustration Board. Illustration board consists of high-rag-content paper mounted on stiff cardboard for greater durability and ease of handling. The paper surface may range from a smooth Bristol to rough watercolor paper. *Hot pressed* board is a smooth surface, ideal for delicate line work and precise mechanical art. *Cold pressed* board has a slightly coarser surface that is suitable for line drawing, opaque renderings, and the normal variety of mechanical art. *Rough* board is generally mounted watercolor paper and should be used for the wash drawing. The cardboard mounting is either *single thick* (1/16 in.) *or double thick* (1/8 in.); the thicker backing minimizes warpage. The facing paper may be stripped from the backing in order to facilitate the pasting-up of the illustration.

Watercolor Paper. The best watercolor paper is produced with a 100-percent rag content, making it capable of absorbing the excess moisture required for the execution of a wash drawing. Watercolor paper is manufactured in rolls, sheets, blocks (pads bound on four sides), or mounted in the form of illustration board. It is available in a number of surface textures. Quality illustration board should bear the imprint of its manufacturer or a reputable art-supply dealer on the back side.

Newsprint. Newsprint, bound in pad form, is economical to use when large quantities of paper are expended for rough sketches or quick layouts. Newsprint is best used with pencil, crayon, or charcoal; it will not accept ink or watercolor.

Kraft Paper. Brown wrapping paper is available in rolls or in pad form and is ideal for sketching in oil. The high absorbency of the paper causes the normally slow-drying oil paint to dry in a short period of time.

Colored Paper. Lightweight colored paper, available in a wide range of printed hues, is used for a variety of art applications, particularly in the preparation of tight comprehensives, packaging dummies, posters, etc. Coloraid paper, long the standard of the industry, has been supplanted by Pantone colored paper (see page 256), largely because Pantone is an integral part of a sophisticated color-matching system.

Mat Board. Mat board is cardboard, either single or double thick, used for matting and sometimes mounting illustrations and photographs. Although it is available in a wide variety of colors and textures, the most popular mat board has an "eggshell" texture and is gray on one side and white or cream on the other.

Mount Board. Mount board is similar in appearance to illustration board, but is surfaced with a cheaper grade of paper. It may be surfaced on one or both sides and does not bear the manufacturer's imprint. Mount board is inexpensive and is used for quantity mounting of photographs or for the construction of dummy boxes and displays.

Foam core mounting board consists of a urethane-foam core sandwiched between two sheets of paper. This middle core will not fade, warp readily, or deteriorate.

Chipboard. Chipboard is a gray, unsurfaced cardboard used when a cheap mounting board or a stiffener is required. Easel devices for counter cards and other displays are usually die-cut from chipboard.

CRITERIA FOR SELECTING PAPER

Paper may be purchased through the printer or ordered directly from a paper house. The paper house is not a manufacturer; it is a mercantile establishment that may stock the products of several manufacturers. Most paper houses employ salespeople who willingly supply samples and cost estimates for their clients.

Paper should be carefully selected; the cost of the paper has a pronounced effect on the total cost of the printed job. When ordering paper, the following factors should be considered:

Proposed Use.   The paper selected should be compatible with the printing process and the kind of ink that will be used. It should be physically adaptable to the intended purpose of the job. Factors such as strength, durability, foldability, permanence, and any physical situations to which it may be exposed should be considered. Opacity may be an extremely important qualification. In the selection of paper, the most essential requirement becomes the deciding factor, because no paper possesses all of these attributes in the exact degree desired.

Quality.   The quality of the paper should also be compatible with its intended use. It is as foolish to purchase excessive quality as it is to purchase inferior quality.

Weight.   The weight of both paper and cover stock should be appropriate. The paper should be heavy enough to stand up to the requirements of the job, but not so heavy as to become cumbersome or difficult to handle. Paper that is heavier than necessary will cause excessive shipping or mailing costs.

Surface and Finish.   The nature of the paper surface should be considered in terms of both the printing process—remembering that halftones are best printed on smooth paper—and the desired aesthetic appearance of the finished result.

Size.   Paper may be purchased in a wide variety of sizes. The size capacity of the press employed, the manner of imposition, and the paper size should all be carefully matched for utmost efficiency of press time and a minimum of waste.

Color.   Paper is manufactured in a multitude of colors. Even so-called "white" paper is available in a variety of shades, many of which will alter the printing characteristics of a halftone. The color selected should be compatible with the aesthetic requirements of the job; the paper is just as important to the job's appearance as any design element. A well-planned job may incorporate the color of the paper as an integral part of its design.

Grain.   All machine-made paper has a grain that is caused by the directional movement of the Fourdrinier screen. Paper tears and folds most easily *with* the grain. Paper may be ordered with the grain running in either direction; grain direction may affect folding, binding, and color registration.

How to Test for Grain Direction

Bend the paper by holding one edge with both hands and letting the opposite edge sag. Do the same, holding the adjacent edge. The greater sag of the two establishes that the grain is parallel to the held edge.

Tear the paper at a right angle to each of the two adjacent edges. The paper will tear more cleanly *with* the grain.

Crease the paper in one direction and repeat at a right angle. The sharper crease will be *with* the grain.

Wet the paper on one side, drape it over an arm—wet side down—and it will roll. The grain is parallel to the roll's axis.

BIBLIOGRAPHY

BRUNO, MICHAEL H., ed. *Pocket Pal,* 13th ed. New York: International Paper Company, 1986. A complete, up-to-the-moment text on the technological aspects of graphic arts production.

COGOLI, JOHN E. *Photo-Offset Fundamentals,* 4th ed. Bloomington, Ill.: McKnight Publishing Co., 1980. A manual of offset lithography.

DENNIS, ERVIN A., and JENKINS, JOHN D. *Comprehensive Graphic Arts,* 2nd ed. Indianapolis, Ind.: Bobbs-Merrill Educational Publishing, 1983. A comprehensive description of the various graphic arts processes.

MANDELL, STEVEN L. *Computers and Data Processing,* 2nd ed. St. Paul, Minn.: West Publishing Co., 1982. An extensive analysis of the entire field of computer technology.

NEBLETTE, C. B. *Photography, Its Materials and Processes.* Princeton, N.J.: D. Van Nostrand, Inc., 1962. An old but extremely comprehensive source of information concerning all aspects of photography. This highly technical text goes into great detail.

Print Media Production Data. Wilmette, Ill.: Standard Rate and Data Service, Inc., 1986.

TIME-LIFE BOOKS, EDITORS OF. *Understanding Computers: Input/Output and Computer Images.* Alexandria, Va.: Time-Life Books, 1986. A well-illustrated examination of the computer's capabilities.

ZANDI, M. *Computer-Aided Design and Drafting.* Albany, N.Y.: Delmar Publishers, Inc., 1985. A thorough exposition of the aspects of computer-aided design.

INDEX